BIG KIBBLE

BIG KIBBLE

The Hidden Dangers of the
Pet Food Industry and
How to Do Better by Our Dogs

Shawn Buckley and
Dr. Oscar Chavez
with Wendy Paris

ST. MARTIN'S PRESS
New York

First published in the United States by St. Martin's
Press, an imprint of St. Martin's Publishing Group

BIG KIBBLE. Copyright © 2020 by Shawn Buckley and
Oscar Chavez. All rights reserved.
Printed in the United States of America.
For information, address St. Martin's Publishing Group,
120 Broadway, New York, NY 10271.

www.stmartins.com

Designed by Donna Sinisgalli Noetzel

Library of Congress Cataloging-in-Publication Data

Names: Buckley, Shawn Richard, 1964- author.
Title: Big kibble : the hidden dangers of the pet food
    industry and how to do better by our dogs /
    Shawn Buckley and Dr. Oscar Chavez with
    Wendy Paris.
Description: New York : St. Martin's Press, [2020] |
    Includes bibliographical references and index.
Identifiers: LCCN 2020024205 |
    ISBN 978-1-250-26005-5 (hardcover) |
    ISBN 978-1-250-26006-2 (ebook)
Subjects: LCSH: Pet food industry—United States. |
    Pet food industry—United States—Quality
    control. | Pets—Feeding and feeds—United States.
Classification: LCC HD9340.U52 B83 2020 |
    DDC 338.4/7664660973—dc23
LC record available at https://lccn.loc.gov
    /2020024205

Our books may be purchased in bulk for promotional,
educational, or business use. Please contact your local
bookseller or the Macmillan Corporate and Premium
Sales Department at 1-800-221-7945, extension 5442,
or by email at
MacmillanSpecialMarkets@macmillan.com.

First Edition: 2020

10 9 8 7 6 5 4 3 2 1

For Simon, Nala, Shadow, and Rey.

Thank you for your inspiration.

Contents

PART THREE

Good Friends Deserve Great Food

Authors' Note

This book is written and published for informational purposes only and is not intended to replace the advice of each reader's own veterinarian or other licensed professional. As a pet parent, you should consult a veterinary professional in all matters relating to your dog's diet, health, and well-being, especially if your dog has existing, or appears to be developing, chronic medical conditions, and before starting, stopping, or changing the medications your dog is taking, or any nutritional or health regimen your dog is following, under the supervision of a veterinarian or other licensed professional.

The intention of this book is to alert pet parents to the issues—and all too often the perils—presented by "Big Kibble's" mass-produced, feed-grade dog food, in order to raise awareness. It is not intended to give veterinary or individualized nutritional advice.

The fact that a veterinarian, medical professional, organization, or website is mentioned in this book, as a potential source of information or products, does not mean that the author or the publisher endorse any particular veterinarian or other professional, or the information they may provide or the food or other nutritional products they may recommend or produce.

Again, pet parents are solely responsible for the health and nutritional decisions they make for their dogs, under the guidance of a veterinary professional.

PART ONE

Four Legs, Full Heart

Introduction

> May you be as good a person as your dog thinks you
> are.
>
> —*Unknown*

Elise Maitland long considered her dog, Michigan, a member of the family. She'd been reluctant to adopt the collie-Labrador mix initially; as a single mom of four, she wasn't eager to take on a fifth dependent. But Michigan, then just a puppy, quickly won her over with his protective nature. He seemed determined to help the Ontario, Canada, mother keep an eye on her kids.

Labradors are the most popular dog breed in America, for good reason. They are loved for their friendliness, and for their affectionate, boisterous, outgoing nature. Collies—the *Lassie Come Home* dog—are known for their loyalty and intelligence, and for being devoted to their human families. Michigan was a perfect combination of the two breeds, and he helped keep his family safe and happy for a dozen years.

But then one day, something upsetting happened. Michigan

suddenly lost control of his bowels. The next day, it got worse, with bloody fluid oozing out of the family's beloved dog. Elise got Michigan into the car after midnight and drove to the emergency clinic, more than thirty minutes away.

The clinic kept Michigan overnight. A few days and more than a thousand dollars later, Elise finally took him home, his diagnosis unclear. He never fully recovered, and died about a year later of kidney failure. What could have caused this otherwise healthy dog to develop kidney disease?

His food, as it turned out.

As Elise later learned, thousands of pet parents throughout North America had been unwittingly feeding their dogs commercial dog feed laced with melamine, a plastic that can lead to kidney disease and kidney failure if eaten. But why would Michigan, or any other dog, have eaten melamine? No pet parent would intentionally feed a dog melamine.

As it turned out, two Chinese manufacturers and a U.S.-based importer were involved in a scheme to add melamine to wheat gluten to boost its apparent protein levels in lab tests. Before they were caught, they'd sold it to a dozen pet feed manufacturers in North America that incorporated it into more than one hundred and fifty different brands, which then got poured into the bowls of tens of thousands of pets around the continent. Finally, this intentional contamination of dog feed was discovered and led to the biggest pet food recall ever, in 2007.

For many dogs, however, the recall came too late. Michigan ingested the melamine in his daily bowl of Ol' Roy, the private label feed sold by Walmart that is one of the least expensive kibbles on the market. On the other end of North America, a very fancy little Japanese Chin, owned by a retiree living outside Orlando, Florida, died of melamine poisoning from more expensive canned feed. The melamine turned up in homes across the continent, from the biggest names in pet food, including Nestlé

But the pet food industry as a whole has served as the repository for waste products of the human food chain practically since its inception, and this poses real threats to our dogs, as we've seen. In recent decades, some players in the Big Kibble machine seem to have grown ever more profit-focused, elevating the bottom line above the well-being of their customers—our pets, who do not have a voice of their own.

While dog food was an amazing invention of the late nineteenth century, today a handful of multinational corporations dominate Big Kibble: Mars Petcare Inc. is the largest, followed by Nestlé Purina PetCare, J. M. Smucker, and Hill's (a subsidiary of Colgate-Palmolive Co.). These corporations own many of the most popular and lesser-known brands, despite the multitude of names and prices on the shelves. Partly in response to the growing concern of pet parents about the quality of the food in the wake of repeated recalls—about one every five days, according to the FDA—these companies have begun gobbling up independent brands, too. Big Kibble sources many ingredients from the same handful of suppliers, meaning one tainted batch of protein, vegetables, or grains can wind up in hundreds of brands of dog food—even those you think are independent or that are labeled "all-natural" or "holistic."

Recalls aside, Americans have grown far more conscious of what's on our own plates in recent decades. Many of us choose fresh, organic, locally grown food when possible, and scientific research continues to demonstrate the benefits of this way of eating. What we feed our dogs has always reflected our concerns about ourselves, and many pet parents are starting to ask what, *exactly*, is in the kibble in their dogs' bowls. The answers have been trickling in, and they're disturbing. Benign-sounding ingredients on the labels can mask some pretty disgusting, and even dangerous, material. The ultraprocessed nature of kibble poses problems, too;

if even 15 percent of an adult human's overall diet comes from ultraprocessed foods, as a recent study shows, the risk of cancer and
chronic disease rises. You wouldn't feed your child—or yourself—
nothing but cheese puffs and packaged cereal every day for life.
Yet Big Kibble would have us believe that this is the best way
to feed our pets, citing the "complete and balanced" nutritional
profile of their product as "proof" that the continual ingestion of
processed food is healthy.

Dog lovers are sitting up and taking notice, waking up to
the fact that we cannot keep feeding our pets kibble as usual. At
this point, the desire for better-quality food for dogs is largely a
consumer-driven phenomenon. We see it as very similar to the
consumer-led backlash against Big Tobacco.

For generations, it seemed as if practically everyone smoked,
and they lit up everywhere: at work, in hospitals, in schools, at
home, in front of the baby. We could smell it in our homes, feel it
in our lungs, but everyone did it. How could it be bad? Seven top
tobacco CEOs testified before Congress in April 1994 that they
did not believe cigarettes were addictive. They admitted that cigarettes may cause lung cancer, heart disease, and other problems,
but insisted that the evidence was not conclusive. The FDA had
oversight of breakfast cereal and pharmaceuticals, but it didn't get
similar authority over cigarettes until forty-five years after the first
U.S. Surgeon General's report linking cigarette smoking to lung
cancer. In other words, our government gave the FDA authority
to regulate tobacco a full half-century *after* there was plenty of
good evidence that smoking was addictive and could be deadly,
and that being exposed to secondhand smoke was unhealthy, too.

The antismoking movement was slow to take root—partly because Big Tobacco blew one of the world's largest smoke screens
of misinformation in our faces. But as more scientists began publishing reports about the dangers of smoking and of secondhand
smoke, the public raised an outcry. The movement away from

cigarette smoke everywhere was irreversible, once people fully understood the dangers.

To us, the similarities between Big Tobacco and Big Kibble are notable in terms of the marketing muscle and profit motivation, and the fact that monitoring and avoiding Big Kibble has been largely a consumer-driven movement, to date. As more and more pet parents hear about recalls and what's in the bag, they are looking for alternatives. When they try feeding their dogs fresh, whole foods, they see dramatic improvements in their health. As we've seen through our work, seemingly healthy dogs with mild issues such as allergies, ear infections, and diarrhea get healthier; seriously sick dogs with advanced diseases thrive.

Big Kibble is aware of this shift in consumer consciousness. The industry trade group, the Pet Food Institute, recently hired a thoughtful, savvy publicist who is encouraging pet food companies to be more transparent with customers. Even if what they're sharing doesn't always look so appetizing, the argument goes, pet parents will find out sooner or later. Many pet parents are already beginning to ask what's really in the bag.

More transparency sounds good to us. Some kibble companies, however, are taking a different approach: launching expensive marketing and advertising campaigns to address the *desire* for real food without actually changing what's in the bag. In one recent, beautifully shot national TV campaign, adorable dogs scramble over countertops toward steak and carrots in a home kitchen, ready to make their own dinner by themselves. Rachael Ray arrives with a bag of food, the implication being that what's in the bag is the same as what's on the counter. Even the voice-over promises the kind of food you'd want to feed your pet: "Simple, natural ingredients, like real meat and wholesome veggies."

There is no T-bone steak, human-grade chicken breasts, or whole carrots in that bag. It's all marketing. Hot air. Or, in this case, hard kibble.

We Americans love our dogs. We increasingly see them as four-legged members of our family. We want the best for them. When it comes to commercial kibble, however, even the so-called "best" is not good enough.

Commercial pet food was an innovation of the late nineteenth century, and one that offered pet parents huge benefits—ease, convenience, and a sense of security. Dog food, at its best, was designed to meet pets' nutritional needs. We admire much of the work of these pioneering dog food companies: creating a new industry revolving around dogs, helping build veterinary nutrition as a science, contributing to veterinary education, launching some truly impressive (and nervy) marketing campaigns. But Big Kibble, as an industry, has stagnated, clinging to midcentury notions about processed food and refusing to acknowledge and incorporate a half century of science, at the expense of our dogs. Human nutritionists and the average consumer know far more about the value of fresh food now than we once did. It's time for veterinary nutrition to evolve.

Through our decade-plus work in the pet food industry, we have come to believe that a diet of nothing but processed feed made from low-quality ingredients suppresses the immune system of dogs. As pet parents around the nation have seen again and again, it can also lead to serious health problems. When that processed food is made from tainted ingredients, it can be deadly.

For years, pet parents lacked the information they needed to make better choices—or much in the way of better options when it came to prepared food. This is beginning to change, which is good news for pets everywhere. Journalists, bloggers, and aggrieved pet parents are sharing news of recalls online, posing hard questions to Big Kibble, and broadcasting whatever answers they can get. Recipes for home cooking for dogs and the nutrient blends needed to balance them are increasingly available in stores and online. And companies such as ours, JustFoodForDogs, are offering pet parents a real alternative—dog food made from human-grade ingredients.

Ours was the first to sell human-grade food for dogs, made in restaurant-style open kitchens. While this isn't a book about us, it is a book about our mission. We're no longer the only company offering pet parents the option of fresh, whole food for dogs. The concept we launched in 2010 has become its own pet food category. We couldn't be happier. As more people learn about what's in the bag, they're searching for alternatives. Brands in our category are scrambling to keep up with the demand.

We are Shawn Buckley and Dr. Oscar Chavez, founder and chief medical officer of JustFoodForDogs, the nation's first company offering nutritionally balanced meals for pets made only from fresh, whole, human-grade food. We buy our meat from the same guy who sells to the restaurant down the street. We use high-quality whole carrots and Granny Smith apples, fruits and vegetables that any of us would be glad to eat—which you can see stacked in piles in our open-to-the-public kitchens that now offer freshly made and fresh-frozen dog food in cities from Los Angeles to New York City.

You might be thinking, "Wait! But you, too, have a stake in the game! You're biased against Big Kibble because you sell fresh, whole foods for dogs!"

We *do* have a stake in the game, but it's far bigger than our own bank balance. It's about our own dogs, and about *all* dogs. We got into this business *after* switching our dogs from kibble to fresh food and seeing the many dramatic improvements that defied anything we'd seen before. After learning about what can be in kibble, we couldn't stand by watching as other pet parents fed their dogs meat in a bag, shelf-stable at room temperature for a year or longer. That's not a description of real food. Pets and pet parents deserve better choices.

We believe so strongly that dogs should eat the same quality food as we do that we've thrown everything we have into bringing nutritionally balanced, fresh, whole food to more dogs. We post our recipes online for anyone to download for free. We speak to veterinarians at animal hospitals around the nation about food and nutrition. We talk to strangers on airplanes about what they're feeding their dogs. We started our own veterinary nutrition program to help teach proper formulation of fresh food to more vets. We have helped fund research. This is how much we were moved by the facts as we learned them, and this is what we want to share with you in this book.

We make our business decisions *first* by deciding what's good for dogs. Profits come second. Our company is part of the movement toward socially responsible, sustainable business. Corporations around the world are adopting standards known as the "triple bottom line," or the "3 Ps: People, Planets, and Profit." The goal is to do well and do good. We totally support this, though we're aiming for a quadruple bottom line: *Pets*, People, Planets, and Profit.

We wrote this book with a sense of responsibility to dogs, and an objective: helping more people truly understand what's in the bowl. We're advocating for our dogs, loving creatures who give so much to us and yet can't advocate for themselves. If, after reading this, you stop feeding your dog ultraprocessed dry kibble or canned feed and switch to fresh, real food—whether you make it at home or buy it from one of the companies now offering it—we will have succeeded in putting your dog on the path to a longer, healthier life.

> **Shawn:** My interest in fresh, whole food for dogs started almost by accident. I'd been feeding my dog, Simon, what I thought was a high-quality, lamb-and-rice dry dog food.

When the store was out of it one day, I picked up a bag of chicken-based dog food and happened to notice that the price was the same as for the lamb.

In my home, my lifelong partner, Andrea, does most of the cooking. But I knew enough to know that lamb meat costs more than chicken. Why did it cost the same in a bag of dog food? And why, now that I came to think of it, was my dog eating little brown pellets that don't actually look or smell like meat, or like any kind of real food? Dog food contains real meat, right?

Wrong. When I got home, I started investigating what actually goes into the bag. I'd been an entrepreneur my whole life and had just sold my third business, so I had some free time. As it turns out, there's very little real meat in dry dog food. Usually, it's meal, a product that comes from a renderer. And even when it is meat, it's not the same quality meat humans eat. When I found out what is allowed to be in dog food, I couldn't believe it. I did not want Simon to eat this stuff.

Andrea and I decided to make food for Simon at home, using the same quality meat, vegetables, and grains people would eat and following, roughly, some recipes for homemade dog food we found online. This small switch—changing his diet—totally transformed Simon. He looked better and had more energy. He was more bright-eyed and sharper. He even seemed *smarter*.

We'd also just rescued an eight-year-old German shepherd, Nala, that had been abused and malnourished. Nala's fur was dry and patchy, and she was so tired, she could barely hold up her head. Of course, we gave her the food we were making, too. It was unbelievable how much better she got, and how quickly. Within months, her ears were standing up like they're supposed to. Her coat was thick and shiny. She had more energy and seemed happy and carefree. She looked like a show dog.

We regularly walked our dogs around the neighborhood, and one day two neighbors, Lance and Gretchen, stopped us to ask what was going on with our dogs. Why did they look so much healthier and happier? What were we doing that they weren't? When we told them that we'd begun making their food, they said they wanted to try feeding their dogs real food, too. The improvements in their dogs, once they stopped eating their bagged kibble and started eating real food, were as dramatic as those in Simon and Nala.

Eventually, I started asking myself some bigger questions: Would all dogs do this much better eating real food? How could more people feed their dogs fresh food, using the same meats and vegetables we eat? Could there be a business here? It was obvious that the current dog food business model was broken. There had to be a better way to feed the world's dogs. This is how I became a disrupter in the pet food industry.

Oscar: I was working at Cal Poly Pomona, teaching veterinary nutrition, when I happened to drive by the new JustFoodForDogs kitchen that had opened in my neighborhood. Curious to see what it was, I stopped in. Shawn, who was there that day, gave me a tour and explained the vision. I'd never seen anything like this in dog food before.

I invited Shawn to come in and share his concept with my students, as I often did with representatives of pet food companies. The students were really interested. No pet food representative had ever talked to them about using human-grade, USDA-certified meat and fresh produce approved for human consumption.

Shawn reached out again a few months later to see if the university could do a feeding trial for his company, a step dog food brands can take to encourage veterinarians to recommend them. The industry-standard feeding trial is very rudimentary, actually. Eight laboratory dogs eat the food being tested for six months. Six dogs have to finish. The dogs have their blood tested for four very basic biomarkers before and after the trial.[4] Shawn is an advocate for dog rescue and did not want to use lab dogs. He proposed feeding JustFoodForDogs to pets of faculty and staff at the university.

The university agreed to do the trial with pets rather than lab dogs, but then upped the ante by requiring a yearlong trial on thirty dogs, with testing for more than twenty-five biomarkers. This was a lot to ask, given the industry standard. But Shawn was on board immediately with this rigorous, expensive, expanded protocol.

I checked with Dr. William Burkholder, a veterinary medical officer and supervisory veterinarian at the FDA, about the plan. That conversation raised some pretty serious questions for me about commercial dog food and the FDA's role in ensuring its safety. He told me, in essence, that the FDA doesn't oversee feeding trials. Companies run them and also interpret the results. Dr. Burkholder said that in his twenty-five years of doing this, he couldn't recall one instance in which a feeding trial got looked at or questioned by a state official. I found myself wondering how "official" or valuable the standard feeding trial is if no one looks at it.

At the time, I had a golden retriever named Rey who had been with me for more than a decade. Rey had recently been diagnosed with kidney disease, and I did what most people do: switched him from his regular food to a veterinary-recommended therapeutic brand designed to slow the progression of kidney disease, this one made by Royal Canin. About six months later, Rey stopped eating the kibble. I was worried. Rarely does a golden retriever say no to food. Could this mean his kidney disease was getting worse? He was also experiencing some signs of senility, staring off into space and forgetting where his food bowl was.

Meanwhile, at the university, the team ran the first tests on the dogs in the JustFoodForDogs trial. They'd been eating the food for six months, and the results were amazing. The dogs were doing great, not merely handling the food well but as a cohort actually doing better on various blood markers than when they'd started. JustFoodForDogs had begun developing veterinary-support diets for specific problems, including kidney disease. I decided to feed it to Rey.

Within weeks on the fresh whole-food kidney diet, Rey's health improved. When we tested his urine, I saw something shocking: his kidneys were working again. This does not happen. Kidney disease, as far as we know, is progressive. But on the real food, Rey was thriving, despite his history with kidney disease.

I knew that JustFoodForDogs was onto something profound for the lives of dogs. When we got the final results from the feeding trials, I decided it was time to change my career. Sure, I was a year away from tenure at the university, but I realized that I could make a far bigger impact on the lives of dogs by throwing my energy behind this new company's mission than by continuing with the status quo. I resigned at Cal Poly Pomona and joined JustFoodForDogs.

HOW THIS BOOK WORKS

How did our relationship with dogs grow so warm that we now bring them with us to the coffee shop and let them sleep on our bed? In part 1, we take a new look at the age-old human-canine bond. This great relationship, stretching back tens of thousands of years, has evolved dramatically in recent decades, for our mutual benefit, we argue. In chapter 1, we visit a physical therapy clinic for animals and meet a dog whose life was saved by the absolutely astonishing medical advances that have been developed for two-legged *and* four-legged mammals in recent years.

Chapter 2 looks at some of the other, sometimes extreme lengths we go to for our dogs today and asks the question, Who is this treat or toy or TV station really for, the dog or the dog parent? Regardless of the answer, caring for dogs helps us become better humans, in some surprising ways. Our own daily devotion to our dogs helps increase our humanity and empathy for members of our own species.

Chapter 3 delves into the history of dog food and shares how one Cincinnati-based entrepreneur concocted the idea of a special food for dogs in the 1800s. It was such a success that those in other industries nosed in, from biscuit bakers to feed makers to horse slaughterers, eager to lap up the dollars of the newly discovered market of pet parents.

Part 2 goes behind the scenes into Big Kibble. Chapter 4 looks at the rise of Big Kibble and shows how economic and social developments of the late twentieth and early twenty-first centuries have shaped what's in the bowl, too often in ways that are dangerous or even deadly to our nation's dogs. These developments include consolidation, globalization, and money in medicine.

In chapter 5, we examine why you can't judge a kibble by its cover—even one labeled and priced as superpremium. Throughout this book, we generally refer to commercial dog food as "dog feed," because, as chapter 5 explains, what dogs eat is regulated as livestock feed, not as food for humans. This distinction allows Big Kibble to legally—and unknowingly or knowingly—include adulterated ingredients purchased from barely regulated factories overseas. They can mix in the scraps from the human commercial meat industry, such as rendered by-products, and include them as protein. They can add minerals laced with heavy metals and purchase spray-on flavor and fat to meet nutritional profiles and boost flavor. The Association of American Feed Control Officials sets the standards for pet feed, with serious input from Big Kibble and the suppliers that profit from it. This structure is riddled with conflict of interest, and its enforcement processes pose grave danger to our pets.

Chapter 6 provides details about the "meat" used in our dog food. For the past half century, our pets have been used as four-legged recycling machines for the waste from human food production. When a pet food company says it's environmentally friendly, it means it's upcycling slaughterhouse discards and feeding them to our dogs. Some leaders in the rendering field, in fact, consider their industry to be the "greenest" one out there. We love the idea of recycling in general. But not at the expense of our pets.

Feed-grade "meat" isn't the only thing that makes its way into the bag. Chapter 7 looks at the problem with grains—mold on grain due to improper storage. The grain-free movement has taken hold, but some formulations of grain-free dog feed are now implicated in the rise of a dangerous disease, dilated cardiomyopathy, in dogs. In chapter 8, we take a look at what else goes into the bag and how it's processed. The carrots and peas, potatoes, and other vegetables aren't necessarily any better quality than the meat. The current system allows the inclusion of vegetable scraps from the human food production chain, as well as vitamin and mineral premixes that can include industrial chemicals and heavy metals.

So what can you do to safeguard your dog's dinner? Part 3 explains the nuts and bolts of what dogs need to eat. (Hint: It's not a bag of kibble labeled as "ideal" for a specific breed.) Chapter 9 shares more of our story and why we decided to throw our energy into creating the first company offering real food for dogs. This chapter looks at the challenges we faced pushing against the status quo of Big Kibble and advocating for pets and the difference real food makes in dogs' lives.

But don't take our word for it. Ask your dog. Try cooking for your pet at home or purchasing premade fresh, whole food for your dog from one of the handful of companies now offering it. Chapters 10 and 11 help you become a better steward of your dog's diet by separating the facts from the fiction when it comes to dog nutrition and offering clear answers to burning questions such as Can my dog eat popcorn?, Why does my dog eat grass?, and Why does my dog chew up my shoes?

The final section, Recipes, shares a handful of our most popular recipes and cooking tips (including how to stir up a month's worth of food at one time and package it for easy freezer storage). This book you're holding will put you in a better position to improve your dog's quality of life and happiness by giving you the real scoop on the one thing he loves most (after you): food. With this book, you're also helping us save the lives of other dogs. As the authors, we have pledged to donate 100 percent of the royalties we receive from this book to pet rescue organizations, another passion of ours. These are the often underfunded groups who save the lives of abandoned dogs and help them find new homes.

Together, armed with knowledge and love, we can improve lives—the two-legged and the four-legged kind.

1

Our Longest Love Affair

Caring for Our Four-Legged Friends

Dogs have a way of finding the people who need them,
and filling an emptiness we didn't ever know we had.
— *Thom Jones, American writer*

WORK IT OUT

Gleaming plateglass windows line the front of the physical therapy center, sparkling despite the marine layer rolling in from the Pacific Ocean a few miles away. Inside the six-thousand-square-foot facility, an airy, state-of-the-art gym is stocked with the latest PT equipment: thick blue Tumbl Trak floor mats, a treadmill, red and yellow core-stabilizer balls, a ramp with stairs. A sheet of paper taped to a white cabinet door lists exercises for specific goals: core strengthening, endurance, and balance and proprioception. It feels like any cutting-edge physical therapy clinic, though if you look around, you can't help noticing an awful lot of dogs on the premises, not just the two curled up on dog beds under desks in an office, but also those sitting in the waiting room and working out in the gym.

This is BARC—Beach Animal Rehabilitation Center, located

in Torrance, California. It's one of a small but growing number of physical therapy clinics for dogs. BARC bills itself as a veterinary specialty clinic offering a holistic approach to healing—addressing the whole body as a system—rather than zeroing in on a bad leg or bum hip while ignoring the other muscle, nervous, and skeletal systems involved. Its official mission is to help animals live longer, healthier lives. The unofficial guiding passion is to use physical means to help dogs regain mobility rather than immediately resorting to surgery—or worse.

Dog PT may sound like an example of indulgent dog owners throwing everything they have at overly pampered pets. After all, why on earth would a dog need a physical therapist? Dogs get plenty of exercise. They don't need to be coerced into working out (unlike some species; we're not naming names). They'll run around a park all day—and roll in the grass and forge in the lake and chase the ducks—if you let them. When it comes to dogs and exercise, the limiting agent is normally the person taking them out. But physical therapists are not like personal trainers, people charged with motivating movement and helping set goals; these are professionals who step in when something has compromised mobility or is causing pain.

As it turns out, many of the same techniques that reduce pain and swelling in humans and increase strength and mobility also work for dogs. Physical therapy can improve a dog's life, and in some cases save that life. As more of us come to view our dogs as fluffy family members, we're questioning the limitations of old-school care—and adapting for our dogs many of the tools proven to make a difference in our own lives. BARC is one example of the thousands of surprising ways that we're updating our relationship with our dogs, for the benefit of both species.

Physical therapist and dog lover Amy Kramer founded BARC in 2016. Dr. Kramer is not a veterinarian. She did her doctorate in human physical therapy at Western University in Pomona,

California; got licensed as a physical therapist; and planned to have a typical career in PT—as in, working with people. But then Dr. Kramer's rottweiler, Lucy, wrecked her knee. Dr. Kramer decided to have Lucy undergo knee surgery. After she healed, Lucy couldn't bend her knee enough to get through the dog door and let herself out while Dr. Kramer was at work.

When Dr. Kramer reached out to the surgeon for help, he told her that Lucy was fine, as far as he was concerned. She was able to walk. "In my mind, she wasn't fine because she didn't have enough range of motion to get through the doggy door, or even to sit down all the way," says Dr. Kramer. "The surgeon didn't have an answer for it other than to say to me, 'Well, aren't you a physical therapist?' I said, 'Why yes I am!' I went home and applied my skills as a PT to my dog, and within a week and a half, she could get through the dog door."[1]

This was a "light-bulb moment" for Dr. Kramer. Surely there were other dogs in need of a licensed physical therapist's rigorous education? After receiving a four-year college degree, a doctor of physical therapy candidate pursues three years of additional, specialized education in anatomy, physical manipulation, treatment techniques, and more. Dr. Kramer decided to learn as much as she could about dog PT and to consider offering it to more pets and their parents. But there wasn't much out there to help her. While some veterinarians have been practicing versions of physical rehabilitation on animals since the 1980s, there isn't a postgraduate degree program offered for vets equivalent to the one for PTs who work on humans.[2]

Physical therapy for humans has been around for about a hundred years. The first professional PT association in the United States, the American Physical Therapeutic Association, was formed in 1921, largely to help injured vets returning from World War I. Today, we often don't consider PT for ourselves until something has gone really wrong. But as our understanding deepens of holistic care and of the idea of wellness more generally, we're slowly seeking out physical therapy for ourselves and for our dogs. In 1993, the American Physical Therapy Association (APTA) endorsed collaboration between physical therapists and veterinarians, and the American Veterinary Medical Association (AVMA) adopted further guidelines around the practice in 1996. These efforts led to new help for dogs (but some conflict between veterinarian and physical therapy groups, both of which claimed the specialty as a subset of their field).

Today, licensed (human) physical therapists and veterinary doctors who want to do PT on dogs can go to one of two training and certification programs in canine rehab offered in the United States. The Canine Rehabilitation Institute, with campuses in Florida and Colorado, began offering classes in 2003 and includes thirteen days of course work in three modules, a forty-hour internship, and an exam.[3] Classes are taught by working practitioners and involve hands-on lessons in anatomy and biomechanics, with dogs on site. The Canine Rehabilitation Institute also offers training and certification options for veterinary technicians (vet nurses) and acupuncture training for vets.[4]

The other option is the University of Tennessee's Canine Physical Rehabilitation certification program, offered not only to veterinarians and physical therapists but also to licensed vet techs (nurses), PT assistants, occupational therapists, and students.[5] It consists of seven modules, including online instruction, a four-day, in-person component in locations around the world, an externship and exam. The University of Tennessee program also offers a Certified Canine Fitness Trainer program, open to vets, PTs, vet techs, dog trainers, and others.[6]

Dr. Kramer decided to attend the Canine Rehabilitation Institute, obtain the program's Certified Canine Rehabilitation Therapist certificate (CCRT), and then combine her course work and college work to help more dogs. In 2007, she founded California Animal Rehabilitation in West Los Angeles. The clinic was a huge hit. In 2014, she sold that practice and then opened BARC a little farther south, in Torrance, to serve families who couldn't make the twice-weekly (or more) drive to L.A. and to work closer to her own home.

On a foggy Friday in April, Brutus, a tiny brown Yorkie with a tan face and feet, lies on his side on a blue Tumbl Trak mat. Dr. Erin Bukofsky, a physical therapist and CCRT, sits on the floor with him, massaging Brutus's left thigh with both thumbs, working in small circles. A young physical therapy aide with tattooed arms and a kerchief around her head, Cat Swisshelm, sits on the floor, too, petting Brutus as he lies on his side. If a dog can smile, Brutus the Yorkie is definitely smiling while getting his massage. Brutus tore ligaments in both of his back knees. This was a result of a preexisting condition called medial patella luxation, in which the kneecap doesn't track in its groove correctly. It's a common ailment in little dogs and one that can lead to ligament rupture. The team here is trying to help Brutus maintain his range of motion while scar tissue forms over the tears. Then they'll reestablish his ability to put weight on his back legs.

At BARC, rehab generally follows the standard of care that physical therapists use for human patients. It's a five-step process that includes reducing pain and swelling, improving range of motion, working on weight bearing, working on strengthening, and returning to function. These aims are achieved through various methods, including hands-on manipulation, LASER, ultrasound, electrical stimulation, acupuncture, hydrotherapy, and controlled, guided exercises.

Swisshelm then carries Brutus to the acupuncture room, a small, private office behind the main gym. BARC's medical director and co-owner, Dr. Debra Voulgaris, joins them. Dr. Voulgaris received a bachelor's and a master's degree in the arts, then went on to earn a doctor of veterinary medicine degree at Ross University School of Veterinary Medicine, followed by internships in equine medicine and anesthesia. While in private practice in New York, she continued to expand her education in animal care, becoming a certified veterinary acupuncturist. She then returned to academia for a three-year anesthesia and pain-management residency at the University of Tennessee, earning her CCRT while there. She has since studied other healing modalities, all of which enable her to take a holistic approach to dogs, bringing a variety of tools and techniques to the patients at BARC.

Today, Dr. Voulgaris is dressed in green and gray doctor's scrubs and wears a stethoscope around her neck, her curly brown hair pulled back into a ponytail. She sits down on the floor behind Brutus, her blue plastic carrying case of needles with her. Within a few minutes, Brutus has a dozen red-tipped needles sticking out of his back. Acupuncture is used here to help reduce pain, improve blood flow, and stimulate nervous system functioning. It may sound new-agey, but this 2,500-year-old Chinese healing art is also commonly used on farm animals around the United States to stimulate estrus, or "heat," which facilitates easier coordination of breeding.

Meanwhile, in another clean, modern room across the hall, a superfluffy poodle mix is strolling on an underwater treadmill. This is Lola, who came to BARC with paralyzed back legs due to a herniated disc in her back, an injury known as IVDD, or intervertebral disc disease. She'd had surgery and now needed PT to regain functional mobility. Lola is walking in a tank of warm water nearly up to her shoulders. The treadmill moves on its own, forcing all four legs to work. The water helps support her body weight, making it easier. Underwater treadmills are also popular with injured human runners, too, because the buoyancy reduces stress on the joints and provides resistance and body support.

In some ways, dogs are better candidates for PT than humans. True, they can't tell you where it hurts, and they may mask a problem for years by shifting their weight off one hurt leg onto the other three. But they can often regain movement, even in paralyzed legs, a turnaround far less common with humans. Through physical therapy, a partially paralyzed dog won't necessarily win any agility contests at the dog park, but as with Kramer's own dog, many dogs will be able to regain much of what they've lost, letting them fully enjoy their lives and resume their roles as daily companions, snuggling buddies, and best friends of their pet parents.

After her session, Lola steps out of the tank onto a rubber floor mat. She looks up with big black eyes, her fluff of a body balancing on skinny, water-soaked legs. As the tech leads her out of the room, her walk isn't perfect. It's a little wobbly, or "drunken" looking. But a family member with a wobbly walk is far better than one who can't walk at all or, worse, no furry family member at all. "We see so many dogs that were told they'd never walk again. The people think they have to euthanize their dog or that it's surgery or nothing," says Dr. Voulgaris. "They are heartbroken. They are just so sad. But more than 80 percent of the time, we can figure out what's going on and address it. A dog that is otherwise healthy can have a new lease on life."

The treadmill-walking Lola and Dr. Kramer's rottweiler wouldn't have been in physical therapy if they hadn't had surgery. Some pet parents try PT first instead of surgery. Physical therapy is part of the growing range of medical care available to dogs. As with human medicine, veterinary medicine has changed dramatically during the past few decades—grown more technical, more specialized, more extensive, more expensive, and in some places more holistic and prevention-focused. Veterinary medicine today can save the lives of patients that would have died in the past.

THE BEST MEDICAL CARE MONEY CAN BUY . . .
FOR YOUR DOG

One day in late March, 2019, a perky orange Pomeranian, a ten-year-old rescue dog named Dee Dee, was bouncing along the sidewalk with her pet parent, Eva Bitter, in Upper Manhattan. Suddenly, a Husky, also out for a walk, lunged at the tiny dog. He grabbed Dee Dee between his teeth and swooped her up. "I was walking with my friends, and none of us saw it coming," says Eva. "I heard her scream and I looked up, and the Husky had her in the air and was shaking her like you see in a nature show. You could just see the flash of her orange fur, back and forth."

Eva froze for a millisecond. Then she screamed and managed to wrench Dee Dee away from the Husky. The tiny dog kept shrieking. She had a huge gash in her inner thigh and another on her lower back. She was bleeding all over Eva's dress. You could lift up the dog's skin and look underneath, seeing clear through to her other side—an injury that veterinarians call a "degloving."

Eva jumped in an Uber and rushed to the nearest animal hospital, where the vets did their best to stitch up Dee Dee on the spot. They also put in drains to remove the fluid that was building up between the muscle and the detached skin. Dee Dee was saved. At least for the time being.

But a day and a half later, she was hiding under the bed in Eva's apartment, refusing to eat or take the medicine the doctors had prescribed. "Her stitches were opening, and you could see her flesh, which was swelling and starting to turn black," says Eva. "She was acting like she was dying." Eva brought Dee Dee to West Chelsea Veterinary, the neighborhood vet she'd been using since adopting Dee Dee from a shelter in Maine a couple years earlier.

West Chelsea is a full-service general practice office and hospital that has been seeing pets in Lower Manhattan for twenty years. With its diagnostic tools and high-tech monitors and treatments, it's a far different office than it was when it opened, and an example of the high-quality care available for dogs and cats around the nation today. Beyond the large waiting room and half dozen general consultation rooms, West Chelsea's hospital treatment center resembles the triage section of a human hospital. Four treatment stations with beds and IV drips branch out from a central "nerve center" of desks and computers, separated by glass walls. A microscope sits on a counter, used for blood and skin-cell analysis. There's an ultrasound room and a separate glass-walled surgery suite. Vets here do more preventative care than in the past, such as blood work on healthy middle-aged pets to screen for kidney and liver function, electrolytes, and red and white blood-cell count, allowing them to catch a potential problem before it starts.

On a typical day at West Chelsea, you can hear the beeping of a monitor and see veterinarian technicians in green scrubs hurrying around—licensed paraprofessionals who function as veterinary nurses. Kennels line one wall, a glass door placed over one to create an oxygen chamber for a small dog needing extra support. An assistant sits on a stool in front of another kennel, monitoring a patient who is coming out from anesthesia. A vet walks past in blue scrubs with a stethoscope around his neck, while a couple other staff members work in the dental suite, cleaning a dog's teeth while it's under anesthesia and keeping an eye on its vital signs—his heart rate, breathing, blood pressure, and oxygen saturation, registering on a tall plastic monitor on wheels attached to the dog.

As a general practice hospital, West Chelsea is the first stop for pet parents whose dog needs a checkup or vaccine or has a minor problem such as diarrhea. It's also where you might take a dog like Dee Dee who has been attacked and isn't recuperating.

When Eva arrived with Dee Dee, veterinary technicians rushed the dog to a bed at one of the treatment stations and quickly gave her fluids through an IV to stabilize her, oxygen for support, and an antibiotic shot. The veterinarian on duty who saw Dee Dee, Dr. Hyla Gayer, said that the tissue under the ripped-off skin had become necrotic; the muscle that was exposed was dying, which is why it was black. She advised Eva to leave Dee Dee for a few hours to give the team time to hydrate her, open up the stitches to clean them, and do some wound care.

"A few hours later, they called and said that when they opened her up, they found more necrotic tissue under the skin. Her fat and flesh and muscles were dying. They said they really thought I should take her to a wound-care specialist," says Eva.

Specifically, the team at West Chelsea thought Dee Dee should see Dr. Philippa Pavia, a board-certified veterinary surgeon working at the downtown branch of Blue Pearl specialty hospital. As in human medicine, excellent primary care doctors for dogs will refer critical patients to specialists with additional training and the latest equipment. A board-certified veterinary surgeon is one of many specialists working in veterinary medicine today. More than half of all vet school graduates complete their eight-year degrees, then pursue more education in one of twenty-two specialties, including veterinary surgery, cardiology, nutrition, and toxicology. These doctors often find work at specialty referral hospitals.[7]

"They said the specialty hospital was her best bet. It was a life-or-death thing. I didn't know how it would pan out or how I would pay for it," says Eva.

Specialty hospitals are another relatively new development in pet care. In the New York City area, there are half a dozen such places, offering advanced care in areas such as oncology, neurology, integrative medicine, critical care, dermatology, diagnostic imaging, ophthalmology, and surgery. For decades in New York City, there was only one option for an animal that needed specialized care, the nonprofit Animal Medical Center, a hundred-year-old institution that began as a shelter and evolved into a leading research and referral hospital. In the past, most cities and towns lacked specialty hospitals. If your dog needed specific, highly specialized care, you might drive to a university with a specialty veterinary program, if there was one in your state or in the next. If not, you had no choice: it was the end of the line for your pet.

Today, these veterinary specialty hospitals are rising around the nation. Both independent hospitals and even corporate chains are part of this evolution. Blue Pearl, for example, is owned by Mars, which manufactures Pedigree, Whiskas, and Royal Canin, and also owns the hospital chains of Banfield, VCA, and Pet Partners. (Read more on consolidation of Big Kibble in chapter 4.)

Eva decided to borrow money from her father for the $2,000-plus down payment required to go to Blue Pearl. Her brother, who runs a successful dog-walking company in Manhattan, offered to have one of his walkers bring Dee Dee over, but the vets at Chelsea wanted to transport the suffering dog themselves for extra safety.

Dee Dee was rushed to the ICU at Blue Pearl, where she wound up staying for six and a half weeks. The skin had been ripped off from 20 percent of her body, Eva learned, and it was continuing to pocket and die. The fat underneath was dying, too. In addition to Dr. Pavia, Dee Dee saw board-certified veterinary surgeon Dr. Sarah Kalafut and board-certified veterinary emergency and critical care specialist Dr. Josh Rosenbaum. This veterinarian team did daily bandage changes, called "wet bandage care," under anesthesia, a demanding, highly specialized process. Every day, they found more tissue dying and removed it. They did ultrasound scans and X-rays. Dee Dee was on three different painkillers intravenously. She also had a feeding tube through her nose and into her stomach, similar to those that doctors use for newborns in the NICU.

Eva went to the hospital every night after work or even in the middle of the night to provide moral support to her dog, and she'd read that a pet parent's presence can help a dog heal. She got to know the doctors and veterinary technicians, all of whom seemed moved by the little dog's heroic efforts to fight for her life. This round-the-clock, highly specialized care was extremely expensive and a relatively exclusive option (though veterinary care in general still costs about one-tenth of human medicine). But this level of care was *possible* because of the advancements made in medicine for dogs.

Eva found the night technicians particularly supportive, helping her feel less self-conscious about caring so much for this little dog.

Then the feeding tube stopped working adequately. The team inserted an esophagostomy tube through Dee Dee's neck. Still, Dee Dee went from bad to worse. She caught pneumonia and lost so much fluid that she needed transfusions of protein serum and red blood cells. Despite the efforts of the vets, fluid kept oozing from Dee Dee's wounds. They finally decided to try something called wound VAC, a vacuum-assisted wound-closure process developed for soldiers and burn victims. This was a final, last-ditch attempt to save Dee Dee's life. "They were always preparing me that she was going to die," says Eva.

The wound VAC worked. It saved Dee Dee's life. The deterioration process stopped. Dee Dee finally began to heal. She eventually was well enough to go home, albeit with the esophageal tube still in place. "When I finally got to take her home, the vets were crying. No one thought she would make it this far. The vets are astounded by it," says Eva, who has remained in contact with the veterinary team. "Whenever I tell Dr. Pavia that I am so grateful to her, she says, 'This is the reason I get up in the morning.'"[8]

The cost for this kind of medical care can be astounding, too. The total ticket for Dee Dee's round-the-clock, nearly two months of cutting-edge medical intervention was close to $90,000. Eva was able to cover these costs because the Husky that attacked Dee Dee was also a rescue dog—just adopted out the week before—

and the organization that had facilitated his adoption paid for Dee Dee's medical bills. Most people don't have those kinds of funds. But most dogs don't need that kind of care. Still, the fact that these treatments are available is part of the overall development in medical care for dogs.

More people today are buying medical insurance for pets than ever before, from companies like Trupanion and Nationwide, another sign of the shift toward pets as family. We think pet insurance is a great idea. It can make a pricey intervention possible for more families, if it is needed. Premiums tend to be small, starting at around twenty-five dollars a month, depending on the age and health of the dog.

In the not-too-distant future, we expect to see pet ambulances racing through the streets to get critically ill or injured dogs to specialty hospitals ASAP. And because these emergency vehicles will be transporting dogs, which tug on everyone's heart, we expect more compassionate hurrying to the side of the road by motorists than is typical with human ambulances (like it or not).

Routine veterinary care, which has also continued to improve, remains relatively affordable—$138 per visit, on average nationwide as of 2016. Nearly 80 percent of pet parents in the United States bring their dog in for routine care at least once a year, according to the American Veterinary Medical Association.[9] Most vets would prefer twice-yearly visits, particularly for dogs under two. In their first two years of life, dogs develop as much as humans do between birth and eighteen. Their aging and development then slows slightly, but a yearly visit is close to a human's seeing a doctor only once a decade.

Today, Dee Dee is back to her old self, taking walks, socializing with other dogs, and eating good food. "Quality food was a big part of Dee Dee's recovery," says Eva. "Dee Dee survived because of the medical intervention, but also because every single person on the staff gave her so much love and attention. It's like she was able to understand that she was wanted here on earth. There was such a context of support for her. We all need that."

All of this specialized medicine brought to the aid of a dog may sound like some futuristic, twenty-first-century luxury of the wealthy, but actually caring for animals as we care for ourselves has a long tradition, rooted in the practical needs of a developing America. In fact, the fields of veterinary medicine and human medicine used to be far more closely aligned, as authors Barbara Natterson-Horowitz, MD, and Kathryn Bowers explain in *Zoobiquity*, their bestselling book about the similarities between humans and other animals.

Throughout the 1800s and into the early 1900s, in many rural towns in the United States, the same doctor who checked in on your animals would also see the people in the family. He might bring a new calf into the world and deliver a baby for Mom. He might look at a horse with a broken leg and at Junior's sprained ankle. The first accredited vet school in the United States didn't open until 1883—the School of Veterinary Medicine at the University of Pennsylvania. (Though the oldest English-speaking vet school actually started a hundred years earlier, the Royal Veterinary College, in London, where Oscar went.) In the early days of U.S. medicine, medical professionals generally saw *all* biological beings, bringing their expertise of the body to anyone with, well . . . a body. Whether the patient had a button nose or a long snout, two legs or four, was somewhat inconsequential.[10]

When it came to four-legged patients, most of these doctors were caring for farm animals. In 1931, three-quarters of all practicing vets focused on livestock—mostly cattle but also horses, chickens, sheep, and pigs. And most of these vets were men.[11]

Around the beginning of the twentieth century, changes in our economy, rising urbanization, and the invention of the automobile all diminished the role that farm animals play in our lives. Horses were no longer our main source of transportation (a fact that also influenced the early recipes for commercial dog food; see chapter 3). As people moved into cities, they had to leave their cows and chickens behind. Many sought dogs or cats to make their urban spaces feel more homey. All of these developments changed the demands on veterinarians. Who needs a horse doc if you live in an apartment?

Medical professionals interested primarily in four-legged animals (and two-legged ones with feathers) had to rethink their careers. Veterinarians near farms and in cities began making less money than doctors who saw human patients. Doctors also garnered more prestige.

By the end of the twentieth century, more than half of all practicing vets were focusing on small animals, such as dogs and cats, rather than livestock. These numbers have held steady into the twenty-first century. As of 2011, more than half of the American Veterinary Medical Association's members, about 44,000 vets, worked exclusively with small companion animals. The student body of a typical veterinary school has changed, too. As recently as the 1980s, only 35 percent of veterinary school students were women. Eight-five percent of vet students slated to graduate in 2023 are women.[12]

As the fields of human and veterinary medicine became increasingly split, the sharing of knowledge between them more or less stopped—making the notion of a dog cardiologist or hip surgeon sound strange or extravagant. But comparative medicine, like learning about human anatomy from frog anatomy, has a long history for good reason. "The fixation on human uniqueness, human exceptionalism, made anything animal 'other,'" says Bowers. "But adaptations over hundreds of millions of years throughout the animal kingdom means humans have many similarities with other animals in terms of physical and mental health.

Organs function roughly the same way across species; a kidney is a kidney is a kidney. Bio-inspiration, looking to the natural world to find patterns and trends that can relieve problems for all species, makes sense."[13]

Today, doctors on both sides of the divide are once again looking for ways that developments in each field can be harnessed for the benefit of all—and insisting that bringing high-quality care to all animals is good medicine. Bowers and Natterson-Horowitz run conferences around the world that bring together highly specialized research MDs and veterinarians. These conferences have led to dozens of collaborative studies in areas ranging from heart health to mental illness to healthy aging.

Even the Nobel Assembly is recognizing the possibilities of reconnecting the fields of human and animal medicine. In September 2019, scientific leaders from a range of disciplines gathered for a conference at the Nobel Forum at the Karolinska Institute in Stockholm, Sweden. The conference, called "Bio-Inspired Medicine—Unlocking Access of Nature for Opportunities in Health," was designed to tap into strategies from the animal world and see if they could be used to help human health.

The existence of this type of conference is an example of how increasing our understanding of nonhuman animals, and improving how we care for them, can benefit us. Pet parent Eva Bitter's experience is another. Some critics of high-quality care for dogs see it as a waste of resources, an anthropomorphizing or humanizing of our four-legged companions. They accuse today's superdedicated pet parents of substitution—using dogs to fill a gap in their lives, squandering money and affection that could better be directed toward people.

We couldn't disagree more. Caring for our pets deepens our humanity. And it's not mutually exclusive; loving your dog will not make you love your mother less. Recognizing the needs of the small, vulnerable creatures in our midst expands our ability to see the needs of our own species. Caring for dogs builds compassion, empathy, and understanding, characteristics sorely in need in our society.

Dogs also bring us together. While it can feel uncomfortable to talk to a stranger on two legs, dogs have no such self-consciousness. They'll bounce right up to a person on the sidewalk—bringing their pet parent along with them. Pet parents will tell you about the neighbors they know and the friends they've made through their dogs. Often people who stop to pet a dog will look up and say to the pet parent, "Thank you. That made my day."

In our own lives, there's no way we would meet people at the rate we do if it weren't for dogs—our own and other people's. Shawn likes to talk about an interesting discussion he had with a family at a mall in Newport Beach, California, called Fashion Island. He was having gelato at an outdoor place and began petting a short, curly-haired dog that seemed to be a combination of a poodle and a dachshund. It was a supercute dog, bouncing around like a puppy.

Eventually, Shawn looked up to see who was holding the leash. It was a father, a recent immigrant from the Middle East, who was at the mall with his wife, two smiling kids, and their dog, Fiona. They started talking about the dog, and the father said, "You know, to be honest, we got a dog because we really wanted to fit in here and Americans all have dogs. But then we fell deeply in love with her. She's seriously a part of our family now."

That choice makes perfect sense to us. There's so much divisiveness in our culture, and this father wanted to convey a sense of unity and connection, to assure his new neighbors that he was one of them. Getting a dog seemed like the fastest route.

And it worked. That dog, and their obvious love for her, instantly created warmth and openness around this family. The kids clearly adored this wiggly, wagging puppy. The whole family was beaming. "It was quite literally the best thing that happened to me that day," says Shawn. "As a student of all things dog, I thought I had considered all the ways dogs improve our lives and make us better people. But this was a new variation for me. It impressed me. I have no doubt that this family will continue to meet people through Fiona, but I also could have predicted their rambunctious puppy would have worked her way into their lives even if that hadn't been their goal. It's part of the magic of dogs."

2

It's a Dog's Life: 2.0

*The Human-Canine Bond,
Growing Closer Every Year*

> The greatness of a nation can be judged by the way its
> animals are treated.
>
> —*Mahatma Gandhi, world-renowned
> Indian civil rights leader*

WORKING LIKE A DOG . . . AND LOVING IT

Back in 1993, girls began showing up at the office once a year in their pigtails and sneakers, clutching dolls or mini briefcases. This was for Take Our Daughters to Work Day, an initiative launched by feminist Gloria Steinem and the Ms. Foundation for Women to give girls a peek into the working world and raise their expectations for themselves professionally. The program was later adapted to include sons, but for many professionals today, every day is Take Our Children to Work Day, and the children in tow are dogs.

On a recent spring day in Santa Monica, California, an earnest-looking millennial with shiny brown eyes and deep red lipstick chatted with a barista at a local café. Her pug-Chihuahua, sitting on the floor near a table in the back, barked. "Pickles!" the young woman admonished, turning toward the dog. Then she turned back to the barista with the quick smile of a busy mother. "I have to go get my little one."

Pet parent returned, Pickles settled down on his green dog bed—brought along for the day—and took a nap. At the next table, a long black dachshund–cocker spaniel named Marshmallow lay stretched out on the floor, his short legs splayed to the side. Human customers had to step around him to get to their seats. A gray whippet wearing a red plaid mackintosh with a hood bounced into the coffee shop, causing a fourth dog to yap from somewhere else in the room. The whippet barked in response. His pet parent, a middle-aged woman dressed in black, responded like any mother reprimanding her wayward toddler. "Quiet! You're in a coffee shop!" Her tone implying, *This is not how we behave in public.*

The number of solopreneurs lugging laptops to coffee shops and co-working spaces has risen steadily in the past two decades, as has the number of dogs tagging along with them. Eighty-five percent of dog owners in the United States currently view their dogs as members of the family.[1] A quick Internet search for "dog friendly cafes in Los Angeles" turns up dozens of places where you can get a cappuccino with your border collie, a pour-over with your poodle (a muffin with your Muffin). You'll also find dog-friendly cafés in cities such as Cincinnati, Austin, Atlanta, and Birmingham. The website BringFido.com lists dog-friendly establishments nationwide. Boris and Horton in New York City's East Village has even been given Department of Health approval for dogs. The café has a separate area for patrons with dogs, complete with an air purifier running to minimize odor (presumably from the dogs).[2]

Dogs are also welcome at many co-working spaces. Walk into pretty much any WeWork, the pioneering co-working company with shared office space around the world, and you'll find plenty of people hard at work on laptops, dogs asleep in their laps. Throughout California, smaller, dog-friendly co-working companies now operate, including Cross Campus, Satellite Centers, and Union Cowork. Individual co-working spaces welcome dogs in sizable cities such as Denver, Austin, Dallas, New York, Chicago, Minneapolis, and Phoenix, as well as places that may be unexpected: Sioux City, Iowa; Lancaster, Pennsylvania; Huntsville, Alabama; and more.

Working with and sipping coffee with our dogs are not U.S.-based phenomena. Tokyo has more than fifty pet-friendly cafés. Countries throughout Europe have long had far more inclusive dog policies than we have. You can bring dogs to restaurants in Switzerland as well as to art galleries in England and even some beaches in Italy.[3]

Career Dogs

Increasingly, large corporations are recognizing the benefit that dogs bring to the workplace. At Amazon's corporate headquarters in Seattle, as many as six thousand dogs were heading to work with their pet parents, as of this writing. Employees at the San Francisco–based game-design company Zynga and the software company Salesforce are also free to bring their dogs to work. Ticketmaster allows employees to bring dogs to its multiple locations, as does the home-care company Bissell, based in Grand Rapids, Michigan. The goal of these companies is not, obviously, to expand a dog's sense of possibility but rather to lure millennial workers and to create a better workplace environment. Many corporations with dog-friendly policies point to research showing that dogs in the office can do everything from reduce stress to promote more positive social interactions

among human workers. These kinds of social benefits help
attract and retain talented employees.[4]

Where the Dogs Are . . . at Work

Looking for a good job with a great dog policy? Rover, the
national pet-sitting and dog-walking company, asked users
about their companies' dog policies, then ranked corporate
headquarters according to a variety of criteria, including
dog-friendly office space, on-site parks and other perks for
dogs, help with dog insurance, and even paid dog adoption
or bereavement leave. Here are Rover's top twelve:

Amazon, Seattle, WA
Procore Technologies, Carpenteria, CA
Trupanion, Seattle, WA
PetSmart, Phoenix, AZ
Airbnb, San Francisco, CA
Nestlé Purina PetCare, Saint Louis, MO
Petco Animal Supplies, San Diego, CA
Zogics, Lenox, MA
Ceros, New York, NY
Uber, San Francisco, CA
Salesforce, San Francisco, CA
Chewy.com, Dania Beach, FL, and Boston, MA[5]

This same line of thinking motivates many solopreneurs to
bring their pups to the coffee shop or co-working space. Starting
and running your own business can be lonely and isolating. As
research shows and anecdotal evidence confirms, dogs can help
spark conversation and create a sense of community. In a survey
of more than two thousand people living in four cities, those with

pets were "significantly more likely" to get to know their neighbors than those without pets—and presumably to know their tablemates at the coffee shop, too.[6]

HAPPIER AT HOME

Of course, plenty of people still leave their dogs at home while they're at work. Some people choose dwellings based partly on options for their dogs, such as a house with a backyard. Or a condo with shared social space. When a twenty-seven-floor luxury condominium building was under construction across the street from Bloomingdale's in Manhattan in 2004, the $50 million project featured double-height ceilings, a lobby with golden-hued granite floors, a fitness center with a mahogany yoga deck, and a sky-high "pooch park" with a view of the East River—offered as an enticement to potential buyers.[7]

Life has gotten even cushier for some dogs since then. What does today's homebound dog do all day? He could watch Dog TV. Founded in 2009 in San Francisco, Dog TV is the first television network with programming designed specifically *for* dogs. The twenty-four-hour network, available on cable channels and through streaming services like Roku, offers programming in three categories: relaxation, stimulation, and exposure. If you feel guilty about your dog having too much screen time, don't worry. The content, produced in conjunction with dog experts, is billed as educational. The exposure videos, for example, help dogs gain comfort with things that might scare them, such as vacuum cleaners and busy streets.

In the past, a stay-at-home dog might gaze longingly after you, then go to sleep or maybe chew through a pair of shoes until you returned. When you traveled, you might have dropped him off at a bare-bones kennel, where he'd sleep in a wire dog pen. He was safe, but probably not very happy. Today, the options for day and overnight boarding have changed dramatically, in many cases resembling facilities for human toddlers. In Paradise Valley, Arizona, outside Scottsdale, the Applewood Pet Resort offers dogs outdoor playtime on its two-acre grounds. We visited on a very hot summer day and drove up the circular driveway to the impressive covered entryway, with vine-covered support pillars and iced water and cold towels for pet parents. Our first thought was, Where do *we* check in?

In New York City, dogs can enjoy "five-star" accommodations at the D Pet Hotels. Located on a busy side street in Chelsea, the Manhattan branch of the D Pet Hotels collection has two floors with supervised play areas and luxury overnight "suites." Some suites have human-size double beds and flat-screen TVs. What do overnight visitors watch on TV? You guessed it: Dog TV. Or sometimes a movie, like *Beverly Hills Chihuahua*. There's also a small gym and the occasional yoga class. During a typical weekday, anywhere from forty to one hundred dogs—day visitors and overnight guests—run around together in three indoor play areas lined with black rubber mats, one with a small slide.

The D Pet Hotels collection has franchises in Austin, Scottsdale, and Los Angeles. The L.A. branch will pick up your pooch in a luxury sports car, for a fee (a perk more likely to wow the pet parent than the pet, who probably can't distinguish between a Ferrari and a Fiat). But for some pet parents, the extra cost is worth it. As New York City franchise owner Kerry Brown says, the hotel concept makes it easier for superbusy, possibly stressed-out urbanites to focus on work without worrying about their four-legged children. "New Yorkers work hard and play hard, and they want a guilt-free, stress-free option. In an urban environment, their dog may be the only family they have," she says.[8]

Today, our dogs are not just family members—they've also become a runaway success as a consumer category. When Dr. Amy Kramer opened her first dog rehab center in Los Angeles, there were only a couple of companies making underwater treadmills for dogs. Now, half a dozen companies manufacture them. Pet parents today buy dog Halloween costumes at places like Petco and Chewy.com, allowing them to dress up their dogs as penguins, say, or hot dogs. You can get a faux-fur orthopedic dog bed from Treatadog.com. You can hire a chauffeur, personal chef, party planner, and pedicurist (paw-dicurist) for your pooch. The monthly subscription service BarkBox will send your dog a "curated" collection of toys, treats, and chews each month. In the United States, we spent $97.5 billion on pet products in 2019 alone, with nearly a third of that going for supplies, over-the-counter medication, and services such as grooming, boarding, training, pet sitting, pet exercise, and pet walking.[9] Globally, the pet-products industry brought in $125 billion in sales in 2018, having risen every year for more than five years.[10]

While enrichment activities such as park time and toys help dogs thrive, not all of these products and services are actually *for the dogs*. Some dogs might enjoy dressing up in costumes, but we've all seen the photos of adorable dogs looking pretty miserable in their tiaras and tutus. Even some of the luxury services ostensibly for the pets probably benefit pet parents—in terms of peace of mind—more than their dogs. High-quality boarding for dogs is certainly beneficial, but even at some of the most expensive doggie day cares / overnight resorts we've seen, the people-facing front areas are far more enhanced than the dog areas.

It's important to ask yourself who this particular outing or treat or toy is really for—you or your pup? If it's primarily for your own amusement or emotional appeasement, ask yourself, At what cost to my dog? If you love taking your dog trick-or-treating, and he enjoys it—or at least doesn't mind—certainly dressing him as a ballerina can be fun. But if he's miserable, we say find another way to celebrate the season.

Those of us who love dogs also love products *featuring* dogs, and probably always have. In 1898, the family-owned candy-maker Gimbal's introduced Licorice Scotties, chewy, dog-shaped candies. Licorice Scotties are still available at places like Target and CandyNation.com. They're so popular that you can find out how many calories they have on the fitness app MyFitnessPal.com (six pieces = 140 calories). Plenty of other dog-themed products have popped up since Gimbal's started. You can buy Scottie-dog pajamas; Scottie-tail coat racks; and plenty of candy molds, cocktail napkins, Christmas ornaments, tote bags, cozies, and bedsheets printed with Scotties or poodles or pugs or black Labs.

Dog-themed products turn up where you'd least expect them, such as at the gift shop of a hotel in Marfa, Texas, an art colony deep in the West Texas desert. Inside the rambling old stone Hotel Paisano, as far off any beaten track as you can get, an entire kiosk is devoted to dog-themed souvenirs—bulldog key chains and pocket pins, silver dachshund paperweights, and a three-piece treat jar with a dog-bone handle and a dog-bone–shaped cookie cutter. Elsewhere in town, artist Lesley Villarreal offers custom "pet pawtraits," soulful, close-up art photography portraits of your dog, shot in-studio or outdoors. David Capron, the photographer at Dogma Pet Portraits in Costa Mesa, California, shot all the art photos of dogs hanging on the walls in our office. He started out doing family portraits, realized that nearly every family photo included a dog, and decided to switch his focus to furry subjects. David has perfected the art of catching a dog's best look or action shot.

Readers love dogs, too. There are magazines about dogs in cities from Houston to Honolulu. In the college town of Las Cruces, New Mexico, the publication *Dog'Cruces* has been informing local pet owners of dog-related events and specials for nearly a decade.

This may sound like our consumer culture on overdrive, a capitalist society inventing "needs" and then creating something to fill them. Does anyone really need a gray wool throw pillow with a shaggy black Scottie-like dog whose yarn fur hangs over the edges? (Well, maybe. It is very cute.) While exact numbers vary, there are some 80 million pet dogs in the United States, with nearly 40 percent of American households including at least one, and certainly plenty of pet parents have the disposable income to splurge.[11] The Internet and developments in manufacturing and shipping have made it easier for businesses catering to niche markets—such as labradoodle lovers—to find customers and flourish. We see this consumer-based focus on our four-legged family members as ultimately beneficial, since it allows us to embrace our love of dogs in fun, lighthearted ways.

FROM DOGHOUSE TO OUR HOUSE

Why has our relationship with our dogs intensified in so many ways? Demographic changes have definitely contributed to today's particular dog-as-family-member ethos. Families have long bought dogs to help kids gain a sense of responsibility or to add some frolicking fun to the household. Coco was part of the Stone family on *The Donna Reed Show*, and Tramp the dog was a beloved part of *My Three Sons*. Lassie, the helpful border collie who first appeared in the 1943 movie *Lassie Come Home*, went on to have her own family television show in 1954 that ran for nineteen seasons, until 1974. In today's ever more complex parenting landscape, a dog can feel like an old-fashioned standby method of establishing a sense of home.

But an entirely new demographic category has arisen in the past few decades—the single urban adult in no rush to partner up or procreate. A person living in this new type of household has different needs, many of which a dog can fill.

More of us are remaining single deep into adulthood than at any other time in recorded human history or not marrying at all.[12] In 2018, only 29 percent of adults thirty-four and under were married in the United States. Even as recently as 1978, 59 percent of adults were married, meaning there's been a thirty-point drop in the number of marriages among young adults in the United States in the past four decades.[13] For an increasing number of people, choosing a home based on how much the dog likes it makes sense; the pooch may be the *only* other living creature sharing the space (with the exception, perhaps, of a few potted plants).

Fewer people are having children, too. Between 2007 and 2013, the birth rate in the United States fell 10 percent, to just over 60 births per every 1,000 women under the age of 30.[14] Many child-free adults want someone to care for, and a dog can fill the void. As Pickles's owner put it, "I do want to have children some day, but for now this is like practice. Especially because he's a Chihuahua. He throws tantrums like kids do."

Urbanization has not only influenced the veterinary industry but also helped create a new style of human-canine closeness. A dog left home all day can lead to complaints by the neighbor on the other side of the wall. "After my landlord told me she was barking all the time and couldn't be left in the apartment, I started bringing Dee Dee with me everywhere," says pet parent Eva Bitter. More together time creates its own virtuous cycle: the desire to sip coffee or watch a movie with your dog leads to more desire to sip coffee or watch a movie with your dog. As anyone with a dog knows, the more time you spend together, the closer you feel. This is partly due to dogs' unique ability to read our emotions and verbal and nonverbal cues (see p. 50). Or, as Eva says, "She's with me every second, and she's become my best friend, like my life partner. I know people say that about romance, but she's my life partner in terms of another being. I just totally love her. She's my favorite being ever."

Urbanization also contributed to the rise of leash laws, which vary state by state and county by county. The legal requirement to restrain dogs rather than let them roam free has created a whole culture of dog-walking humans.[15] In the 1970s, many suburban families simply let their dogs out. As that behavior was replaced with having to walk the dog, the intimacy between person and dog grew.

Since living with a dog can lead to hair on the couch and red eyes on human residents with allergies, there has been a rise in the number of engineered dogs that don't shed. We've been breeding dogs to help with specific tasks for centuries—hunting, swimming, following small animals into a narrow burrow, grabbing on and refusing to let go. Today's doodle-type dogs, bred to take advantage of the hypoallergenic fur of poodles, have a different kind of job. They work indoors, for one thing, and are charged with being good family members who can sleep in the bed, remain loyal and devoted, and snuggle—without causing sneezing, itching, or too much extra cleaning.

Snuggling—part of the job description for many dogs today—is one obvious reason for the age-old human-dog bond. Dogs are just so cute and fluffy. This full-body longing to hug something fluffy is well expressed in the 2010 children's animated comedy *Despicable Me*. Agnes, the youngest of three orphan girls (voiced by Elsie Fisher), sees a fluffy pink-and-white unicorn at a fair. In a now-classic movie moment, she yells, "He's so fluffy I'm going to die!!" Dogs, too, trigger our desire to cuddle up, *now*!

But unlike a stuffed unicorn, dogs love us back, totally and unconditionally. Your dog is never too busy on his smartphone to greet you when you arrive, nor is he likely to stand you up for a walk because someone better looking came along. Dogs' abiding love of us is a big piece of the human-dog bond.

A hilarious series of public service announcements encouraging dog adoption emphasizes dogs' unconditional love. These spots ran on TV in the 1990s, sponsored by the animal rescue organization Companion Animal Placement. In one, a tired-looking businessman comes home at the end of the day and is greeted by his small white spaniel-like dog. The spaniel gazes adoringly at the man as he slowly takes off his business jacket and formal shirt. Elegant piano music plays in the background. The businessman picks up a bra and puts it on. He then puts on a wig, a skirt, and a lady's shirt. The spaniel wags his tail. The man pets the dog and heads out for the evening in full drag. These words appear on the screen: "That's the great thing about pets. They really don't care."

We'd rephrase that to say: "That's the great thing about dogs. They really *do* care. But they *don't* judge."

Like humans, dogs can read facial expressions and body language. For a study published in *Learning and Behavior Journal* in 2018, researchers recruited twenty-one healthy, food-motivated domestic dogs of various breeds and ages, then showed them photos of humans displaying different emotions. In one set of photos, for example, a human subject's eyes were wide with fear. In another, her teeth were clenched and her eyes narrowed in anger.

For the experiment, each dog entered the room hungry and was led to a bowl of food in the middle of the room. The researchers illuminated an image displaying one emotion on both sides of the dog's head. The dogs consistently and notably focused on the image to their left when it showed anger, fear, or happiness. Of course, dogs are known to tilt their heads back and forth with a quizzical expression all the time. But looking left is a sign of action in the right hemisphere of the brain, the side involved in expressing and processing intense emotions. To researchers, this study showed that dogs are "sensitive to emotional cues conveyed by human faces" and that their brains can "process basic human emotions."[16]

This study followed other research also showing that dogs can process human emotional cues.[17] Of course, you probably don't need a study to tell you that your dog knows how you feel. Many dogs seem to understand when we're sad and need to lie on the couch together. (They certainly can read cues suggesting that you're about to leave the house without them.) They read our moods, and many respond accordingly.

Dogs can also see and understand pointing, the only species besides humans that can do so with flexibility and nuance. In one famous, oft-repeated experiment called the "object-choice task," a treat is hidden under a cup, but under a second cup no treat is placed. When a researcher points to the cup with the treat, the dog will go get the treat, even if the researcher stands next to the other cup or points and then drops his arm. Dogs also understand if we point with a foot or our chin. Some very socialized wolves and chimps can understand pointing, too (and even some bats raised by humans), but not with this degree and subtlety of understanding, and not as easily or naturally.

As dog researcher Julie Hecht puts it, this one little gesture, "in all its complexity, could be a core feature of the intimate bond we share with dogs."[18] Why does pointing matter? Because it shows that dogs grasp our mental state; they know we want them to think about whatever we're pointing at. We are communicating to them, and they are understanding. In another study, researcher Amy Cook and colleagues found that dogs respond better to their owners' pointing than to that of a stranger, further cementing the idea that reading this gesture says something important about our connection.[19]

Dogs learn our commands and create their own ways of communicating. Your Labrador won't tell you to "Sit!" but he might stare at his toys and then back at you to tell you that it's time to play. A paw hover or turn of the head can be a request for food. In a recent study from the University of Salford, published in the journal *Animal Cognition,* dogs used at least fourteen different gestures just to get a belly rub. Dogs rolled over, rested their paws on people, and nudged the human handlers with their noses, all different methods of saying, "Hey! It's time to scratch my belly!" If the human handlers failed to get the message, the dogs in the study tried other forms of making themselves understood.[20]

HOW DOGS MAKE US BETTER PEOPLE

We use dogs' remarkable ability to connect and communicate with us for all kinds of canine professions. We train dogs to sniff out drugs, help the armed forces, and detect changes in a human companion's body chemistry that could signal an oncoming epileptic seizure or disease.[21] Think about that: some people pay huge amounts of money for full-body scans to detect early tumors or other internal shifts. Dogs have that ability within them. Dogs can even be trained to disobey their owners for safety, as those who go through the two-year rigorous process of becoming Guide Dogs for the Blind learn. These guide dogs will defy a command to cross the street, for example, if they see a speeding car coming.

Dogs have other, lighter jobs, too. The Chihuahua Gidget worked as a spokesmodel for Taco Bell from 1997 to 2000. In the original ad, Gidget is running down the sidewalk, ears wide, salsa music in the background. When she arrives at a taco stand, her thoughts are voiced by actor/stand-up comedian Carlos Alazraqui, "Yo quiero Taco Bell." More recently, Tinkerbelle, a five-pound rescue dog, has found work as a paid model for Target, Ralph Lauren, Febreze, and Swiffer, among other companies. As her pet parent Sam Carrell says, "With everything that happens, I think, 'Wow, this is a big deal!' And then something else happens, and I think, 'Wow, this is an even bigger deal!' The bar keeps rising, so who knows what's next."[22]

Many people feel that living with a dog improves their health. As the notion of "wellness" has grown and taken root, some health-minded humans see getting a dog as one more way to be well. A recent publication, *Get Healthy, Get a Dog,* from the Harvard Medical School and the Angell Animal Medical Center, shares a slew of studies showing that dog owners have lower blood pressure, healthier cholesterol levels, and a lower risk of heart disease than nonowners.[23] Dog owners are also less prone to loneliness, anxiety, and depression than nonowners, the report shows, and having a dog can be like getting a live-in mindfulness coach, it turns out. Your dog encourages you to be in the present moment and notice the joys around you (Squirrel!). The Harvard publication offers advice for using your daily walk as a mindfulness meditation: "When you notice that your mind has wandered—and it undoubtedly will—gently bring your attention back to the sensations of the moment, including your dog's delight at being with you and outdoors."

A 2015 study showed that humans who gazed into their dogs' eyes had increased levels of oxytocin, the "love hormone" that rises when two people are having a loving connection, such as nursing mothers.[24]

We've all probably heard (or experienced the fact) that petting a dog can lower stress. For those with "white coat syndrome," people whose blood pressure rises in front of a doctor about to take their blood pressure—merely picturing a dog can slow their heart rate. A 2017 entry into the dog-as-stress-reducer literature, published in the journal *Social Development,* shared the results of a study of 101 children aged seven to twelve. For those who had a pet dog present, that fact "significantly buffered the perceived stress response" in comparison to the children without a dog— even if the child's parent was there. Certainly, having a dog with behavior problems or medical expenses can be stressful, but for most pet parents, the perceived health benefits outweigh these factors.[25]

Because they love us so steadily and can read our emotional cues, dogs are regularly called in to help people overcome emotional obstacles. We all know people who have gotten dogs to replace or perhaps inspire connection with other humans. A landscaper in central California who describes herself as having "trust issues" got a dog at her therapist's recommendation. "She told me to start with a dog, and worry about human companionship later." Using a dog as a gateway to human trust worked for her, and for countless others who find themselves more comfortable and more outgoing in general since getting a dog. The dog makes it easier, since people will stop to pet a stranger's dog and then look up and greet the human on the end of the leash, too. Some universities have taken to "hiring" dogs to work in the student health center because research shows that coming in to visit with a dog can help these fledgling adults feel less homesick, less depressed, and less in need of medical attention.

Still, despite all these ways dogs assist us, we think the most significant thing dogs do for us is *let us love them*. A dog enables us to express our innate desire to care for another and to feel deeply. We humans have a need not only to be loved but also to give love. Dogs allow us to love them easily. A human being? Not always so simple. Will that person love you back? Will he take your love and use it against you? Will he cheat? Will he lie? Will he steal your stuff? (Will she wreck your car, run off with your best friend, then criticize your faults by text from Costa Rica?) But a dog always has your back. You can love a dog, risk-free. Letting us love them may be the most magical thing they do. It's also key to dogs' amazing ability to help make us better humans.

Bailey, a fluffy cream-and-white goldendoodle, had a good life in Carroll Gardens, a leafy, historic neighborhood in the tony section of New York City known as Brownstone Brooklyn.

Mornings, he'd trot along with his pet parent, Orna Le Pape, to a nearby coffee shop called Henry's Local. As Orna later told *The New York Times,* he'd sit quietly outside, looking around, his leash looped around a metal chair while she ordered, then spend his days at home in her townhouse while she worked.

But one morning, a noise startled Bailey when he was sitting outside the coffee shop. He jumped, knocking over the metal chair he was tied to, making more noise. Bailey bolted, the chair clattering behind him. The chair finally broke loose, and he took off with all the might of his poodle / golden retriever heritage. Orna ran after him, but the dog was faster. In no time, Bailey was around a corner and gone.

Orna spent the day looking for him. Her teenage son designed a flyer to post around town. All that day and the next, Orna looked for Bailey, growing desperate. The dog seemed to have disappeared. What did turn up, however, was completely unexpected: a sense that the entire neighborhood was coming together to help her find her dog. This is New York City, where you can live next door to someone for two decades and never exchange a word. But now strangers were going out of their way to help find this dog. The owner of the copy shop didn't charge to print the flyers. Strangers posted the flyer on their streets and posted photos of it on Facebook. Some people reportedly offered to pray for her dog in church. The owner of a winery in Red Hook, Brooklyn, offered a free tasting and tour as a finder's reward.

After three days, a woman who knew about the lost-dog story caught site of Bailey running in the neighborhood. She took off after him, calling Orna as she ran. She eventually lost site of Bailey, but other strangers saw him, calling Orna with his location.

Finally, sixty hours after he first bolted in fear, a starving, scraggly-looking Bailey made it back to his own stoop, one paw bleeding, but otherwise fine. Orna had her dog back—and a first-hand view of how much a dog can bring out the best in us. As a friend of Orna's later told *The New York Times,* "At a time like this, when there's so much turmoil . . . here's this story that everyone can latch on to and be on the same side. Everyone wants a lost dog found."[26]

There are so many examples of how dogs bring us together. We love a viral video on the Animal Bible's Facebook page called "A Dog in Raging Waters." We've watched this video literally dozens of times. An ordinary-looking black dog finds himself standing in the raging waters of a man-made dam, struggling not to be swept off his feet and over the edge. A group of strangers in the grassy embankment above jump the fence and form a human chain, gripping each other's wrists to lower one man down the steep, sloped concrete wall. He lets go, forges through the water, and grabs the dog, but when he makes his way back to the wall, he can't reach the men above. For a few breathtaking minutes, he keeps trying to throw the dog up to the men, or scramble up himself. But to no avail. Finally, the group flags down a fifth man, who instantly scales the fence, joins the chain, and ultimately saves the dog. It's impossible to watch this video without choking up. (The tense music edited in doesn't help.) As these strangers show, a dog in peril touches us deeply. We can relate, and we drop our guard to pitch in and help.

Learning to care for animals helps us develop compassion for those who are vulnerable, including other people, perhaps without our even realizing it. Nowhere is the humanizing effect of animals clearer than at a place like the Gentle Barn, an animal sanctuary and foster-youth therapy program.

Ellie Laks founded the Gentle Barn in California in 1999 and has since opened barns in Saint Louis and Nashville. The Gentle Barn is a refuge for abused and abandoned animals, including dogs, horses, cows, llamas, and more. The staff spends months or even years helping animals recuperate physically and emotionally and then "recruits" them for the organization's ten-month, hands-on therapy program for kids in foster care or in the criminal justice system. The human program is designed specifically to reach kids who are too injured and shut down to respond to traditional therapy.

Laks describes one session in which a seventeen-year-old boy came to the Gentle Barn after a history of jail time and affiliation with gangs and drugs. He had a teardrop tattoo under one eye, a shaved head, and piercings. He walked into the group with what Laks describes as a "gangster swagger." When Laks asked him for a word that described him, as she does with all kids at the start of each session, he said, "I'm cool."

When Laks brought the kids down to the horse barn to groom the horses, she paired the boy with a beautiful, silvery quarter horse named Caesar. He'd been a Hollywood horse, used in the movies. "This boy was bouncing up and down, being loud, making jokes, and performing for the other kids. He was very inauthentic. Caesar walked to the back of his stall and wanted nothing to do with this kid. A lot of teens who have been affiliated with drugs or gangs or who live in the inner city have learned to be tough and to look and act fake, to have this hard exterior. That may be fine in the inner city, but a horse will have nothing to do with you if you act like that.

"I said to him, 'Look, Caesar has been through really hard times. He's been through a lot of abuse. He always had to play a part, and no one cared what he actually felt or thought. He had a very fake exterior and kept his interior hidden.' I told this boy it took us three years to heal Caesar and to show him that his likes and dislikes are safe with us. 'Now that he's in a real place, he's looking to make connections with other people who are in a real place. He's sizing you up, trying to find out if you're good to hang with. I wonder if there's anything you can do with your voice and your body to make him think you're safe to hang out with?'"

The boy looked at the horse and then dropped his tough act immediately. He quieted his body, and stopped making jokes and performing. The boy approached Caesar in a gentle way, using a quiet voice and calm body language. The horse instantly responded. "Caesar stood still and let himself be brushed. A hush fell over the barn as all five boys focused on their horses, whispering to them, trying to communicate kindness and gentleness and safety to these huge, vulnerable animals.

"After about fifteen minutes, I said, 'In this moment, right now, what is the word that describes who you are? He looked up at me with tears in his eyes and said, 'Gentle.' I said, 'I want you to know that's who you really are. You're gentle, kind, thoughtful, and real. You can see that Caesar wants to be with you.' The boy had tears streaming down his face. When he left, he hugged me goodbye. He was never cool or fake or gangster again. When he left that program, he was a completely different person."

Laks has dozens of similar stories about suffering children connecting to their softer side by caring for the animals. "A lot of people say animals are healing because they're not judgmental or because they love us unconditionally. But I think they're healing because they connect us back to the love that's within ourselves. We feel loving, nurturing, compassionate, and full of empathy. Those things make us feel good about ourselves."

Feeling worthy improves one's life and one's relationships, a reality that underlies the work of psychologist and author Steven Stosny, founder of CompassionPower in suburban Washington, D.C. Stosny has helped thousands of people overcome resentment, anger, abuse—and even violent behavior that landed them in maximum security prisons. As Stosny puts it, "Resentment and anger make you feel more powerful, but not more valuable. It's a tragic substitution of power for value. Compassion and kindness make you feel more humane and more valuable. Then you don't feel as vulnerable and you don't need the resentment. The world looks very different when you are creating value than when you are devaluing."[27]

Those of us with dogs get to see ourselves as valuable, nurturing, and awesome every single day.

WHERE, OH WHERE, IS NUTRITION IN ALL THIS?

Despite our growing awareness of the value dogs add to our lives, and what we can do for them, one part of our relationship with dogs has not kept up: the food we feed them. Even many of the most educated, dedicated dog owners have a gap in their knowledge when it comes to dog nutrition.

The modern dog began to evolve away from a now-extinct type of gray wolf sometime between ten thousand and thirty thousand years ago.[28] While researchers continue to debate when and where, exactly, this evolution took place, they all agree that dogs are biologically and temperamentally distinct from wolves. Behaviorally and nutritionally, dogs are more similar to humans than to wolves in many ways. Dogs' digestive systems are more like ours than like wolves' in terms of the ability to process carbohydrates.

In a classic experiment comparing wolves to dogs, all of the canine participants could figure out how to get food out of a trick box. But when the box was then changed so that the door to the box would no longer open easily, the dogs looked to their human handlers for help. They wanted the treat, and they wanted the people to get it for them. The wolves, however, when faced with the locked-box problem, never once gazed at the human handlers. They kept working at the box until they figured it out.[29]

For wolves, finding food on their own is part of survival. But for our pet dogs, we run the kitchen. They rely on us and give us so much in return. It's up to us to take our job as Nutrition Manager seriously.

Still, dogs can't eat exactly what we eat. Just as dogs are not floppy-eared, friendly wolves (despite the dog feed commercials suggesting otherwise), so too are they not fluffy, four-legged humans. Dogs have unique characteristics and abilities—and they need a high-quality, dog-specific diet for optimal health.

As more and more of us are choosing fresh, whole food for ourselves, we are questioning the wisdom of feeding our dogs ultraprocessed food for their entire lives. We know that an unhealthy diet can cause health problems for humans. Pet parents are saying to themselves, "Dogs do so much for us, but are we really doing the best by them with these little brown pellets in a bag?"

Today's super high-tech specialty hospitals can do so much for dogs. Many pet parents pay for health insurance and shell out hundreds, if not thousands, of dollars for medical treatments once something has gone wrong. Pet parents often will spend whatever they can to extend or save a dog's life. But as specialty veterinarians practicing in oncology, dermatology, internal medicine, or other areas note, by the time they're called in, it's usually very late in a disease progression. They're in repair mode, trying to make up for what went wrong. The best time to protect your dog's health is before he gets sick, including by exercising him properly and feeding him real food.

When it comes to dogs, food matters to them as much as it does to us, if not more. Like humans, dogs are what they eat. Nutrition affects everything about dogs—their ability to behave, their personality, their energy level or lack thereof, the development and persistence of illness, their coat, their teeth. We believe that delicious, high-quality food is *more* important for dogs than for us because their lives are simpler than ours, meaning food plays a much larger role. In one day, your dog will eat, sleep, play, eat, wrestle with his toys, try to get you to pet him, and . . . eat. Sure, his life is enriched by other things such as going for a walk or taking a car ride and sticking his head out the window. But he isn't going to school or to work. (Or, if he is going to the office, he's lying around while you work, probably thinking about food.) He doesn't date, plan to lose five pounds, train for a marathon, or draft a new business plan. Food is one reliable source of joy, a high point of every single day.

What your dog eats is also more controllable than what you eat, because you provide that food; he doesn't have to rely on his own willpower to stick to a healthy diet. Feeding our dogs is not only our duty and a main point of connection with them but also an opportunity for us to treat them as well as they treat us. Think about how much your dog loves you, and then imagine if your dog were making *your* meal choices; wouldn't he find the most delicious and healthy options he could?

But dogs don't choose our meals, of course, or theirs. Over the thousands of years of living with us, dogs have learned to rely on us. If turned loose in the woods, your dog would not become a hunter. He'd find his way back to your house and wait for you to fill his bowl. Yes, dogs will also eat pretty much anything dropped on the floor or street. Some dogs will gobble up items left on the counter, too—a plate of half-eaten chicken, pancakes, a scarf. But what they *will* eat and what's nutritionally optimal are not the same thing. We make the food choices for our dogs, and since no dog we've met will reject fresh, whole food, there's no reason for them to suffer the consequences of a poor diet.

Dog food as a distinct category was an invention of the late nineteenth century. The idea of a special food for dogs, one that is highly processed and superconvenient, was a business inspiration that boomed into a multibillion-dollar industry.

We give those early inventors a lot of credit for the idea, and for recognizing that dogs have their own nutritional needs. But as business opportunities grew, globalization made outsourcing cheaper. And, as the wealth of pet parents increased, the industry took on a life of its own—ignoring some of the latest nutrition science and, as you'll see, at times ending the lives of the very animals it was designed to nourish.

3

A Biscuit in Every Bowl

The Invention of Dog Food

> If you pick up a starving dog and make him prosperous, he will not bite you. This is the principal difference between a dog and a man.
>
> —*Mark Twain, American author*

To you, morning may sound like the coffee maker gurgling. To most dogs, it sounds like hard kibble hitting the bowl. This was not always the case. The idea of premade, packaged food for dogs was a flash of business creativity of the late 1800s, made possible by the manufacturing capacities and wealth that had been growing ever since the Industrial Revolution. Dog feed was an early start-up, and when it arrived, it took off like a greyhound at the track.

What's in the bowl and how it's marketed has changed along with other key shifts in our economy and society, in peacetime and in war. You can trace the major economic and social transformations of the past 150 years by following the trail of dog food—or dog *feed,* as we call the commercial product now regulated by the feed industry.

For centuries, dogs ate what we ate—our leftovers. Pets of the ultraprivileged, the kings and those in their courts, might have dined on roast duck or foie gras. Dogs of the working class might eat meat scraps, if their pet parents had the means to buy meat. If not, they'd scarf down the same boiled vegetables and rough bread their human companions ate or forage for food wherever they could find it.

But a dog's dinner started to evolve from the purely pragmatic to the philosophical. Already in the mid-1800s, what you fed your dog was a question not only of wealth but also of which prevailing philosophy of nutrition you followed—for yourself and for your dogs. Without much in the way of good, solid nutritional studies, so-called "experts" of the day were left to issue opinions about what dogs—and humans—should eat. One British dog expert insisted that meat was bad for dogs, causing physical and behavioral problems, such as making a dog too amorous.

But then all that changed. Around 1860, as the most widely known story about the invention of dog food goes, an American electrician visiting England had an entrepreneurial vision that transformed the daily diet of dogs around the world.

James Spratt of Cincinnati, Ohio, traveled to England for work. While there, he saw street dogs in the northwestern seaport of Liverpool scarfing down hardtack. Hardtack is a dry, puck-like foodstuff made of flour, water, and sometimes salt that sailors carried on long ocean voyages to curb hunger because it was practically nonperishable. Bland and barely nutritious, hardtack served as a superefficient way to quiet hunger pains in the absence of fresh food.

To hungry street dogs hanging around the docks, hardtack was a treat. Watching these dogs gobble down biscuits, Spratt suddenly had a business inspiration. What if he created purpose-made biscuits for *pet* dogs, such as those kept by wealthy English gentlemen for hunting? Wouldn't an avid sportsman buy a special food for his dogs?

Spratt created a beefed-up version of hardtack, literally, blending flour with beef blood, as well as beetroot and vegetables.[1] In a move that future dog feed makers would follow, he outsourced the production to a factory churning out other commercial food products, in Spratt's case, a biscuit company called Walker, Harrison and Garthwaite.[2] Spratt unveiled his creation in England in 1860: Spratt's Patent Meat Fibrine Dog Cakes. His new company, Spratt's Patent Limited, became the first large-scale commercial dog biscuit operation in the Western world.[3]

Pet parents sat up and took notice. As Spratt had guessed, wealthy pet parents were willing to shell out the shillings for a special food for their hunting dogs. By 1900, Spratt's Patent Meat Fibrine Dog Cakes were sold throughout Europe and the United States.[4] The company then unveiled varieties for dogs with real and imagined special needs, a step future kibble companies would also adopt. Spratt's offered Patent Charcoal Dog Cakes for canine sour stomach, Patent Cod Liver Oil Old Dog Cakes, and Pet Dog Cakes, which, according to Spratt's ads, were "especially valuable for pets kept in the city."

OTHER INDUSTRIES NOSE IN

For a few decades, Spratt had the corner on the dog biscuit market. But then other types of businesses began to notice the new market of dog owners. Biscuit makers were an obvious entrant into this newly invented industry. Walker, Harrison and Garthwaite, the baker for Spratt's, introduced its own dog biscuit.

In the early 1900s, a small bakery on Manhattan's Lower East Side called the F.H. Bennett Biscuit Company began mixing up dough for dogs. It introduced to the market a bone-shaped dog biscuit called Milk-Bone (which contained cows' milk, hence the name).[5] Milk-Bone was a huge success stateside, and many of us grew up with red cardboard boxes of Milk-Bone dog treats in our cupboard. When Milk-Bone was introduced, it was more than a treat; its makers envisioned it as a complete meal.

In Boston, a company called Potter and Wrightington had been canning Boston Baked Beans and Boston Brown Bread since the late 1800s.[6] Potter and Wrightington moved into milling whole-grain flour for health-conscious humans, which it sold under the name Old Grist Mill. Old Grist Mill introduced two types of doggy dough: a hardtacklike Boston Terrier Biscuit and softer loaves sold as Old Grist Mill Dog and Puppy Bread.[7]

A popular industry around the turn of the century was the patent medicine business, for humans and dogs. "Patent medicine" is a term generally referring to elixirs and cure-alls of dubious utility that were marketed aggressively with outrageous claims in the mid- and late 1800s. Many of these were not actually patented.[8] The patent medicine craze existed for animals, too.[9] Around 1900, the Boston-based A. C. Daniels Company, one of the most successful makers of veterinary patent medicine, introduced Medicated Dog Bread, targeted at owners of ailing dogs.[10]

One of the most significant entrants into the dog food business was yet another thriving U.S. industry—livestock feed producers. Feed producers were essential to the success of American farmers, creating reliable products to feed cows and chickens, pigs and horses. Purina began in 1894 in Saint Louis, Missouri, and quickly became a leader in the animal feed industry. It soon branched out into people food with the introduction of a cracked wheat hot breakfast cereal. In 1902, Purina's president and cofounder, William H. Danford, decided to align the cereal more closely with good health by securing the endorsement of a well-known (though, as it later turned out, deeply flawed) health food promoter of the day, going by the name of Dr. Ralston. Danford changed the company's name to Ralston Purina to reflect the new focus on health. In 1926, Ralston Purina introduced a pellet-style, grain-based feed for dogs.

Dog food started out as animal feed, and it remains regulated as such to this day. Feed and food are very different things. Feed, then as now, is, made from different ingredients than the food we eat and produced under different conditions. As safety regulations evolved to protect the human food supply, animal feed was not subject to these same rules. Feed is regulated, certainly, but for the needs of livestock—or, rather, for the needs of the farmers who raise livestock. Livestock animals are "grown," to use the industry term, for quick slaughter. These animals live anywhere from thirty days to about a year before they are killed.

Increasingly, veterinarians and food scientists believe that some health problems in dogs and cats under regular veterinary care stem from eating nothing by processed feed for ten or twelve or fourteen years. Despite the amazing advances in veterinary medicine, dogs still don't live much longer than they ever did. The life span of golden retrievers, for example, is commonly believed to have dropped from about fifteen or sixteen years in the 1970s to more like ten or twelve years now.

The nonprofit Morris Animal Foundation recently launched a long-term study designed to track the health of three thousand pet goldens to record incidences of cancer over the years, which has grown common in the breed.[11] Some professionals point to processed feed as a potentially leading cause of dogs' stagnant or even declining life span. Livestock eating feed only live a handful of months or years—not enough time to manifest long-term, diet-related issues.

Another difference between feed and food is its point of sale. Feed is sold at feedstores, not the grocery store. Before the 1930s, dog food was, too. In many homes, dogs still occupied a role closer to horses than housemates, making the feedstore a logical location to buy dog feed. Also, animal feed is made from leftovers of human food production, the scraps and bits deemed inedible for humans. Selling this stuff next to the noodles and fresh produce in the grocery store (also a relatively new invention) just seemed unsanitary.[12]

Dog feed is still made from the scraps of the human food chain, but it's sold, of course, right next to real food in grocery stores everywhere. This change in venue happened as a result of industry pressure. In 1931, the National Biscuit Company purchased F.H. Bennett Biscuit Company, makers of Milk-Bone. National Biscuit was a Manhattan-based conglomerate of commercial bakers that sold its products in grocery stores; it had contacts with grocery store buyers, the people responsible for filling the shelves. The National Biscuit Company pushed grocery retailers to carry its new offering, bone-shaped dog biscuits. National Biscuit succeeded in this effort, and Milk-Bone became the very first dog feed to be sold alongside human food. This opened up the world of grocery stores to other dog feed manufacturers, giving them easier access to urban pet parents, who did not have livestock hanging around the barn. This transition also made sense with the shifting demographics of the nation. As more people moved from farms to cities, they bought dogs as pets to have animal companions.[13]

The National Biscuit Company later became Nabisco, and the change of sales venue it pushed through stuck. But the actual rules and regulations around dog food didn't change. It's still considered feed, and still made from some pretty disgusting ingredients that you would not want the rest of your family to eat. In a recent FDA video called "Pet Food and Treats in Your Home," available on YouTube, a nutritional scientist from the FDA warns viewers that humans can become ill, or even die (if they're immunocompromised), from touching contaminated pet food. She cautions pet parents to wash their hands after touching pet food, as well as to use warm water and soap on any surfaces and utensils it came in contact with, to protect against potential salmonella poisoning.[14]

A BUSINESS BUILT ON BRANDING

From the beginning, marketing drove the success of commercial dog feed. Since dogs can't share their precise opinions about this blend or that and since actual information about dogs' nutritional needs was scarce, early dog feed purveyors made all kinds of claims about their products.

Purina's first president, William Danford, was known as a hard worker and something of a marketing genius. After World War I broke out, Danford heard returning soldiers referring to their food rations overseas as "chow."[15] Patriotism was high. Americans at home proudly contributed to the war effort in various ways, including by buying federally issued Liberty bonds and thrift stamps.[16] Danford began marketing Purina's livestock feed as "animal chow," the name suggesting that our farm animals, too, were helping us battle "the Hun" (the Germans) and needed rations for the fight. When Ralston Purina introduced its own version of feed for dogs, in 1926, it named this food "Dog Chow." Because feeding a dog is part of fighting for freedom.

Before Purina came up with the notion of dogs as defenders of the American way, Spratt, too, was paying careful attention to the language he used to market his food. From the start, he went for snob appeal, promoting his Meat Fibrine Dog Cakes as a "superior" way to feed pets. The biscuit maker he used, Walker, Harrison and Garthwaite, also pursued an elite market for its own dog products, commissioning such beautiful, full-color illustrations for its ads that the vintage images are still sold by auction houses, archive services like Getty Images, and on eBay.

Spratt's ads were also attractive. Oscar was so captivated by a poster of an elegant art nouveau Spratt's ad in deep orange and mustard yellow that he saw in Paris on vacation during his first year of vet school that he bought it, framed it, and hung it on his wall. "I was drawn to it and thought I'd put it up in my office when I graduated. I had no idea that it was the first-ever dog food."

In the United States, Spratt advertised at one of the nation's very first dog shows. The dog show was a new amusement, dreamed up largely by a group of sportsmen who used to meet in a bar at the Westminster Hotel in Manhattan. They'd get together to boast about their hunts and their hunting dogs, calling themselves the Westminster Breeding Association. In 1876, when preparations were being made for the nation's upcoming centennial and the Centennial Exposition being held in Philadelphia in its honor, the Westminster Breeding Association decided to launch a huge dog show in conjunction with the exposition.[17] For Spratt, what better place to attract the attention of people with time, money, and concern with the perfection of the *Canis familiaris*? He advertised his cakes at the show. The Westminster Breeding Association, meanwhile, went on to become the Westminster Kennel Club and, in 1884, to establish the American Kennel Club.[18]

From the early days, what we fed our dogs reflected not only our economic landscape but also our concerns about ourselves. Health food was on the mind of many Americans around the turn of the twentieth century—healthful grains, in particular. In Michigan, John Harvey Kellogg, who was working at a sanitarium, introduced Kellogg's Corn Flakes as a health food in 1894. The Boston-based mill Potter and Wrightington proffered what it called, "hygienic health foods for family use." What's good for the parent is good for the pup, many dog feed companies reasoned. Early ads stress the health benefits of the advertised brand and, often, the inferiority of other options.

A. C. Daniels, the veterinary patent medicine company, claimed that competitors' blends could cause, "constipation, indigestion and skin ills." Its Medicated Dog Bread, in contrast, was made with "the best winter wheat, rice meal and fresh meat."[19]

A Potter and Wrightington ad appealed to grain-focused pet parents:

OLD GRIST MILL DOG BREAD
It Is Better Than Beef[20]

An early Spratt's ad goes after table food. It shows a Scottish terrier trying to climb a tree, from which hangs table scraps and soft food. In bold letters, the ad proclaims:

Barking up the wrong tree!
Spratt's dog biscuit foods are specially baked to a degree
of hardness that suits a dog's teeth and digestion. Spratt's
Biscuits provide, in concentrated form, energising and
sustaining ingredients in correctly balanced proportions.[21]

Certainly some early dog feed makers strove to create truly healthy foods for dogs. Some, like JustFoodForDogs and others, still put a dog's health first. But commercial dog feed was—and is—largely assembled from scraps of the industrial food business. These get processed, packaged up, and peddled to diners who can't complain and aren't in charge of choosing their meals.[22] Dogs get fed what we no longer need—such as, in the early days of the dog feed industry, horses.

CAN DOGS EAT HORSE?

Americans don't eat horses. While there have been dark moments in U.S. history when horses were slaughtered and sold like steak, "chevaline," or horsemeat, has never been a truly popular "other brown meat." Since the founding of the United States, horses have been our co-workers and companions. They're part of our national origin story. Horses are loyal, beautiful, and *fast*. Horses are our second-best friends (after dogs, that is).

These "living machines," as they were sometimes called, carried laborers and their supplies across the nation. Before the invention of the car, the horse was the major form of transportation. Horses helped build other forms of transportation, too—railroads, canals, ferries, and ports.[23] They hauled heavy tilling equipment to create new farms and helped settle the West.

In the cities, too, horses played a critical role. In New York City alone, 150,000 horses trotted through the streets at the end of the 1800s. Horses pulled the earliest public transportation, two at the helm of each twenty-person "horse car" that served New York City back then. Horses were also the first bike messengers and shipping trucks, carrying documents between offices and trotting manufacturing materials and goods from railroad docks to factories and from factories to shops.[24]

Horses also created early urban blight; each of these massive, four-legged creatures let loose some twenty-two pounds of poop a day on the crowded streets, a problem that plagued residents and the street-cleaning commissioner at the time. This was long before the invention of the now-ubiquitous plastic poop bags dog owners carry. (And horses would need very large bags.)[25]

But then the horse car began going the way of, well . . . the horse and buggy. Motor cars began edging horses off the road in cities and in rural areas (the might of their engines measured in horsepower). The Ford Motor Company sold its first Model A in 1903.[26] By 1912, cars outnumbered horses in New York City. The city's last horse car made its final run in 1917.[27]

The automobile was conquering the West, too. As early car dealership magnate Charles Howard put it in 1908, "The day of the horse is past and the people in San Francisco want automobiles."[28] By the end of the 1920s, there were 23 million registered automobile drivers.

We still depended on horses for some things. In 1914, when World War I broke out, draft horses and mules were needed to transport munitions to soldiers. In Missouri, Guyton and Harrington became the largest mule supplier in the world, breeding and selling nearly two hundred thousand mules and nearly the same number of horses to the British army between 1914 and 1918.[29] The Veterinary Corps were responsible for the health of the small cavalry, and some early veterinarians got their start caring for those horses.

After the war, all the horses being bred to ship overseas found themselves stuck at home, without a job. They weren't needed for war and were no longer so valuable for transportation. Horse racing was becoming a popular pastime, but even this amusement left hundreds of thousands of horses hanging around eating hay without a purpose—at least from the perspective of those who bred and fed them. After centuries of helping lead the charge in peace and in war, our long-standing four-legged partners were effectively tossed on the discard pile.

What to do with all those animals? What about dog food? Horse kill factories soon became yet another industry to see a new market in dog feed. One of the most successful horse slaughterers turned dog feed maker was The Chappel Brothers, located in Rockford, Illinois.[30] The Chappel Brothers created a horsemeat-based canned dog feed that they named Ken-L-Ration. After some initial resistance from pet parents and feed suppliers, the idea of dogs eating horsemeat took off.

In the early years of the Roaring Twenties, Ken-L-Ration became one of the first canned dog food brands, and the first widely distributed horsemeat-based blend. The company paid horse wranglers to bring it ingredients, as in horses. In one memoir of those years, a horse wrangler describes buying "killer horses"—those purchased specifically for slaughter—to supply to a dog feed factory at ten dollars a head.[31]

A few other companies soon offered versions of horsemeat-based canned dog feed. The U.S. horse and mule population in total had peaked at nearly 30 million in 1915, due to the demand for horses on farms and to convey equipment on the battlefield. But mechanized tractors and other equipment soon pushed horses off the farms, and the end of World War I meant no more horses were needed to help fight.

Throughout the 1920s, the number of horses in the United States began declining at a rate of about five hundred thousand a year, most sold to meat-packers to be made into dog feed, bone-meal, leather, or glue, according to the Humane Society Institute for Science and Policy. By 1960, there were only about three million horses left in the United States.[32] The number of dogs? Within a decade or so, about 35 million pet dogs lived with us.[33]

The massive changes in our economy and society had in some ways shrunk the size of our animal companions. The move from farm to city or suburb and from horse to automobile didn't end our connection to animals; it just changed it. We still loved our four-legged friends—just shorter, cuddlier, fluffier ones.

The dog feed industry grew like a golden retriever puppy—fast and furious, stumbling over itself. Canned dog feed was a huge part of its success. Even during the Great Depression, when so many other industries collapsed, pet feed stayed strong. Some of these sales were probably due to hungry humans prying open cans for themselves. The need to find protein at a low price—even if it came from horsemeat—accounted for as much as 20 percent of sales, by some estimates. Some analysts consider pet care, including dog feed, a consumer staple, and one that has remained relatively recession-proof.[34]

By 1934, American pet parents purportedly were spending $40 million a year on dog feed. The numbers continued to sky-rocket. By 1936, Americans spent more than $100 million on pet feed a year, most of it canned.[35] Within a handful of years, canned dog feed accounted for 90 percent of the market.[36]

The Chappel Brothers horse-to-feed business was so successful that Quaker Oats bought the company in 1942.[37] (It was eventually sold to H. J. Heinz Co., in 1995.)[38]

Meat-packers that slaughtered and processed animals for human food took note of this new market and saw in it a way to utilize their discards. Some, including Armour and Swift, began using the remains from the meat production process in their own canned varieties.[39] In Chicago, a dog feed company called Rival began relying on grade B beef purchased from area meat-packers to make its own canned feed.[40] By 1936, the robust pet feed industry was the nation's second-biggest user of tin cans.[41]

Then World War II broke out. Our Allies, and later our own troops, needed all the metal they could get. The properties that make tin particularly good for canning—waterproof, long-lasting, lightweight—made it great for shipping supplies needed to fight a war. It's hard to imagine a shortage of packing materials now—with Amazon boxes arriving by the hour pretty much everywhere—but at the time, metal shortages led to metal rationing. In 1942, the U.S. War Production Board ordered a reduction in the use of metals for packaging consumer products. If you wanted to buy a canned good, such as a tin tube of toothpaste, you had to turn in the old tube first. The manufacturing of all kinds of daily products also came to a stop, including radios, metal furniture, vacuum cleaners—and canned dog food, which was considered a nonessential item.[42]

But pet parents had grown used to the idea of buying a special feed just for their dogs. What could they feed their dogs now?

Dry dog food! The young and growing pet feed industry responded to the crisis in canning by churning out more dry feed and promoting a slew of supposed benefits to feeding dry. One upside of dry was easy to talk about: the ease for humans. In the midst of the challenges of war, from casualties overseas to food shortages at home, dry dog feed was refreshingly pleasant and simple. It was also less messy and smelly. As a satisfied Spratt's Patent Cat Food customer put it, dry food was "both handy and cleanly."[43]

Dry dog feed soon overtook canned as the industry leader. But the use of horsemeat in dog feed didn't completely fade away. A newspaper advertisement in *The Toronto Blade* from July 1950 features a cartoon dog and cat talking about how they used to argue about what to eat. But not anymore:

One day our master brought home some Ken-L-Ration. We both love it because it's made with LEAN, RED MEAT and is good for us too! Every can of this famous food is packed with choice cuts of lean, red meat—nutritious, U.S. government inspected horsemeat.[44]

Very early television ads, which you can still see on YouTube, feel so sweet and old-timey, it almost makes you nostalgic for the days of horsemeat in cans. Almost. In one TV commercial, three small children each hold a floppy puppy and sing about how "My dog's better than your dog" because he's bigger, faster, and shinier because he gets Ken-L-Ration.

Horsemeat was again (briefly) on (some) tables in the United States in the early 1970s. Horse slaughterers continued to kill and ship horsemeat overseas until 2007, when our nation's last horse-slaughtering outfit closed.[45] But horsemeat can still be imported, and there is no federal law preventing its use in dog feed. It certainly seems risky for a company to use horsemeat in dog food today. But as recently as May 2015, the state of Illinois filed a formal complaint against an Evanger's plant in Wheeling, Illinois, citing unlicensed use of horsemeat, along with other violations. The Illinois inspection and complaint came after a report of unsanitary conditions at the plant. The plant's records, according to the Illinois complaint, showed a pet food for sale with horsemeat listed as its main ingredient, despite the fact that it lacked a license to process horsemeat. This lack of license was the violation cited, *not* the use of horsemeat itself. That Evanger's dog feed plant obtained a license to process horsemeat the following year, although reportedly it has since let the horsemeat license expire.[46]

THE CRAVING FOR CONVENIENCE

The productivity of U.S. factories was a decisive factor in winning World War II. After the war, those same factories kept going, churning out low-cost consumer items. Many economists point to postwar mass production as intrinsically tied to the rise of the American middle class. Factory workers earned good salaries, and foremen even better ones. Incomes rose while prices dropped. The GI Bill allowed unprecedented numbers of Americans to buy homes and go to college, both of which helped sustain the economic boom. More people moved to the suburbs, and supermarkets sprouted up: aisle upon aisle needing to be filled—with more stuff.

The postwar years marked the beginning of an era of abundance, and the pet food industry capitalized on the growing wealth, rise of consumerism, and increasing attachment to the family dog. It was no longer only English gentlemen with hunting dogs who could afford a special food for their dogs. Many average pet parents could, too. The dog feed of choice soon became kibble.

For many American families, after the war years of scraping by and making do, *ease* became the new ideal. In dog food, the convenience of dry feed was very alluring. As the anthropologist and social historian Mary Elizabeth Thurston, author of *The Lost History of the Canine Race*, asserts, while many people used dry dog feed out of necessity during the war, it now became a strong preference: "The notion of a mass-produced, machine-processed pet food—inexpensive, easy to serve, and touted as superior to home cooking—was increasingly appealing to busy urban consumers, and commercial pet food became part of the new status associated with being 'modern.'"[47]

Pet feed manufacturers emphasized the convenience of kibble in their ads, such as one by a company called Kasco:

Feeding a dog is simple today. It is unnecessary to cook special foods, measure this and that. Why bother when it takes less than a minute to prepare a Kasco meal for your dog?[48]

Gaines introduced its super-speedy dry dog feed Gravy Train in 1959. Its commercials told pet parents that adding water would "Gravy it up!" Because making gravy out of real meat takes too much time. (Gravy Train, now owned by J. M. Smucker / Big Heart Pet Brands, has $40 million in annual sales. It was also tied to a pentobarbital recall in 2018.

Even Ken-L-Ration got in on the convenience craze, promising:

No Thawing—No Cooking—Ready to Serve.

Once again, what people fed their dogs reflected what was happening in their lives, and what was on their own plates. People, too, were gorging on processed food, eagerly whipping up and shoveling down the latest, fastest, foodlike invention. Such as Cheetos, introduced in 1948—like cheese, only crunchier.[49] While families had been buying Kraft Macaroni and Cheese since 1937, now they could also serve up precut slices of cheese, soon known as the individually wrapped Kraft Singles.[50] Presliced cheese was followed by an even faster cheese: Cheez Whiz.

Because processed food lacks the flavor of fresh—despite the added sugar, salt, and fat—some early ads for convenience foods resembled those of dry dog feed. Many companies ignored those aspects of food previously considered of utmost importance, such as nutrition and taste, focusing on speed and ease instead.

Soon, many American home chefs were coating their chicken and fish with Shake 'n Bake, serving it with a side of Rice-A-Roni or Minute Rice, and baking Betty Crocker's chocolate fudge brownie mix for dessert. We grew accustomed to being unable to pronounce many of the words on the ingredient label, let alone find them in our gardens. While a simultaneous interest in fresh, local produce began sprouting in the 1960s, particularly in Northern California, the desire for convenience above all took root in households across the nation, and it continues today.

Convenience food for two- and four-legged Americans got a huge boost from another invention: the extruder. What the internal combustion engine was to transportation, the extruder was to food, and then to dog feed. Extrusion changed the nature of what we consider food.

THE BIRTH OF KIBBLE

To extrude means to push out, like Play-Doh through a plastic die or toothpaste through the tube. But extrusion technology when applied to foodstuffs also involves cooking, either in the extruder, out of the extruder after passing through it, or at both times. Extrusion technology existed to some degree in the prepared food industry before World War II, of course. The first extrusion machine was a piston-and-ram type that squeezed out sausages. This was followed by a continuous pushing process that created the noodles for Kraft mac and cheese and the crunchy bits of Wheat Chex, Ralston Purina's breakfast food bestseller.[51] But extrusion technology made huge strides after World War II. Better methods and machines expanded the number and variety of convenience foods exponentially.

In the midst of the extruded food frenzy, two Purina executives had an insight: Chex cereal was so crunchy and appealing to people, wouldn't dogs also enjoy munching on fun shapes of crunchy food?[52] In 1954, these two employees borrowed an extruder from Purina's breakfast cereal group; packed it with ingredients dogs might like, such as meat scraps, meal, soybeans, and grains; and cooked it up.[53] The mixture came out hard and crunchy and apparently pretty flavorful. "It tasted similar to popcorn," one of these kibble creators later wrote. The dogs who tried it also approved. Kibble as we know it was born.[54]

Purina's marketing team decided that this special foodlike feed should be sold in the grocery store alongside human staples, rather than in the feedstore. In 1957, Purina Dog Chow in its new, extruded form appeared alongside Milk-Bone on the grocery shelves. Pet parents were soon hooked. Kibble by Purina—a "distinctively shaped" dog feed, as Purina describes it on its website, quickly outpaced Gravy Train to become the bestselling dry dog food in the world.[55]

THE FIGHT AGAINST FRESH FOOD

From biscuits to cans and from cans to kibble, the dog feed industry had become a commercial force. By the mid-twentieth century, the market for pet food was firmly established, and lucrative. More companies moved into the business, such as Carnation. Founded in Kent, Washington, in 1899 to sell condensed milk to gold prospectors en route to Canada's Yukon Territory, by the 1960s Carnation became a pet food industry leader with its Friskies brand.[56] Liggett and Myers, makers of Chesterfield, L&M, and Lark cigarettes, perhaps sniffing the winds of change, entered the dog feed business.[57] The tobacco company bought the Allen Products Company, makers of Alpo, in 1964.[58]

In 1958, pet feed makers formed their own trade association, the Pet Food Institute, which remains active today. But then something interesting happened. Almost immediately after the Pet Food Institute formed, news and feature articles began appearing touting the superiority of commercially sold dog feed over home-cooked food. In newspaper after newspaper and magazine after magazine, the supposed benefits of commercially sold dog feed were being explained. Why did so many journalists suddenly have an interest in commercial dog feed?

In *The Lost History of the Canine Race*, Thurston describes reading the minutes of a meeting of the Pet Food Institute in the early 1960s. As she tells it, one PFI member was talking about the success of the group's ongoing PR campaign against home-cooked food. This effort, as Thurston writes, had yielded placement of a kibble-and-cans-only message in articles appearing in a thousand daily and weekly newspapers and in magazines such as *Good Housekeeping* and *Redbook,* as well as on nearly a hundred radio stations.[59]

Certainly, there are risks to feeding your dog nothing but table scraps. For one thing, some human foods are toxic to dogs, such as onions and garlic (see chapter 9). A family's dinner of meatloaf laced with onions is not a meal for a pup. Other foods are too fatty for dogs, such as steak trimmings, pork belly, or fried chicken skin, and can cause digestive issues. Additionally, a dog's nutritional needs differ from a human's. As we explain in chapter 11 and the recipe section of this book, and in all of our recipes online, "people food" needs to be nutritionally balanced for dogs, ideally with a vitamin mix designed for them. But we don't believe that the pet feed industry was strictly trying to steer dogs away from onions. This sounds to us like a marketing move designed to convince pet parents that dogs must eat commercially made feed, processed, packaged, and sold by pet feed makers, and nothing else. It was an (admittedly pretty brilliant) PR effort to corner the market on the bowls of hungry, four-legged Americans.

And it worked. In 1959, the *Sioux Falls Argus-Leader* ran a piece entitled "Killing with Kindness?" It included this advice:

> According to the Pet Food Institute, authorities in the field of canine nutrition are unanimous in their agreement that the regular feeding of nutritionally inadequate table scraps or other foods meant for human consumption will shorten a dog's life.

The piece goes on to tell readers:

> If you wish your dog to live longer, be healthier and more intelligent, it becomes essential to provide him with a regular diet of either canned or dry dog food (or both), one that is sold by a reputable manufacturer.

And finally, the article notes:

> Fortunately, modern dog foods are as palatable as they are nourishing, and most dogs eat them even more eagerly than they gobble up leftovers.[60]

Articles like this, often citing the Pet Food Institute as a source, appeared around the nation, and for years. Some were part of otherwise warmhearted features about our love for dogs, such as the *Tallahassee Democrat*'s feature about National Dog Week. The article warned against human food for dogs and offered this plug for kibble:

> Prepared pet foods are scientifically balanced to provide the nourishment a dog needs for good health and good looks.[61]

Perhaps the biggest early PR coup was a 1961 holiday article put out by United Press International, a wire service that supplied articles to some six thousand newspapers, magazines, and TV and radio stations at its peak. The feature was about buying dogs for Christmas, and included these lines:

> The puppies given for Christmas—some 700,000 of them by the Pet Food Institute's estimate—will take a lot of care for the next year.

Then, later:

> A quality, prepared dog food will supply the necessary balance of protein, carbohydrates, fat, minerals and vitamins.
>
> Begin by mixing the dog food—canned or dry—with warm milk and cereal, gradually increasing the portion of dog food until weaning food is eliminated.

And don't forget:

> Most puppies are beggars, but try to resist the temptation to give them table scraps and snacks. Too many 'people-food' treats and table-scraps make for an overweight, finicky dog.[62]

By the late 1960s, the voice of the pet feed manufacturers had been heard—and heeded. Within a few decades, as Thurston puts it, perhaps a bit dramatically, "A whole generation of consumers now could not recall a time when pets ate anything but commercial dog food, and the campaign to discourage alternative food sources had been so successful that some consumers were fearful of feeding their dogs even a piece of soda cracker."[63]

In our business today, we still hear this concern about fresh food for dogs, from consumers and from some vets: "But I thought dogs can't eat people food!" It's frustrating to us that this belief persists, as dog lovers and as purveyors of fresh food for dogs.

By 1974, more than half of all U.S. households had pets. Pet food sales reached an estimated $2 billion a year, surpassing sales of coffee and baby food. Pet feed had become the best-selling category in the dry grocery market.[64] By 1991, pet feed sales reached a peak of more than $8 billion a year. Kibble and canned food took up more shelf space in many supermarkets than breakfast cereal.[65]

The pet food industry kept morphing, impacted, as always, by broad economic and social forces in the human world. Beginning in the mid-1980s, a few major trends began changing the face of the business: consolidation, globalization, and money in medicine. These developments wound up hitting dogs hard, paving the way for commercial dog feed larded with unhealthy, adulterated, and even deadly ingredients.

Big Kibble had arrived.

PART TWO

The Kibbles and Bits

4

The Rise of Big Kibble

Consolidation, Globalization,
and Kibble Cash in Vet Schools

> The better I get to know men, the more I find myself loving dogs.
>
> —*Charles de Gaulle,*
> *President of France, 1959–1969*

Do you trust the kibble in that bag on the shelf? If you're like a growing number of American pet parents today, you probably don't, at least not entirely. In a recent survey conducted by the market research firm Packaged Facts, nearly 60 percent of dog parents said that when choosing dog food, fear of contamination or of unsafe ingredients was a key consideration. Nearly 70 percent of dog parents expressed at least some concern.[1]

The relative low cost of most kibble, which for a long time seemed like an unmitigated good, now points to part of the problem. The fact that we can feed a thirty-pound, four-legged member of our family on less than one dollar a day should—and increasingly does—make many people worry. What must happen in the supply chain and processing today for so-called food to be this cheap?

Conversely, a higher price doesn't always mean better quality.

Even as the price of processed pet feed has steadily risen, particularly for "premium" brands that charge upward of one hundred dollars a bag, many pet parents worry about the frequent news reports of tainted commercial pet feed and "killer kibble," even among some of the most expensive brands.

How did we get here?

For starters, consolidation, a trend that has swept through business at large and contributed to some dire circumstances for dogs. After the early days of individual entrepreneurs from Cincinnati making biscuits for dogs and Lower East Side baking companies following suit, big companies began gobbling up little ones like a hungry dog let loose at a Fourth of July picnic.

TASTES LIKE CONSOLIDATION

On a hot June day outside an Austin Walmart, the blacktopped parking lot radiates heat, like a grill primed for searing meat. Pet parents turn off their air-conditioned cars and hurry through the heat into the supercooled store to pick up supplies. Texans have big choices when it comes to feeding their dogs, or so it seems.

Here in Cedar Park, a bedroom community spread out between downtown Austin and the Texas Hill Country, you might swing by the closest Walmart to pick up a bright red bag of Ol' Roy kibble, stacked up for the taking, fifty pounds for $19.98, as of 2019. Ol' Roy is one of the least expensive and top-selling dog feed brands in the country, a private label product sold in Walmart, named after Sam Walton's dog, Roy. Private-label feed, like private-label clothing or food, is that which has been manufactured in a third-party plant, usually one that produces for many customers on the same production lines, perhaps with the same basic ingredients. The feed is then packaged and labeled with the name of the company selling it, in this case Walmart.

Most private-label pet feed factories finish one order, then go on to churn out kibble for the next client.

On the other end of the price-per-portion spectrum in Cedar Park is Natural Pawz, a store for boutique pet products located near a big, airy Sprout's and a natural cosmetics retailer, around the corner from the popular barbecue restaurant Smokey Mo's. Here's where health-minded pet parents able to spend more come to do well by their good dogs. At Natural Pawz, that same twenty dollars gets you four pounds of dry dog feed—if you choose a bag of Merrick Backcountry Raw Infused Great Plains Red Recipe with Beef, Lamb and Rabbit. Or, for close to thirty dollars, you can buy four and a half pounds of Orijen's Regional Red Dry Dog Food. If you do the math, you realize that fifty pounds of either of these brands would cost you upwards of two hundred dollars.

Some in the pet feed industry point out that premium brands go further than budget ones because they pack more calories per cup. But that's still a pretty big price difference among bagged kibble at two different stores.

Somewhere in the middle, from the point of view of price and exclusivity, is PetSmart, offering everything from the bestselling budget brand Pedigree to celeb-founded pet feed by Rachael Ray, which costs less than Merrick but still about five times as much as Ol' Roy.

Well, you might think, *it must be worth it. It's superduper premium. Plus, Rachael Ray! She's so trustworthy.* Surely, Merrick and Rachael Ray are independent brands, hand-cooked by chefs in airy kitchens? After all, look at the price. And the commercials.

Look in the bag, however, and what you see and smell and touch (washing your hands afterward) is all the same—hard brown pellets that are shelf stable for years. Even when the ingredients listed on the bags sound exotic—ostrich! highlander beef!—those "premium" proteins are not generally the same cuts humans eat, nor those shown in the photos on the bag. And they've generally been processed at kibble factories. (Though some brands now add freeze-dried bits, the base is still processed feed.)

There are also a growing number of nonkibble options at pet specialty stores, including fresh, whole-food brands like JustFood-ForDogs, smaller companies offering dehydrated options, and truly independent brands. But these remain small players relative to Big Kibble. While today you see what looks like a huge variety of dog feed brands on the shelves, this apparent diversity masks an industry dominated by six major multinational corporations.

Rachael Ray's Nutrish, for example, was bought in 2018 by J. M. Smucker, one of the five largest kibble companies in the world. Merrick, that Texas-born maker of natural and organic pet feed, was bought by the multinational powerhouse Nestlé Purina PetCare in 2015, a year after the megacorporation gobbled up another small, boutique brand, Zuke's Performance Pet Nutrition.

Consolidation in pet feed isn't new. By 1974, five corporations already controlled most of the product on the shelves: Ralston Purina, Quaker Oats, General Foods, Liggett and Myers, and Carnation.[2] But in the latter part of the twentieth century, consolidation accelerated across industries. More nonpet multinationals threw in billions to get in on the kibble craze. In 1984, Switzerland-based Nestlé bought industry powerhouse Carnation for $3 billion, the largest acquisition outside the oil industry at the time.[3] A decade later, H. J. Heinz bought the classic brand Ken-L-Ration from then-owner Quaker Oats. In 1999, Procter and Gamble bought the premium brand Iams for more than $2 billion. The industry contracted again in 2001, when Nestlé purchased Ralston Purina for $10.3 billion, renaming its new pet division Nestlé Purina PetCare Company.

Another consolidation trend emerged: multinationals pursuing ownership of premium-priced, independent brands to attract pet parents avoiding budget-priced, seemingly less safe kibble.

In 2018, for example, General Mills bought the boutique brand Blue Buffalo for $8 billion.

In 2018, there were at least fifty-one announced mergers and acquisitions by pet feed producers, equipment makers, and suppliers—and companies outside the pet feed industry. Some of these were major players swallowing up other companies, large and small, such as J. M. Smucker's purchase of Ainsworth Pet Nutrition (Rachael Ray) and Nestlé Purina's purchase of the majority of custom dog feed maker Tails.com. Cargill bought a private-label pet food manufacturer called Pro-Pet. Tyson, the Arkansas-based multinational that is one of the world's largest producers and sellers of chicken, beef, and pork, bought a way to dispose of the unusable chicken bits and turn them into dog feed. It acquired American Proteins's poultry rendering and blending facilities and American Proteins's subsidiary, AMPRO products, which makes animal protein feed supplements.[4] (Chicken feces and parts such as beaks and feathers can go into dog food, as it turns out. See chapter 5.)

Private equity firms swallowed up pet feed makers, and companies of one type of pet product or service bought others, such as Mars Petcare purchasing a DNA diagnostics company focused on eye problems in dogs called OptiGen, veterinary corporations, the veterinary laboratory Antech Diagnostics, and several other veterinary service providers.[5]

For pet parents, all of these mergers and acquisitions mean you don't really know who's making the feed in the bag, where they are making it, or with what ingredients it is being made. There are certainly some truly independent kibble brands on the shelves, but you often can't tell who they are by reading the label. The pace of consolidation means that an independent brand today might be a multinational tomorrow. Certainly, some multinationals buy boutique brands and allow their once-independent subsidiaries to continue operating as usual. Nestlé, for example, has said that its new "premium" brand, Merrick, is still made in separate factories and never with any ingredients sourced from China. But not all purchasers preserve the suppliers and/or manufacturers of their acquisitions, and even when they do at first, they may change these unique practices over time to conform to those of their other brands.

Small does not necessarily mean safe when it comes to kibble. In May 2018, Merrick recalled five different types of treats under the Merrick Backcountry and Castor and Pollux names after a dog got sick from them. Also, we worry that some independent companies' formulations may be questionable. Some of the boutique grain-free kibble brands have been implicated in a recent uptick of diet-related dilated cardiomyopathy cases, and we suspect that the formulations may be at fault.

The Kings of Kibble

It may look as if you're buying a premium brand from a small company, but a handful of international conglomerates own nearly all of the brands on the shelves today. The pace of consolidation means that who owns what keeps changing, but here's a look at the top Big Kibble companies and their earnings, as of the most recent numbers compiled by PetfoodIndustry.com.[6]

Kibble King #1: Mars Petcare

Annual Revenue: $18,085,000,000. Production plants: 63

Mars Petcare's parent company, Mars Inc., is the world's seventh largest private company, with annual sales of more than $33 billion. The Petcare division is huge, and hugely profitable. Mars Petcare owns forty-one different brands, including five brands worth at least $1 billion each. In

2014–15, Mars Petcare bought 90 percent of Procter and Gamble's pet food business for $2.9 billion. Mars sells pet feed throughout North America and Latin America, as well as in Australia, Eastern and Western Europe, Africa, the Middle East, and Asia.

Mars owns Pedigree, Iams, Whiskas, Royal Canin, Cesar, Eukanuba, Sheba, and Temptations, Banfield, Blue Pearl, and VCA pet hospitals, and Antech Diagnostics, one of the few veterinary laboratories in the country.

Kibble King #2: Nestlé Purina PetCare

Annual Revenue: $13,200,000,000. Production plants: 46; total facilities: 58

Purina may seem like Good Old American chow, but Switzerland-based Nestlé bought Ralston Purina in 2001, making it part of one of the largest multinationals in the world. Nestlé Purina operates pet food factories in nineteen countries and has three global headquarters, including just one in the United States, in Saint Louis.

Nestlé owns Purina, Purina ONE, Purina Pro Plan, Alpo, Bakers, Beggin', Beneful, Beyond, Busy, Castor and Pollux, Cat Chow, Chef Michael's Canine Creations, Deli-Cat, Dog Chow, Fancy Feast, Felix, Friskies, Frosty Paws, Gourmet, Just Right, Kit & Kaboodle, Merrick, Mighty Dog, Moist and Meaty, Muse, Pro Plan Veterinary Diets, Second Nature, Waggin' Train, and Zuke's.

Kibble King #3: J. M. Smucker / Big Heart Pet Brands

Annual Revenue: $2,900,000,000. Production plants: 6

J. M. Smucker makes many classic-sounding brands of pet feed and snacks, and runs processing plants in

Alabama, Kansas, and New York and distribution centers in Kansas and Pennsylvania. In addition to its own brands, J. M. Smucker manufactures private-label pet products for other companies. In 2015, J. M. Smucker bought Big Heart Pet Brands (formerly the pet division of Del Monte Foods, after a merger with Natural Balance Pet Foods in 2013). In 2018, J. M. Smucker acquired Ainsworth Pet Nutrition and Rachael Ray's Nutrish.

J. M. Smucker owns Meow Mix, Kibbles 'n Bits, Milk-Bone, 9Lives, Natural Balance, Pup-Peroni, Gravy Train, Nature's Recipe, Canine Carry Outs, Milo's Kitchen, Snausages, Meaty Bone, Rachel Ray's Nutrish, and Dad's.

Kibble King #4: Colgate-Palmolive / Hill's Pet Nutrition

Annual Revenue (Hill's): $2,318,000,000. Production plants: 6; total facilities: 7

A subsidiary of Colgate-Palmolive, Hill's sells more than three hundred pet care products. The pet care division accounted for 15 percent of Colgate-Palmolive's worldwide net sales in 2017. Hill's operates manufacturing and warehousing facilities in Kentucky, Kansas, and Indiana, as well as the Czech Republic and the Netherlands. Its primary research center is in Topeka, Kansas.

Hill's owns Science Diet, Prescription Diet, Ideal Balance and Healthy Advantage.

Kibble King #5: Diamond Pet Food

Annual revenue: $1,500,000,000. Production plants: 5

A privately held, family-owned company, Diamond makes three brands of feed for dogs and cats. Based in

Meta, Missouri, Diamond has factories in South Carolina, California, and Arkansas.

Diamond owns Diamond, Diamond Naturals, Diamond Naturals Grain-Free, Diamond Care, Nutra-Gold, Nutra-Gold Grain-Free, Nutra Nuggets Global, Nutra Nuggets US, Premium Edge, Professional, Taste of the Wild, Bright Bites snacks, and others.

Kibble King #6: General Mills / Blue Buffalo

Annual revenue: $1,300,000,000. Production plants: 1; total facilities: 5

Now a subsidiary of the multinational corporation General Mills, the Blue Buffalo Company started in 2002 as a maker of high-quality, superpremium dog food. By 2012, it had reorganized into the Blue Buffalo Pet Products Corporation, and it continued to gain market share. In 2014, Purina sued the brand for false advertising, causing Blue Buffalo to pay a hefty settlement. Blue Buffalo in turn sued its pet food ingredient broker and supplier. But the promise of superpremium feed continued to attract customers. By 2015, Blue Buffalo raised $677 million in its initial public offering. In 2018, General Mills acquired Blue Buffalo. Blue Buffalo now has about 6 percent of the U.S. pet food market.

General Mills / Blue Buffalo owns Blue Buffalo Basics, Blue Buffalo Wilderness, Blue Buffalo Freedom, Blue Buffalo Life Protection Formula, and Blue Buffalo Natural Veterinary Diet.

Consolidation exists down the entire chain in the pet feed industry, from the ingredient suppliers to the manufacturers to the sales representatives visiting the stores—or not visiting. Consolidation can make it harder than it used to be for a person selling dog feed at a small, local store to get good information about what's in the food and to pass on those facts to pet parents.

Chase Champlin is owner, along with his parents, of Newtown Feed and Supply. This independent pet and wild bird supply store, known for its award-winning custom birdseed blends and birding products, sits in a 120-year-old clapboard house, painted a fresh, pale green. The historic structure is located next to a dairy bar and a small, leafy park in Newtown, Ohio, a farm town turned four-way crossing on the outskirts of Cincinnati. Inside the two-story feed supply store, it looks like time has stood still ever since the buggy parked on the narrow-plank oak floors was operational and ruled the roads.

The Champlins bought Newtown Feed about a dozen years ago. A lot has changed in that short time, it turns out. When they took over the store, Chase says, they purchased dog feed from a local supplier. "The rep would come in and check on me. He'd bring samples and toys for my dog. It was a sales pitch, sure, but they kept you up to date on what was happening in the market."

Then, that supplier got bought by a larger distributor, which in turn was purchased by another one. Today, the Champlins buy dog feed for their store from Pennsylvania-based Phillips Pet Food & Supplies, a company with fifteen distribution centers around the country that prides itself on its convenient online ordering process. No sales rep drops by to chat about the feed. "The reps cover Indiana, Ohio, and Kentucky," says Chase, who used to have the feed representative's number saved on his phone. Now he places his order online. "Without the personal contact directly from feed manufacturers, I am left to personally research the products I sell in order to keep my customers current on market changes."[7]

For the pets who eat the feed, consolidation can have even more troubling consequences. A megacorporation can reap huge savings by sourcing the same ingredient from one supplier to use in hundreds of different brands. If that ingredient is toxic, it can show up in dog feeds as seemingly different from each other as Alpo and Zignature. This has proved deadly for dogs in part because of another major trend in manufacturing and business that has emerged in the past few decades: globalization. As international trade has grown, so has the ease with which dangerous ingredients can find their way to consumers around the world, including our nation's dogs.

WHEN "MADE IN THE USA" MEANS SOURCED FROM CHINA

Investigative reporter and mother of two Katherine Eban is a big dog lover, and a lover of big dogs. Romeo was her second Newfoundland. If you've ever seen a huge black animal lumbering down the sidewalk and thought, "Is that a bear on a leash?!" you've seen a Newfoundland.

Romeo is a massive, sweet-souled, 187-pound bundle of fur who likes to sit on the stoop of the family's brownstone and watch over the neighborhood. "It's like *Sesame Street* where we live, and he's like Snuffleupagus," says Katherine. "I hear people walking past, saying, 'Hey, Romeo. How are you?' He's like the hood ornament for the whole block."

Katherine's kids were six and eight when she brought Romeo home. Newfies are considered great family dogs despite their size, because they're so gentle and quick to learn. Most Newfies, that is. Romeo was a wild puppy, chewing everything, "impervious to training, indifferent to direction. Not in a willful way. Just in a relaxed sort of way." It took him months to grasp the concept of house-training. "Our wood floors were buckling because he'd pee inside, and he's like an oil tanker; he's so huge. When we walk him now, he'll go for ten minutes, just standing there, creating a giant lagoon of urine." But the family loved him immediately. So when Romeo became violently ill at fifteen months, Katherine was determined to save his life—and to discover what had gone wrong.

It was December 2015, and Katherine had left town for a few days for a work-related research trip. When she returned, Romeo was acting very strange, in a frightening way, drooling, panting, and chewing frantically at the fur on his front legs as if he wanted to rip it off. The skin underneath was fire-engine red, and raw. "It was really scary," says Katherine. She rushed him to the vet, who induced vomiting. The vet put in an IV drip and announced that Romeo was having an extreme allergic reaction, possibly life-threatening.

But to what? What could have happened during Katherine's short trip? What could be so toxic as to cause an allergy that could possibly kill a 187-pound dog?

The vet ran some lab tests, which turned up antibiotic residue in Romeo's urine. This residue suggested that he'd eaten something laced with a particularly toxic type of antibiotic, or a type that he, at least, was highly allergic to.

Katherine contacted the dog sitter to find out what, exactly, had happened while she was away. Nothing out of the ordinary, the sitter assured her. Romeo had gone to the dog park, played outside, and also eaten a *lot* of treats that she'd brought along. Dogswell treats. She still had the bag. It said, "Vitality for Holistic Wellness Duck Strips" printed right on the front and included salt, molasses, and flaxseed as part of the recipe.

Was it the treats? Katherine spent the day calling the L.A.-based dog-treat maker Dogswell to find out if there had been other reports of allergic reactions to the treats, but she was unable to get a live person on the phone. She also turned to the Internet to do some research.

As it turned out, the FDA had been investigating pet jerky

treats since 2007. In 2012, the agency had issued a consumer warning about jerky pet products imported from China—not specifically those sold by Dogswell, but rather those from all brands. By the end of 2015, the time that Romeo got sick, the FDA had received complaints about some 6,200 dogs falling ill after eating chicken, duck, or sweet potato jerky treats; 1,140 dogs had died from them. The illnesses and deaths were most often, though not always, linked to jerky pet treats sourced from China.[8] In 2019, the FDA was still researching these illnesses and deaths, and trying to identify the exact ingredient in the treats that caused them. As of this writing, the precise cause remains unknown.

The New York State Department of Agriculture and Markets had also been looking into problems with jerky treats from China, Katherine discovered. During testing in July 2013, the New York department had found traces of an antibiotic that is illegal in the United States but not in China in treats made by Dogswell.[9] Dogswell had issued a voluntary recall of its Happy Hips chicken and duck treats, and seven other varieties of treats made from those same fowl, including Vitality, which is the kind Romeo had eaten.

But a voluntary recall does not mean that all of the product immediately disappears from circulation, or from pet parents' homes.[10] Nor does it mean that the media necessarily hears about it, or that the company has changed its suppliers or practices.

During her research, Katherine came across the blog Poisoned Pets, run by blogger / pet food "detective" Mollie Morrissette. Eban reached out to Morrissette, who stepped in to share her own research and offer support and advice. Morrissette said she'd been looking into just this kind of life-threatening reaction to treats and suspected sulfonamide poisoning, a dangerous allergic response some dogs have to a class of antibiotics called sulfa drugs. Sulfa drugs are illegal to use on livestock in the United States but are commonly used in countries like China.[11]

When Katherine ran the sulfonamide theory past her vet, he said it had merit; Romeo's reaction looked a lot like sulfonamide poisoning. For Katherine, this news was deeply upsetting and surprising. How could Dogswell be sourcing its duck treats from China when the package has an American flag right on the front and the words "Made in the U.S.A." printed on the bag?

As it turns out, a label on dog feed or treats that reads "Made in the USA" does not guarantee that *every single part* of that product comes from this country. As the FDA explained in an official 2018 release about the treats, "Manufacturers are not required to list the country of origin for each ingredient used in their products."[12] The Federal Trade Commission mandates that "virtually" every part of a product with this label must be made in the U.S., but the agency has never established a precise legal limit for "virtually," meaning companies are left to decide on their own how much to outsource from (probably cheaper) overseas suppliers.[13] This is true, as Katherine learned, even when the label clearly reads, "Made in the USA."

In practice, this loose use of the phrase "Made in the USA" is beginning come under fire, and as of 2020, a number of lawsuits challenged companies using this language on products with ingredients sourced globally. Still, plenty of pet parents have unknowingly fed their dogs products riddled with ingredients sourced from China.

Anyone with an Internet connection can access the New York State and FDA news releases about jerky treats, and even internal memos from FDA inspectors who have toured dog feed plants. But most pet parents don't peruse internal government memos before handing out a treat. Katherine knew companies could use low-quality ingredients from industrial-scale operations, and she considered herself a savvy consumer. But Chinese fowl being plied with antibiotics prohibited in the United States? That possibility hadn't been on her radar. Despite her job as a professional sleuth and industry skeptic, and her love of dogs, Katherine hadn't come across the FDA's 2012 warning about jerky treats from China. She hadn't heard about the Dogswell recall or read the FDA's end-of-2015 summation. Before Romeo got sick, she, like so many other pet parents, believed that the supposedly high-quality commercial dog feed and treats on offer would be safe.

Romeo got better, but many other dogs were not so lucky. And even for him, it took time. He had to have a round of steroids for the inflammation. The redness didn't go away, and his fur was slow to grow back. The experience left Katherine deeply suspicious of the pet feed industry, yet still unsure if the brand of feed she finally chose is truly safe.

JERKY FROM CHINA? WHAT IS GOING ON?

Globalization in big business isn't new or unique to kibble. Nor is it inherently a bad thing—for business or for consumers. Our global economy has brought products, ideas, and real income to people living all over the planet and increased profits of American businesses greatly.

U.S. companies have long operated factories overseas, to some degree. In the 1980s, globalization really heated up. The growing strength of European and Asian economies—and import tariffs in those lands—made producing products for foreign markets economically advantageous. Many U.S.-based companies opened factories within those countries to better meet the needs of these new markets. This was true in all kinds of businesses. In 1989, Oren Shaffer, the then chief financial officer of Goodyear Tire and Rubber Company, shared this view with a reporter in *The New York Times*: "If you really want to be a player, you have to be inside foreign markets. You can't export."[14]

But then globalization began to change once again. More and more U.S. companies began manufacturing goods in overseas factories to sell to consumers back home in the United States.

The low cost of manufacturing in places like China, along with ever-improving communication technology, better trade routes, expedited shipping, and free trade agreements led many of our favorite brands to buy huge numbers of parts from overseas to import for use in factories here and to do the assembling overseas, too. Despite plenty of talk from politicians and businesses about keeping manufacturing jobs in America, many corporations began seeking the cheapest possible place to purchase supplies and produce products—and still do. By the time the FDA issued its first warnings about jerky from China, globalization had long been standard operating procedure for many U.S.-based businesses, transforming the supply chain of entire industries from automobiles to zippers.

When it comes to pet feed, many classic brands that seem as American as apple pie, or as *Lassie Come Home*, began operating basically as assemblers of finished products, sourcing ingredients from all over the world to make into pet feed here. In 2012, global imports of pet feed ingredients had reached about $4.5 billion. This was double the amount from a decade earlier, according to the USDA.[15]

Of course, the United States is not only an importer of pet feed products but also a huge exporter of pet feed to the growing number of pet parents around the world. Overall, the value of the U.S. pet feed export market grew by nearly 30 percent between 2007 and 2013, reaching a record $1.3 billion in 2012. Globalization obviously has benefits, and when it comes to overseas factories, the jobs they provide can raise the standard of living for communities in developing nations. Factory work offers steady employment and income for things like nutritious food, health care, and education—particularly in factories adhering to good labor practices. Certification programs for factories, which are similar to Fair Trade or Organic certification for coffee, are helping spread safe practices to factories around the world. The Worldwide Responsible Accredited Production Program, or WRAP, for example, sets workplace standards for things like pay, hours, benefits, and health and safety of employees that are aligned with the International Labour Organization's conventions.[16] Factories that seek and obtain the WRAP certification are subject to lengthy third-party audits to check for compliance.[17]

But not all factories are certified or safe. Lack of regulations and oversight can be bad for workers and for the consumers of the products they make. When manufacturing overseas is cheaper due to lax regulations, unsafe and unsanitary conditions, and/ or substandard ingredients, globalization can be a disaster. From 2014 to 2016, multinational pet feed manufacturers were discovered to be linked to slave labor in the production of fish meal, a calamity that they likely knew nothing about but that was possible due to unregulated factories and a variety of unsafe practices overseas.[18] Nestlé admitted in 2015 that seafood caught by forced labor had entered its supply chain. As the Associated Press noted, reports had "tied brutal and largely unregulated working conditions to their shrimp, prawns and Purina brand pet foods." Fish caught by slave labor was tracked into the production of Fancy Feast, Meow Mix, and Iams.[19]

At the time of the Newfoundland Romeo's run-in with duck treats, pet parent Katherine Eban was deep into research about the generic pharmaceutical industry for what would become her *New York Times* bestselling book *Bottle of Lies*. She was investigating manufacturing plants in China and India, taking photos of conditions that could lead to truly dangerous and even lethal drugs for humans, as well as reviewing the factories' internal documentation about purchasing and other practices. She was appalled by what overseas manufacturers can get away with when it comes to products created for *people*. "These plants I was touring are a catastrophe, and much more heavily regulated than those supplying ingredients for dog food. If these plants were such a disaster for humans, what does that tell you about less-regulated plants making food or treats for dogs?"

It tells you nothing good.

It may seem totally illogical that pet feed manufacturers today would risk the health of their own customers by sourcing ingredients from China after thousands of dogs grew ill and died from Chinese-sourced jerky. After all, don't recalls and dog deaths damage their brands? And also, don't people enter this business because they at least *like* pets? Why start a dog feed company if you don't care about dogs? This is an argument we often hear in defense of Big Kibble or in support of a particular person's favorite brand: "Kibble can't be as bad as people claim because no company would kill off its own customers. Also, dog lovers go to work for dog feed brands."

Of course, people throughout the Big Kibble supply chain love dogs. And as we are seeing, both those within the industry and pet parents are beginning to look harder at the supply chains of even these established brands. But from a legal perspective, deterrents against unsafe sourcing aren't in place. And without serious legal repercussions, dangerous practices still happen. As Joan Schaffner, a law professor at the George Washington University Law School and an animal rights activist, explains, all animals, including dogs, are considered "property" under U.S. law. If a dog dies, the responsible party traditionally only has been liable for what's called "fair market value"—the dollar cost of replacing the dog. "Unless you have an expensive show dog," says Schaffner, "most people's pet companions maybe cost $150 if adopted from a shelter. Thus, it's not worth the effort to sue, and thus, the industry is not held liable."[20]

In the last few years, some courts have been adjusting the compensation given when a companion animal is killed—by kibble, say, or by a crazed neighbor. Tennessee and Illinois now have statutes that allow for more than fair market value in the loss of a pet, and some individual courts around the country have informally or even formally recognized that "fair market value" is a small amount of money that seriously underrepresents the true value of a dog to a person. Losing a dog that cost $150 is very different from losing a table lamp that got knocked over and broke. Courts have some discretion when awarding damages, and some have adopted "value to the owner" as the proper standard. Still, most courts around the nation don't allow for noneconomic damages—those that represent the companionship value of the dog to the owner.

Another big problem with the fair-market-value doctrine for dogs is that tort laws, which these are, are designed to influence behavior. No real punishment means no legal reason to behave admirably. "Tort laws," (which are civil laws, as opposed to criminal laws), "are designed to regulate conduct—to set a standard of care to avoid harm," says Schaffner. "If someone knows the law and knows what it will cost if they violate it, they will behave in a manner to not be held liable. But how carefully they act is a function of the potential damages they'll have to pay. As a practical matter, if a manufacturer knows that damages for harming an animal are $150, they're not going to care, especially since most people will not sue for such a small amount of money. However, if it costs the manufacturer $10,000 for every animal harmed, they will take a lot more care to make sure that the product they place on the market is safer."

Of course, class action suits can cost companies real money—or their insurance companies, rather—when they harm thousands of animals. But individual pet parents still don't get much, and overall the current fair-market-value doctrine doesn't adequately protect our pets or pet parents from harm.[21]

If the law changes to acknowledge the true value of pets, that could have other ramifications, such as raising liability and insurance costs, not only for manufacturers of dog feed but also for others, such as veterinarians, dog walkers, and groomers. These costs could be passed on to pet parents. But when it comes to dog feed, this cost is likely small when spread across all pet parents, and we believe that recognizing the true value of dogs more generally is for the greater good.

When it comes to sourcing from China, Big Kibble continued outsourcing as usual, even after a far *worse* contamination scandal rocked the pet feed world, a full decade before Romeo got sick.

KILLED BY KIBBLE

In 2007, something very strange and upsetting started happening in the United States. Happy, healthy dogs were gobbling up various brands of commercial pet feed, then dying. What could be going on?

The dogs were ingesting melamine in their feed, it turned out. Initially it seemed as if the melamine had just gotten into canned pet feed. But then it turned up in kibble. At first, it seemed to be just mass-market, less expensive dog feed, like Alpo. But then it showed up in higher-end brands, too.

If melamine sounds weirdly familiar—like maybe plastic?—that's because it is. Melamine is the material used to make durable tableware: plastic plates with images of flowers and sturdy plastic forks and spoons. But melamine, which is largely nitrogen-based, can also register as protein in lab tests because of the nitrogen, it turns out. If dogs and cats eat melamine-laced food, it can lead to kidney disease and kidney failure.

The melamine-tainted ingredient was introduced into pet feed as early as December 2006. Two Chinese suppliers to the dog feed industry—a processor/exporter of plant proteins and an export broker—were responsible. In 2008, a federal grand jury indicted them on 26 counts for intentionally adding melamine to wheat gluten to boost the protein levels in lab tests. As the FDA reported, "The indictments allege that more than 800 tons of purported wheat gluten, valued at nearly $850,000, were imported into the United States between November 6, 2006, and February 21, 2007."[22] A third company, the Las Vegas–based importer ChemNutra, was also indicted.

Twelve different manufacturers in the Big Kibble supply chain unknowingly purchased the contaminated gluten from ChemNutra, including Hill's, Mars Petcare, Nestlé Purina PetCare, and Procter & Gamble. This contamination led to the biggest pet food recall in history, from budget options to so-called premium ones. The Canadian-based company Menu Foods manufactured nearly two hundred brands of wet and dry dog feed using the contaminated ingredient, including Natural Balance, Science Diet, and Royal Canin. Melamine was also found in rice protein imported from China and incorporated into pet feed.

ChemNutra pled guilty to two misdemeanors. About one hundred class action lawsuits were filed, and consolidated into one, in which more than thirteen thousand people said their pets had died from eating melamine-laced feed. Another nine thousand said their pets had become sick from it. Pet parents eventually won $12.4 million in the class action suit, though the individuals generally received less than one thousand dollars.[23]

It's illegal in the United States to boost protein content with little plastic pellets. But it had become a little too easy, as it turns out, to buy adulterated products from China and then incorporate them into tens of thousands of cans and bags of dog feed sold here. The melamine scandal was a consolidation-meets-globalization disaster. It was a wake-up call for many pet parents—and even for some people in the pet feed industry. Melamine testing is now required for some human food processing, but as of 2019 testing for it was still not required in pet feed.

What happened in the wake of the melamine scare? Lots of flurried action. Congressional hearings. New pet food safety initiatives. And more contaminants in commercial pet feed—even in feed that U.S. brands *sold back to pet parents in China*—leading to more illness, more death, and more recalls. In April of 2014, exactly seven years later, melamine and its derivative, cyanuric acid, were found in "premium" U.S. brands sold to pet parents in Hong Kong, including Solid Gold, Purina Pro Plan, and Iams. The toxin aflatoxin was found, too.[24]

China's pet food exports kept growing, even after the melamine scare. By 2012, China had become the leading pet food exporter to the United States, supplying nearly half of the U.S. import market of $691 million, with chicken and jerky treats among the drivers behind this growth.[25]

Today, more and more consumers are aware of problems with pet feed ingredients from China. Some pet feed companies are stepping up to address those concerns and protect our dogs by sourcing domestically. Other brands are addressing the *appearance* of safety. One way is through clever wording on the bag. If you picked up a bag of Rachael Ray's Nutrish Real Chicken and Vegetable Recipe in the summer of 2019, say from the Petco in Cedar Park (or plenty of other places), you'd see a bright blue, silver-dollar-size label on the front and one on each side, proclaiming:

Safely USA cooked.

The "USA" is in huge letters. The word "cooked" is much smaller, and in harder-to-read cursive. That word "cooked" is key. All of the ingredients could be sourced from China, and yet J. M. Smucker has not technically lied on the label. But even the most concerned pet parent could easily glance at the bag, feel reassured, and grab it—especially since navy blue is the color most associated with trustworthiness, according to marketing research.

Running along the bottom of the navy blue seal, also in a small font, are the words "world's best ingredients." Does this mean the ingredients are sourced globally, like from China? Also, you have to wonder, Best for whom? Are the ingredients best for our dogs?

Still, if commercial kibble is really so risky, you might be wondering, *Why do veterinarians recommend certain brands of it? And why is kibble sold at veterinary offices and even hospitals? Also, my doctor cautions me against too much processed food; why doesn't my vet?*

One reason veterinarians don't warn pet parents about Big Kibble is that they generally trust it. Veterinary curriculums have historically not offered extensive courses in canine nutrition. Big Kibble, meanwhile, has been long on funding of veterinary programs. Big Kibble supports everything from student scholarships to discounts on pet food. This combination can leave veterinary students, who then become veterinary professionals, with very positive feelings for Big Kibble and less than ideal nutritional education to make them question what's in the bag.

KIBBLE CASH IN VET SCHOOLS

Veterinarians love dogs. Most veterinarians enter the field for very personal reasons. Some veterinarians point to a role model—a father who was a veterinarian, perhaps. Or they cite a childhood experience with a favorite pet. Whatever the reason, most chose this field because of a passion for pets. Being a vet is a calling.

If you ask your local vet, she might tell you about one specific dog or cat. Perhaps she was given an adorable, floppy golden retriever puppy when she was young. It got hit by a car, and the family vet miraculously saved the dog's life. She was so moved by this experience that, years later, she committed herself to the field of veterinary medicine. Or maybe that local vet was unable to save the golden retriever. The little girl decided she'd save other people's dogs as soon as she could. Today, she works at a specialty hospital, saving the lives of seriously injured dogs.

Oscar got his first dog in college. When that dog got sick, he found his purpose. "My freshman year at Berkeley, I was lonely. I just wanted a dog. I knew nothing about pets or veterinary medicine or what puppies need, such as vaccines," he says.

Oscar bought a solid black Lab/dalmation mix from a woman selling pups in the Bay Area and named her Shadow. Shadow went everywhere with him, *before* being vaccinated. Then she started having really bad diarrhea and vomiting. At the emergency clinic, the diagnosis came in: parvovirus, the leading killer of unvaccinated puppies. The vets gave her an injection of antibiotics and fluid under the skin and said they could keep her there overnight, but it would be double the price of standard hospitalization since it was an emergency clinic. For Oscar, on an undergraduate budget, the cost of this treatment wasn't an option. "I brought her home, and the next day started calling around to veterinarians, trying to find another option."

All the vets said the same thing: four to five days in the hospital, minimum, to save her life, and at least two thousand dollars in bills. Shadow would still only have a 50 percent chance of surviving. For Oscar, the cost of this treatment just wasn't an option. Finally, the eighth or ninth phone call yielded a different answer. Dr. Beth Philipson at the Banfield Pet Hospital also said that Shadow would likely die if she weren't hospitalized but that there was one other option: take her home and dispense fluids every four hours under her skin with a "fluid administration set" and inject her with syringes preloaded with antibiotics. "She said she could sell me the equipment and show me how to do it. I was a freshman in college—not yet a vet student—and I hadn't really grown up with dogs. I literally knew nothing about caring for animals. I got a couple frat brothers to wake up with me at 4 a.m. to restrain Shadow while I administered subcutaneous fluids and antibiotic injections."

Shadow got better and would be his best friend for the next fourteen years. Oscar had found a major. He registered in premed and went on to veterinary school. "She's the reason I became a veterinarian."

Being a vet is a calling, but the practice of veterinary medicine can be very stressful. For many vets, much of this stress comes from pet parents, people who love their animals, but don't always remember that their vet does, too. A pet parent might yell at a vet who can't save a dog's life. Or who can help a dog, but only with very expensive interventions. Vets also must see animals suffer and die, year after year, despite the many lives saved. These workplace stressors can add up. The website "Not One More Vet," named after the suicide of a well-known, popular veterinarian, acts as a support group for vets to vent about the challenges they face.[26]

For many aspiring veterinarians, the stress of the job starts with paying for school. The cost of attending vet school, including living expenses, as of 2018, ranged from about $150,000 to upwards of $400,000, depending on the state and the school.[27] Of that year's graduates who'd taken out student loans, the average loan debt upon graduation was more than $183,000, according to the American Veterinary Medical Association.[28] That's a huge bill to bring into the start of one's professional life, especially considering that the median salary for vets was just over $90,000 in 2018.[29] This economic pressure can make vet students grateful for any kind of financial aid. Some of that aid comes from Big Kibble.

Kibble cash flows to veterinary students in a variety of ways, both obvious and less so. Nestlé Purina pours a huge amount of money into vet schools, even promoting this fact in its company literature as proof of its commitment to veterinary education and the human-animal bond. This is a real contribution to veterinary medicine, in many ways. Purina offers cash-strapped, animal-loving vet students (and staff and faculty) at many schools discounts on feed for their own pets. The feed is sold through a structured fundraising program by a university's chapter of the Student American Veterinary Medical Association. Sales of feed help Student AVMA chapters raise money to provide scholarships, cover research conference fees and externship expenses, and help pay for surgical packs for third-year surgery courses.

Other brands offer food discounts, too. At UC Davis, the nation's top-ranked veterinary school, as ranked by *U.S. News and World Report,* students can get discounts not only on Purina but also on Hill's, Royal Canin, and others.[30]

Proponents of these programs say that discounted feed allows students to test different brands on their own animals and develop more knowledge about them. This may be true and also fine—when the food on offer is actually nutritious and safe and when students get real access to options other than kibble. There are many options for feeding dogs today, and it's time for students to experience all of these different kinds of food, not just kibble and cans. Our company is looking into similar ways to give students hands-on experience with fresh, whole foods in order to provide them with at least one alternative to Big Kibble.

Critics say that these structured programs can also "buy" loyalty from future vets for ultraprocessed feed riddled with recalls, biasing these hardworking students—dealing with hefty tuition and future debt—toward pet feed companies with some seriously troubling practices. At Louisiana State University's School of Veterinary Medicine, Purina funded the renovation of the food-preparation room / kibble commissary in 2015, which was then renamed the Purina Nutrition Center. The University of Tennessee has a similar sign over its food-preparation room, and these types of Purina nutrition centers exist at more than one-third of the veterinary schools in the nation. While Purina does not demand exclusive use of its kibble in these centers, certainly their presence and branding create a connection in the mind of vet students between Purina and the concept of good nutrition. It's like a billboard on the grounds of an academic institution and can easily be perceived as an endorsement by the university.

Big Kibble gives money directly, too. Between 2006 and 2016, Purina gave U.C. Davis's vet school a gift of fifty thousand dollars a year, every year.[31] Purina funds biannual lunch lectures, guest speakers, and laboratories at Louisiana State University's School of Veterinary Medicine. All of these (very helpful) efforts create more commitment to Purina. LSU's dean of the school of veterinary medicine, Joel Baines, expressed this reality at the opening of the new Purina Nutrition Center in 2015: "The LSU SVM values its corporate partners like Purina. Partnerships like this one have a direct, positive impact on our faculty, staff, students and patients, and we are grateful to Purina for their generosity and their commitment to veterinary education."[32]

Mary Thurston, author of *The Lost History of the Canine Race*, says she asked vet students about their nutrition classes twenty years ago while on her book tour. "I went to Texas A&M University for a book signing at Borders Books and More. A bunch of vet students came in. I asked them what kind of coursework they had on veterinary nutrition. They said, 'We have none.' A Hill's representative would come in and scare the shit out of them, give them the line about not feeding table scraps, tell them to push Hill's Science Diet cradle to grave, and to stock their waiting rooms with Hill's Science Diet products. Many other kibble brands do the same.

"Back in the 1940s and '50s, the tobacco industry would send doctors to medical schools and do the same things. I really feel the pet food industry was taking its cues from the tobacco industry, touting the health benefits of it or having it be 'doctor recommended.' When I go to my veterinary clinic today, it's still filled with bags and cans of Hill's Science Diet."[33]

Veterinary students and practicing vets often resent the notion that they can't remain objective while accepting scholarships and food discounts. But a slew of research in the field of human medicine raises some questions about this likelihood. One study, published in *JAMA: The Journal of the American Medical Association*, showed that medical students are influenced by money in medical school. The study authors found that med students often feel entitled to freebies by drug makers, value the information presented by these pharmaceutical companies, and believe they can remain objective about what they hear, while their peers likely can't. The study authors conclude that this combination of attitudes means med students are likely influenced by the gifts they receive.[34]

In another study, published in *PLOS ONE* in 2014, researchers sent an online survey to 1,388 doctors, asking about their interaction with pharmaceutical sales representatives and their perception of their own prescribing habits. Researchers then cross-referenced the responses against data about the doctors' actual prescriptions over the course of a year. Researchers concluded that doctors who avoided industry-sponsored continuing education classes had more rational prescribing habits than those who attended such classes and that "gift acceptance and the belief that one is receiving adequate information from a PSR (pharmaceutical sales representative) are associated with changed prescribing habits."[35]

As with medical students and doctors, the concern is that veterinary students and working vets may be influenced by industry. The feed programs on campus could mean that a veterinarian may start with a brand in college and continue to recommend it throughout his professional career. Years later, even as evidence mounts against Big Kibble, that doctor can feel an abiding sense of loyalty to and even personal identification with the kibble brand, and a real reluctance to upend all he knows to make a change. We've talked to thousands of veterinarians through our work who absolutely are open to embracing a new way of feeding dogs, and have joined the mission to bring fresh whole food to dogs. But the concern about long-standing bias remains.

Meanwhile, nutrition education in veterinary schools can be surprisingly thin. The field of veterinary medicine has made amazing strides in the past hundred years. In the past couple decades alone, technology has helped veterinarians make lifesaving early diagnoses and perform high-tech interventions unimaginable to the country vet of the past. The nation's thirty accredited vet schools offer a rigorous four-year medical training, plus a variety of postgrad specialization programs. But veterinary nutrition has lagged far behind.

At the College of Veterinary Medicine at the University of California, Davis, students take a first-year course that includes one subsection on nutrition in the fall and a subsection on "gastrointestinal" in the spring. Students also do one clinical rotation on nutrition in their fourth year.[36] This amount of nutrition education is deemed suitable and is the gold standard for veterinary education of the accredited schools in the United States.

If you look at the four-year curriculum for Cornell University's College of Veterinary Medicine, the second-ranked vet school in the nation, you'll see no required courses on pet nutrition. The program does cover physiology and the gastrointestinal system as it relates to health and disease, and there is one elective on pet nutrition offered, though not everyone will have a chance to choose that elective. This means a veterinary student graduating with an Ivy League degree from one of the top two veterinary schools in the nation may not have received detailed instruction on canine nutrition.[37]

Tufts University's Cummings School of Veterinary Medicine, in North Grafton, Massachusetts (ranked number 12), has a class called Gastrointestinal Pathophysiology.[38] The University of Tennessee at Knoxville's College of Veterinary Medicine (number 19) has one required animal nutrition course and one elective for small animal nutrition.[39]

Some point to kibble cash in vet schools as the reason nutrition education lags behind other areas. But it may just be a question of time. There's a lot to cover in vet school. And just as we don't expect our primary care physicians to also be nutritionists, it's probably unfair to assume an average veterinarian will have the nutrition knowledge needed to effectively question kibble or to formulate food. Nutrition is actually a sought-after specialty in veterinary medicine, taught through two- to three-year postgraduate residencies, which culminate in a board exam. These residencies are competitive, and certainly dogs would benefit from more opportunities for veterinary school students to do these residencies.

At JustFoodForDogs, we too help promote nutritional education, but with a focus on whole food rather than dog feed. In collaboration with Western University's veterinary school, our veterinary toxicologist and our staff nutritionist have developed a four- to six-week nutritional education program to train fourth-year veterinary students in the formulation of whole-food diets. (See chapter 8 for more on our veterinary nutrition program.)

As far back as 2011, some vet schools began implementing new policies calling for transparency about who's funding what, and even limiting the amount and the kinds of gifts they'll take from the industry. The Association of American Veterinary Medical Colleges approved an ethics document in 2011 that established principles for schools seeking to create conflict-of-interest policies.[40] U.C. Davis was one of the schools that adopted an ethics policy. Still, that policy does not prevent Big Kibble from offering discounted food to vet students in the form of a fundraising program for scholarships.

Consolidation, globalization, money in medicine—these fac-tors directly affect the safety of the little brown pellets that most Americans rely on today to nourish their dogs. Meanwhile, the regulatory agencies can't, or won't, keep up. Pet feed's history of being regulated as feed rather than food has made it possible for Big Kibble to include all kinds of substandard, disgusting, and even outright toxic ingredients, including, as Oscar learned in 2014, essential minerals laced with heavy metals.

5

You Can't Judge a Kibble by Its Cover

Misleading Labels, False Advertisements,
and Lax Regulations That Let It Slide

> If you want a friend in Washington, get a dog.
> —*Often attributed to President Harry Truman,*
> *based on a Truman character in a 1975 play,*
> Give 'Em Hell, Harry, *written by Samuel Gallu*

The Hyatt Regency hotel in downtown Sacramento looks onto the impressive California State Capitol building and its gleaming Grecian columns, massive rotunda, and life-size statue of George Washington standing high atop, overseeing the action below. It feels like the ideal place to hash out official policy, and in July 2014 the Association of American Feed Control Officials (AAFCO) held its annual meeting at the hotel.

JustFoodForDogs was still small back then, and since Sacramento is not so far from our headquarters, Oscar headed up to Sacramento to see how the organization works and to meet some of the people charged with setting the standards for what our dogs eat. This was Oscar's first-ever AAFCO meeting. To us, being at that AAFCO meeting in 2014 at the state capital felt very "big league." But by the end of it, he came to a very disturbing conclusion: AAFCO can operate at cross-purposes with the values of many pet parents—and even, at times, with the health and safety of our pets.

The three-day conference was organized like these kinds of events generally are: big group sessions held in a ballroom with carpeting, padded chairs, and too much air-conditioning, with smaller breakout sessions. At 8 a.m. on Friday morning, Doug Lueders, manager of the Minnesota Department of Agriculture, kicked off the AAFCO meeting with opening remarks.[1] AAFCO members sat at a boardroom-style table on a raised platform facing the hundreds of attendees. Despite the size of the crowd, the AAFCO meeting had an intimate feel. The attendees, sitting in chairs facing the platform, took turns standing and introducing themselves. These were the major players in pet feed: Petco, PetSmart, Purina, Hills, Blue Buffalo, Mars, and Big Heart Pet Brands.[2] And then there was us, a little upstart fresh food company from Southern California.

AAFCO was formed in 1909, and for the past hundred-plus years has actively shaped feed laws and regulations for commercial livestock growing. When it comes to feed, each state is responsible for setting its own rules and regulations, but since these products are sold nationally, states need consistency to facilitate interstate trade. This is where AAFCO comes in, setting model regulations that state legislators reference when they set their laws. Uniformity in regulatory language is a key purpose of AAFCO. As the group states itself, it works "to provide a level playing field of orderly commerce for the animal feed industry."[3]

Dog food was categorized as animal feed from its beginnings, rather than food, and the federal government gave responsibility for defining its ingredients to AAFCO, rather than setting up one federal agency specifically designed to oversee and regulate companion animal food. Today, the FDA has a "memorandum of understanding" with AAFCO that expressly gives AAFCO the job of maintaining the definitions of feed ingredients, publishing them, reviewing requests for new ingredients, and adopting them, in concurrence with the FDA. In 1959, realizing the might and scale of the burgeoning pet feed industry, AAFCO established a separate Pet Food Committee.[4] But the decisions of this committee, sixty years after its founding, still reflect the group's agricultural roots, allowing dogs to eat the same ingredients as livestock, including plenty of things you'd never feed a family member.

AAFCO doesn't have actual enforcement authority over its model regulations. That power is shared between the states and the FDA's Center for Veterinary Medicine. On the FDA website, you'll read that the agency regulates the cans and bags of cat and dog food and the treats that are sitting in your pantry.[5] The Federal Food, Drug, and Cosmetic Act (FFDCA) states that, "all animal foods, like human foods, must be safe to eat, produced under sanitary conditions, contain no harmful substances, and be truthfully labeled."

In actual practice, however, AAFCO sets the standards for what ingredients can go in and what they can be called—and publishes them in a fat, spiral-bound guide called the *Official Publication.* AAFCO's members include each state, the FDA, Puerto Rico, Costa Rica, Canada, the USDA, and several universities.[6] Companies cannot be members, but these model regulations are endorsed by key stakeholders in feed and pet feed, including the American Feed Industry Association, the National Grain and Feed Association, and the Pet Food Institute. As the *Official Publication* states, "From the start, the association has made concerted efforts to work with industry in every way possible, while realizing their primary duty of protecting the consumer."[7]

The collaborative approach of AAFCO means that the pet feed industry offers serious input into the crafting of the very rules designed to curb its behavior. As AAFCO's executive director, Sue Hayes, says, "Our members see themselves as collaborating on feed laws and regulations to maintain uniformity in interstate commerce. The definitions of ingredients are proposed by industry, many times. It's best that it's done that way."[8]

Anyone can attend an AAFCO meeting, if they pay the fee and register online. (The fee can be hefty; $550 for a nonmember who registered early for the 2020 midyear meeting.) The first two days of the AAFCO annual meeting in Sacramento were devoted to the group's main concerns—livestock feed and its related subgroups. There were meetings of the Ingredient Definitions Committee, the Education and Training Committee, and the Inspection and Sampling Committee. The Pet Food Committee meeting was slated for the very last day. Like us, there were a handful of other attendees at that 2014 meeting who had come specifically to hear about pet food and wound up sitting in on the other meetings while waiting for it to start.

Oscar began to feel as if the interests and priorities of the pet food people attending the meeting were somewhat different from those of the main group. The pet food people wound up finding each other and sitting together for most of the three days. "By the end of the conference, I felt like we were the outcasts in high school," Oscar says. "Like no one really wanted to sit with us at the lunch table."

The gap between the pet food people and others at the meeting became most apparent on Saturday, during the Ingredient Definitions Committee meeting. The committee had a whole list of proposed new ingredients. It was going to vote on including them, and how they should be labeled. A representative from Southeastern Minerals stood up. Southeastern Minerals serves the feed industry, as well as other industries, blending trace mineral premixes and other products that are added to feed.[9] (See chapter 8 for more on chemical premixes.) A company representative proposed that zinc hydroxychloride, one of its blends, be approved as an ingredient in pet food and used as a source of zinc.

Zinc is an essential trace element for all animals and a common supplement in pet food. Zinc supports the immune system, helps with cell growth and repair, and aids breakdown of carbohydrates in the body. Zinc hydroxychloride, however, is another substance entirely.

At the Ingredient Definitions Committee meeting, a slide went up with the properties of zinc hydroxychloride, including its chemical formula. As the definition clearly showed, it must contain at least 54 percent zinc, but it also allows for the possible presence of a lot of other things that aren't zinc, such as arsenic, lead, cadmium, and mercury. As Oscar tells it, he and the other veterinarians in the group were shocked.

Wait a minute! Doesn't that definition spell out a bunch of heavy metals? Lead? Arsenic?

To Oscar, feeding this chemical to dogs was a horrifying proposition. He stood up and objected, as did both of the other veterinarians in attendance that day. Zinc hydroxychloride wasn't a safe zinc supplement, these medical professionals insisted. It would mean pet owners would unknowingly be feeding their dogs dangerous heavy metals.

Who would benefit? Oscar wondered. *The mineral company selling the chemical? Big Kibble, which could label the feed as having "zinc" without paying the price of a higher-quality form of this trace element?*

The AAFCO Ingredient Definitions Committee members let the veterinarians speak. But they didn't seem particularly swayed by the health argument, as Oscar recalls. Susan Thixton, a blogger covering the pet feed industry, who then sat on the AAFCO committee as an adviser, also objected to this ingredient. She was pushing for cleaner ingredients in pet feed, not dirtier ones. She said her readers and followers would think it was "heavy metal soup."

As Oscar watched, the committee rebutted, saying that the heavy metal limits meant that only a tiny amount could get into any one dog; the amount was small enough that it didn't really matter. The veterinarians objected again: these heavy metals could also leech into the environment through the animals' waste and impact humans. The committee expressed the belief that any environmental impact would also be minimal, Oscar remembers. Plus, good news—using this chemical as zinc for pets would free up the more expensive natural resources for other applications.

Oscar, in frustration, decided to voice a business-based argument: Isn't this going to look bad? AAFCO and the pet food industry already suffer from a massive PR problem. Why court a PR disaster?

Well . . . the committee held a vote. The members approved zinc hydroxychloride as an ingredient in pet food. This was just a preliminary approval. After the Ingredient Definitions Committee votes to approve a new ingredient, that decision is sent to the AAFCO board for review. Then the board submits it to the entire membership at the annual midyear meeting, generally held in January.

According to AAFCO's Sue Hayes, there's plenty of time built into the system for objections. "We do not move quickly on purpose," she says. "It's intentional, so that businesses and consumers can find out what we're talking about and understand it."

In this case, the "heavy metal soup" was approved, and then adopted in 2017. You can read its definition in the *AAFCO 2020 Official Publication*, the feed makers "bible" of accepted ingredients, nutrient profiles, and practices. Zinc hydroxychloride is right there in the big red book, on page 418, including the heavy metal limits:

It must not contain more than 20% chloride, 90 ppm lead,
15 ppm chromium, 10 ppm arsenic, 10 ppm cadmium
and 0.2 ppm mercury.[10]

Oscar walked out of the 2014 meeting, stunned. Later, an
AAFCO member approached Oscar and thanked him for speaking up and making him think harder about this issue. This was an
encouraging conversation, but still the overwhelming experience
of that meeting for Oscar was one of frustration. This seemed to
be a group of people with real power, largely set in their ways.
The committee dismissed the very genuine concerns of animal
doctors, and—as we see it—of millions of pet parents around the
country. They seemed convinced that their outlook represented
the values of most pet parents and that only a small group of people shared our concerns about what goes into the bag.

FEED VS. FOOD

The craving for better food for dogs is neither a fringe concern
nor a preoccupation of so-called "coastal elites." This is not about
people with too much time on their hands illogically humanizing
dogs. Pet parents across the nation are seriously troubled by what
they're learning about Big Kibble. We Americans care deeply about
our dogs—and about what goes into the food that *all* of us eat.

Of course, plenty of people associated with AAFCO and the
pet feed industry know this. A handful of years after that AAFCO
annual meeting, the director of the FDA's Center for Veterinary
Medicine, Dr. Steven Solomon, spoke at a different convention—
the tenth annual National Grain and Feed Association–Pet Food
Institute's Feed and Pet Food Joint Conference, held in Kansas
City, Missouri, in October 2019. Dr. Solomon stood on stage
and cited a statistic worth noting: some 95 percent of Americans
see their dogs as members of the family.

Still, old ways are hard to change. Later, at that same 2019 Feed and Pet Food Joint Conference, Sue Hayes, who came to AAFCO after a long career working in the feed industry, responded to a question about the appropriateness of regulating dog food as feed. As she put it, "It makes perfect sense if you understand that dogs and cats are animals. They are not people. We work with many species, and dogs and cats are among them."[11]

But to an increasing number of pet parents, dogs and cats are not just two animal species among many; they are family members.

When it comes to what we put in our bodies and what our pets are crunching in their bowls, feed and food are as different as cats and dogs. Whatever gripes you may have about the nutritional inadequacies of processed food for people, the fact is that our food supply is safer, more sanitary, and more nutritious than what gets thrown to chickens and cows destined for quick slaughter. While there are plenty of reasons to worry about factory farm practices, including antibiotics and hormones fed to feed-lot animals that get passed on to us, the animals themselves generally don't live long enough to see the adverse effects on their own bodies.

When they do, it can be heartbreaking. At the Gentle Barn animal sanctuary in Santa Clarita, California, families can come on Sundays to pet the rescued animals, including a three-thousand-pound cow named Forgiveness. On one sunny Sunday, Forgiveness lies calmly on his side in the yard while little kids toddle up to him to brush his fur and try to wrap their arms around his huge middle. After a tragic start of being taken from his mother at birth—she'd been impregnated to give milk for the dairy industry, then had her calf whisked away—Forgiveness had been put in a veal cage too small for him to move. His leg muscles softened, and by the time he was sent to slaughter, at eight weeks, he was too sick to be used. The Gentle Barn adopted him. He arrived with pneumonia, a skin fungus, a hacking cough, and an extremely high temperature. After months of good veterinarian care and love from volunteers and staff, he recovered and learned to walk. Today, though, twelve years past his original slaughter-by date, his girth is too massive for his own legs to support.

Genetic modification and factory farm practices such as those experienced by Forgiveness are clearly not designed with an animal's well-being top of mind. The feed that livestock eats is not designed to promote healthy longevity. A recent study published in the journal *The Professional Animal Scientist* looked at zinc hydroxychloride as a feed supplement for yearling feedlot steers. The study's stated goal was to help nutritionists formulate less expensive trace mineral supplementation programs for cows that are slaughtered before they're two years old.[12] Like genetic modification, the zinc hydroxychloride was shown to be effective for this specific meat-industry goal.

But dogs live to be twelve or fifteen, or even older. What is the impact of zinc hydroxychloride and its heavy metals on a dog over time? And this zinc supplement is just one of many synthetic vitamins and minerals in dog feed that can include heavy metals.[13] When heavy metals accumulate in the body, their risk increases. What happens if an animal continues ingesting these heavy metals year after year? We don't know.

We do, however, have plenty of evidence showing that toxins can contribute to disease in *humans*. As one recent article on canine cancer in *Whole Dog Journal* put it, the best anticancer suggestions for humans and dogs right now involve maintaining an optimal immune system through good nutrition, weight control, and exercise. As Dallas-based holistic vet Dr. R. H. Anderson told the magazine, "I have my clients work up to feeding their dogs at least a 50 percent natural diet. I clean up the dogs' livers, and I make sure their immune systems are functioning normally.

Every dog is different, but these three things seem to work pretty well."[14] Certainly, ingesting supplements containing heavy metals is not anyone's idea of an immunity-boosting diet.

The goals of the feed industry just don't always align with those of today's concerned pet parents. Nor do some of the other differences between feed and food, such as:

- What can go in it.
- What those ingredients can legally be called on the bag.
- What happens when problems, such as pentobarbital, are found on the factory floor.

THE ART OF CREATIVE WRITING AKA
PET FEED LABELS 101

If you head to the pet specialty big box store, or a boutique, you'll find some bags of dog feed with pictures so appealing, you might be tempted to taste it yourself. But don't. The bag may show a photo of a juicy chicken breast with real grill marks on it, a T-bone steak, bright green peas, carrots, and rice. But that is not what's in the bag.

If you think the photos should accurately depict the ingredients, you're right. AAFCO publishes a second, practical guide specifically for the pet feed industry and its regulators to use, further clarifying the information in its *Official Publication*. This second book, called the *AAFCO Pet Food and Specialty Pet Food Labeling Guide*, details the labeling guidelines for pet feed, and what, exactly, the words on the bag mean. Here's what the labeling guide says about pictures:[15]

A vignette, graphic, or pictorial representation on a pet food or specialty pet food label shall not misrepresent the contents of the package.

We recently stopped in a boutique pet food emporium in Manhattan Beach, California. It was a small upscale place located across the street from our JustFoodForDogs kitchen. We wanted to see what else neighborhood pet parents were being offered. We picked up a package of Zignature Lamb Formula kibble. The photo on the front showed a full rack of lamb. On the back, it lists lamb as the first ingredient. But the lamb used by kibble companies is likely not the prime cut shown on the front. (See chapter 6 for more information on the meat in the bag.) Nor does a bag of Lamb Formula dog feed need to contain much actual lamb to meet AAFCO's guidelines.

The word "formula" in this product is considered a "descriptor" by the same *AAFCO Pet Food and Specialty Pet Food Labeling Guide*. If the name on the front has a "descriptor," the feed inside the bag only needs to contain 25 percent of named meat—in this case, lamb. The rest of it can be anything else legally allowed to be included. This rule, known as the "25 percent rule," is explained in the AAFCO guide:

> If any ingredient, or combination of ingredients, forms part of the name of a pet food or specialty pet food, and there is an acceptable descriptor included with the product name that indicates the presence of other ingredients, the named ingredient or ingredients must compose 25% of the weight of the product.[16]

Other acceptable descriptors include words like "dinner," as in "Beef *Dinner* Dog Food," or platter, as in "Tuna *Platter* Cat Food." Each of these words means the bag needs to contain only 25 percent of the meat listed.

But wait, there's more! If water is added for processing, as happens with canned food, and there's a descriptor (like "dinner" or "platter"), the feed only needs to contain 10 percent of the named meat (by weight).

Do pet parents know that this expensive Lamb Formula Dinner has only one-quarter lamb in the bag—or 10 percent, if it's canned, with added water? Well, now you do. But the average shopper probably doesn't. The ingredient list also includes "lamb meal," a product of a renderer, definitely not shown on the front.

At the same store, we picked up a small bag of treats by Betsy Farms Bistro called "Sushi Roll Recipe Homestyle Treats for Dogs." The bag's full-color photo showed four pieces of fleshy, pink salmon sushi nestled on a white plate, a fifth piece being lifted up by a hand holding chopsticks. But "recipe" is also considered a descriptor word. Because of the word "recipe" on the label, there only needs to be 25 percent salmon in the treat, clearly not what the image shows. We could also see the treats themselves through a clear plastic window: little brown disks of ultraprocessed material. The juxtaposition between the marketing image and the actual treats would be almost comical if our dogs' health weren't at risk.

The AAFCO guidelines give a great deal of credence to tiny nuances of language. Take the word "with." If a pet feed bag uses the word "with" in the title, it only has to contain 3 percent of that ingredient. Because, you know, "with" clearly means a tiny amount—or, actually, not so clearly, if the pet feed industry is being honest about how most people read labels. This is called the "3% or 'With' Rule."[17]

The "With Rule" applies to all kinds of brands you see in the store. Blue Buffalo's "Grain-Free Coastal Blend" dry dog feed "prepared *with* Dry and Raw Wild-Caught Pollack, Halibut, Sole, Nutrient Rich Organs and Cod," only needs to have 3 percent of each of those named types of fish. Taste of the Wild's "Pacific Stream Canine Recipe *with* Smoked Salmon" need only contain 3 percent salmon. Purina's "Pro Plan Chicken & Rice Formula *with* Delicious Shredded Pieces?" Three percent "delicious shredded pieces" is fine. (Shredded what?)

As with "dinner" or "platter," if added water is used in the processing, the amount of the listed ingredient needed to be in accordance with the "With Rule" drops. If it says "with" and water is added for processing, the amount of that ingredient required is negligible, listed as "N/A" in the AAFCO guide.

On the flip side of this language issue, state regulators in a few states have rejected *other* types of qualifiers on the label—such as, in our case, "USDA-certified ground beef 85/15" and "premium fish oil from Iceland." At JustFoodForDogs, we've been prevented by the occasional regulator at the state level from listing these specifics, an intervention we believe comes from the desire to prevent companies using human-grade ingredients to boast about this fact, thereby calling attention to the *lack* of such ingredients in other products. How can customers choose something they don't know is there?

The much larger AAFCO *Official Publication* contains incredibly detailed descriptions of other things your dog might be eating in his kibble. The 746-page book gives some examples of what can be considered dietary fiber, such as ground pecan shells: "Ground Pecan Shells is obtained by grinding the hard outer shell . . . It is to be used as a source of dietary fiber."

"Distressed Pet Food" can go in, as in pet food that can't be sold in stores because the bag is torn, the feed is past its sell-by date, or it has been returned.[18] This line in the *Official Publication* means that, among other things, if a warehouse is stocked with kibble past its sell-by date, that kibble can be reincorporated as a new ingredient in the kibble production chain. Pet feed companies can buy and use this old kibble and not break any rules.

The *Official Publication* lists all kinds of ingredients that can be used as "crude protein." Among the acceptable crude proteins is "Dried Poultry Waste (DPW)," which the *Official Publication* defines as an animal waste "product" that's primarily "feces from commercial poultry, which has been thermally dehydrated to a moisture content not in excess of 15%."[19] Dried Poultry Waste must not contain more than one percent feathers. (A reassuring limitation? Not really.) Waste products, just to be clear, are not good sources of calories for dogs, and can actually be harmful—a truth about waste-as-food in general (even if your dog has been known to eat rabbit poop while walking through a park).

All of this disgusting and inedible material can and does get shoved into the kibble maker or canning machine and repurposed as dog food. Our dogs, whose lives revolve around making us happy, unknowingly gulp down chicken poop and sawdust served out to them by those they love. The feed manufacturers shovel in shit, literally, often while operating in strict accordance with the AAFCO guidelines.

Is AAFCO trying to make it easy for Big Kibble to lie to its customers? That's what it looks like to us. But perhaps some feed control officials simply don't believe that pet parents take the words on the bag very seriously. At the 2014 AAFCO meeting in Sacramento, Dr. William Burkholder of the FDA, who currently sits on the AAFCO Model Bills and Regulations Committee, told Oscar's small "out group" of AAFCO skeptics that pet parents don't really believe the photos on the label.[20]

During one of the breaks, the blogger Susan Thixton asked a woman who was working at the hotel registration desk to come over and share her experience with Dr. Burkholder. The woman said she was feeding her cat canned feed and seemed surprised when Susan said that the chicken in that feed was not the same quality as the meat she might eat herself. Another representative from the FDA who was also sitting with the group asked if she'd eat that cat food herself. She said no; it's for cats. Then Thixton asked her if she *really* believed that the chicken in the canned cat food was the same quality chicken that she eats. She said that she assumed it was, of course. Thixton explained a little bit about feed-grade chicken. "She was appalled," as Oscar remembers, "The FDA folks seemed genuinely surprised by the fact that she took these labels so seriously."

But people do take the labels seriously and expect them to be reliable, in part because we've become accustomed to poring over the nutritional profiles on human food and trusting them.

When it comes to advertisements for food and dog feed, we expect them to be true as well.

A PICTURE IS WORTH A THOUSAND WORDS . . . OR BILLIONS OF DOLLARS

Of course pet parents know that advertisements are designed to sell something. They're meant to be persuasive, rather than objective. Still, while newspaper advertisements included plenty of false claims during the early days of dog feed, most people assume that there are laws around truth in advertising that protect us today.

This is only partly true. "You sort of imagine that there's this overarching 'truth in advertising' law that governs everything, but there just isn't," says consumer expert Bob Sullivan, author of the *New York Times* bestselling book *Gotcha Capitalism* and host of the podcast *So . . . Bob?*[21]

The Lanham Act, often called the False Advertising Act, was passed in 1946. It only applies to companies making false statements about other companies. Consumers can't bring a case under that act. And as Sullivan explains, there's a legal term, "puffery," that gives companies wide berth to exaggerate, as long as they avoid citing specific numbers or false stats. "Puffery is what it sounds like—like a bird puffing out its chest. You're allowed to do that. You can say, 'There's no better coffee than Starbucks!' or

'Dogs love it!' As long as it's an opinion, not a fact, you're fine," says Sullivan. "Plus, what does 'favorite' mean? It's vague. If a company defends a statement as puffery, it's fine. If you say, '72 percent of New Yorkers drink Starbucks,' you could be sued."

Except, even if you're actually lying, you may well not be sued. The Federal Trade Commission Act of 1914, which created the Federal Trade Commission, is intended to offer consumer protection. The FTC has authority to prevent unfair or deceptive acts in or affecting commerce. The commission lists three main truth-in-advertising guidelines: "Advertising must be truthful and nondeceptive, advertisers must have evidence to back up their claims, and advertisements cannot be unfair."[22] Deceptive advertising, according to the government agency, means an ad contains information, either explicitly or through implication, that misleads a reasonable consumer. It can also be deceptive by omission, as in it misleads a viewer by not mentioning certain important facts that would impact a consumer's decision-making process.

This sounds good, but the FTC's actual enforcement capabilities are weak, for a few reasons. For one thing, the FTC is not set up to handle consumer complaints about deceptive advertisements. "It's not like you can call up the FTC and say, 'I bought this dog food and it turned out to be a lie! Isn't that a crime?' You can't do that because they don't answer the phone and talk to an individual consumer about an individual concern. You can file a complaint on the website, but they won't talk to anybody about anything until they've filed a lawsuit," says Sullivan.

Even when the FTC does file a lawsuit, as a civil agency it can only file civil lawsuits, not criminal ones. Basically, if a company lies about its dog feed, that action is not a crime but, rather, a violation of the FTC Act, section 5. "To pursue criminal charges for false advertising, even if the feed killed dogs, the FTC would have to make a referral to the Justice Department, and the Justice

Department would have to step in. This almost never happens," says Sullivan. Also, the FTC does not have jurisdiction over all business sectors and tends to focus on national ads. It leaves disputes about local ads to the Better Business Bureau.[23]

Finally, the FTC has limited people power. It's a federal agency with just over one thousand employees, as of 2019, many of whom are focused on other things.[24] They only pursue a small number of cases each year relating to advertising. As a consumer, you can pursue claims about dog feed through your state attorney general, which is often how these cases start.

Still, the FTC does file *some* lawsuits, and has famously sued both food and dog feed makers for making health-related claims that could not be proved. In 2016, for example, the FTC charged Mars Petcare U.S. with false or unsubstantiated health claims in ads it ran for Eukanuba brand dog food the year before.[25]

One ad had this to say:

Ten years ago, we launched a long-life study. What we observed was astonishing. With Eukanuba and proper care, dogs in the study were able to live beyond their typical lifespan.

In the ad, viewers saw a dog named Iowa who was seventeen years old. "The typical Labrador lifespan [is] 12 years," a voiceover stated. The FTC alleged that this pairing of dog and statistic implied that Iowa had lived 30 percent longer than expected, and that this longevity was due to eating Eukanuba. This claim could not actually be proven through scientific evidence, the FTC said.

Mars Petcare settled in 2016, admitting, basically, that the ad had little foundation in reality. But the details of this "settlement" are pretty discouraging. Mars agreed to stop making these false longevity claims or any similar ones in its ads for one month, during which time the case would remain open for public comment. Mars also had to monitor its ads for similar deceptive claims. After one month, the FTC would decide whether to make this "proposed consent order" final.

In September 2016, the FTC's final ruling came down: Mars could not claim that Eukanuba could extend a dog's life by 30 percent or make similar claims, for a period of twenty years.[26] If Mars violated this consent order—essentially running similar ads again—it would have to pay $40,000 for each violation. That's it. This $18,085,000,000 company was told to stop lying, or else! If it lied again, it would have to pay what is, to it, a pittance. That's the extent of the punishment for lying to pet parents loud and clear, repeatedly, on TV, on the Internet, and in print.

In other words, when it comes to the beautiful, promising ads you see on TV, an awful lot of filler can get in.

ENFORCEMENT, OR LACK THEREOF

While the FTC monitors advertising, sort of, the FDA and each state's feed control or agriculture department oversees granaries and kibble factories. Many of the pet feed recalls we've seen in recent years have resulted from state inspections, including the 2013 recall of Dogswell treats after routine testing by the New York State Department of Agriculture and Markets.[27]

But these state officials have plenty of other jobs, too, and not necessarily enough staff to regularly visit every single player in the pet feed industry. FDA officials also do visit plants and issue reports. You can read these reports online. But when it finds violations, even serious ones that could potentially kill dogs, such as pentobarbital in canned feed, the government gives manufacturers time to fix problems instead of immediately shutting down factories in clear violation. And, like state enforcement officials, the FDA lacks resources and even authority to do everything it should. It has historically lacked the power to impose recalls and

punishments and has been lax about following its own recall protocols.[28] They have enforcement discretion, which means they
pursue and enforce some situations, but certainly not all.

Still, because of the joint federal and state-level regulatory approach, people in the pet feed industry like to claim that kibble is
more heavily regulated than human food. After all, the argument
goes, pet feed companies are required to follow the rules of every
single state in which they want to sell—essentially the AAFCO
guidelines—and also submit labels, and in some cases samples,
to each state's governing authority. This sounds like a lot of work,
and it is, as we've discovered. It's so onerous that some companies
have sprung up offering to help pet food makers outsource the
task of registering and renewing their labels in every state. This
is a bureaucratic protocol that makers of human food do not
have to follow. As Big Kibble defenders say, both federal and state
governments cast a huge net of rules over the pet feed industry.

In practice, though, this net, like all nets, is full of holes.

While the current system creates a lot of red tape for pet feed
makers, the fact is, there is no one single agency fully invested in
pet food safety. The primary focus of AAFCO is livestock feed
and interstate commerce ease; the main concern of the FDA is
people. At the 2019 Feed and Pet Food Joint Conference, Dr.
Solomon talked about "One Health," an approach informing
the FDA, and other federal agencies. This is a vision of animal,
human, and environmental health all being linked. One idea of
One Health is that what animals eat matters and must be safe—
because *we eat them*. While we're hopeful that this will translate
into better-quality animal feed all around, the FDA's focus on
safe feed is still part of its main commitment to protect humans.

Who falls short in this equation? Our dogs. The system gives
dogs and their food supply short shrift. No one at the regulatory level is primarily and solely focused on what's in the bowl—
leaving Big Kibble to essentially monitor itself.

FOOD FIGHT!
FEED MAKERS ON THE ATTACK

In 2014, a strange thing happened in the world of Big Kibble. Blue Buffalo, the supposedly superpremium brand, found itself on the wrong end of a lawsuit concerning its ingredients. According to the suit, Blue Buffalo lied about what's in the bag; pet parents were paying high prices for the advertised high-quality meat and no by-products, when in fact Blue Buffalo had used poultry by-product—a low-price ingredient sold by renderers. (See chapter 6 for more on rendering.)

A Big Kibble company potentially misleading pet parents does not surprise us. But what might have seemed unusual to some was the plaintiff in the case. It wasn't a government agency suing Blue Buffalo. Instead, another Big Kibble player, Nestlé Purina PetCare, was on the attack. Lawyers also filed class-action suits on behalf of pet parents. This is what is happening today; the government is not pursuing Big Kibble for unfair business practices; instead, competitors and consumers are doing that work.

Blue Buffalo's initial response? To file a suit against Purina for defamation.[29] Media outlets around the country reported on this fight. Who would win? The court battle dragged on. In 2016, Blue Buffalo paid $32 million in a settlement.[30] Blue Buffalo also settled the class-action lawsuits in 2015, paying out another $32 million. The company had, it turned out, included poultry by-product in feed labeled otherwise.[31]

Here's another reason why we compare Big Kibble to Big Tobacco: the federal government allowed Big Tobacco to continue lying for profits, even as evidence about its risks mounted. But consumers led the charge for change. With pet feed, the federal and state agencies are letting far too many problems slide, but pressure is mounting on Big Kibble nonetheless. In this case, both consumers and other Big Kibble companies are calling out some of the problems.

Kibble companies attacking each other may well be thinking about profits more than pets; Blue Buffalo was edging into the larger company's sales. But these lawsuits are also shining light on some of the excesses of the industry, inadvertently educating consumers about what's really been going on, and hopefully acting as a lever of change.

In 2016, the Pet Food Institute hired the public relations firm Inspire PR Group, based in Columbus, Ohio, and headed by Hinda Mitchell. Mitchell spoke at the 2019 Feed and Pet Food Joint Conference, cautioning the various industry representatives against publicizing crises faced by competitors. "Crisis is not a competitive advantage," she said. "We are a crucial part of the food supply and we are feeding 89 million companion animals. We have a great story to tell." As she pointed out, when one company goes after another, the whole industry suffers a PR blow.

Mitchell makes a good point. But we see this as potentially good news for dogs. When business as usual can include lying about what our pets eat, a fight between competitors will hopefully lead to one clear winner: our dogs. Big Kibble needs to do better by our best friends, and highlighting the problems can be the first step toward more consumers demanding better food for dogs.

There's a third group doing the watchdog-type work that regulators aren't, and one that didn't exist in the days of the cigarette trials: social media and bloggers.

BLOGGERS BITE BACK

Susan Thixton, the blogger Oscar met at the AAFCO annual meeting in 2014, runs one of the most widely read blogs critiquing the pet feed industry, called Truth About Pet Food. Thixton started her blog in 2006, about five years after her own dog, Sam, died of cancer. On her blog, she writes that her vet told her the cancer likely came from chemical preservatives in Sam's food. This set her on a quest to uncover abuses in the industry.

Today, Thixton's blog shares news about pet food recalls, lawsuits, and AAFCO and FDA actions. It's one of the first resources that pops up when pet parents search the Internet for information about recalls in dog feed.

In 2013, Thixton cofounded the Association for Truth in Pet Food, an advocacy organization that frequently petitions the FDA and AAFCO for better pet food safety regulations. As Thixton writes in her blog, she doesn't accept money or sponsorships from pet feed companies for either the blog or association.

Thixton is also known for "The List," a compendium of pet food suppliers she trusts, which she updates each year and offers to readers for a small fee. The List is so influential among pet parents that some pet food suppliers announce their placement on it. As pet feed company Raw Bistro stated in a 2019 press release: "We're honored to be chosen by Susan Thixton to be on her 2019 List . . . That's high praise for anyone familiar with this very select list!"[32]

Thixton's blog has amassed a loyal following. It not only provides pet parents with information that was much harder to find in the past but also offers proof of the very real concern that pet parents have about what's in the bag.

Another popular pet feed blogger/industry critic is Mollie Morrissette, who runs the blog Poisoned Pets (which pet parent Katherine Eban discovered while researching a dangerous allergic reaction in her dog; see chapter 4). Morrissette posts pet food recalls, safety alerts, local news stories about pet deaths that owners claim are linked to pet food, and news about class action lawsuits. She also researches issues that concern her and shares her philosophy, which is that, broadly, the pet food industry needs tougher regulations and higher-quality ingredients. Like Thixton, Morrissette refuses to take funding from Big Kibble or sponsorships from the industry. All of this makes Poisoned Pets a popular clearinghouse for information in the public record relevant to concerned pet parents.

Morrissette, who had a career as a fashion illustrator and art director in New York City before returning to her home state of California, came to pet food blogging after her own cat got sick.[33] About ten years ago, as she writes, her beloved cat Blackie collapsed at her feet. She rushed Blackie to a veterinary hospital. The vet saved Blackie's life but gave Morrissette some disturbing information: Blackie had likely collapsed because of something in her cat food, which was wreaking havoc on her kidneys and urinary tract.[34]

Morrissette was shocked. Like many pet parents, she had always assumed that the friendly pictures of chicken and fish on the pet food package meant she was feeding Blackie high-quality food made from, well . . . chicken and fish. And nothing a cat shouldn't eat.

This incident started her on what has since become a calling. "For me, it's about false advertising," she said. "You cannot put a picture of lovely roast chicken on a bag if you're using rendered material as your main ingredient. Don't mislead the consumer into thinking this is some fancy, all natural product when it's not."

In 2015, Morrissette began researching a spate of allergic-like reactions in dogs eating jerky treats.[35] She discovered what she believed to be the culprit: antibiotics that are illegal in the United States but used in China that can cause extreme allergic reactions in some dogs. As she writes, she contacted the FDA's Center for Veterinary Medicine about her findings. She was told that her theory was sound, but that the FDA couldn't test it in a study on dogs without feeding them potentially toxic treats. Her information did not prompt the kind of regulatory action for which she hoped, but because of her blog, she was able to share it with concerned pet parents directly.

In 2019, after much petitioning of AAFCO for membership, the association granted Morrissette a role as a "consumer advisor," allowing her to participate in AAFCO meetings and advocate on behalf of pet parents and pets.

These bloggers and others like them are creating real pressure on Big Kibble to do better by our dogs, as are the continual recalls, news reports about problems in pet feed, companies suing each other, and the options presented by fresh, whole-food companies like JustFoodForDogs, The Farmers Dog, Ollie, and Pet Plate. Pet parents are bombarded today with blog posts, videos, social media gatherings, and even invitations to live protests about recalls of kibble and other issues. As publicist Hinda Mitchell told attendees at the 2019 Feed and Pet Food Joint Conference, "Activists are watching and engaging." Mitchell encouraged companies to be more transparent about their practices as a way to build trust and define themselves on their own terms.

We'll see if they heed her advice. Transparency sounds like a smart plan; consumers *do* want to know what's in the feed and how it got there. When it comes to Big Kibble, however, even the most popular brands may face some serious reckoning if they truly show everything that goes into their products. Pet parents are not going to like what they see.

Such as, what's really in the so-called "meat" in the bag.

6

When "Meat" Is a Four-Letter Word

Using Our Pets as Four-Legged Recycling Machines

> The average dog is a nicer person than the average person.
>
> —*Andy Rooney, American radio and TV writer/ personality,* 60 Minutes *commentator*

As the year 2017 dawned, many Americans still recuperating from their New Year's Eve hangovers got another shock to the system: KATU News, the ABC affiliate in Portland, Oregon, aired a report about canned dog feed that sent a chill down the spine of pet parents.[1]

On New Year's Eve, Washington state pet parent Nikki Mael had bought a special treat for her four pugs, Evanger's Hunk of Beef Au Jus canned dog food. It was a pug-size celebration of the dawning year.

Within fifteen minutes of scarfing down the special meal, the usually cheery, muscular little dogs were convulsing, falling over each other, and running into the walls. Nikki rushed them to the emergency vet. One of the dogs, a wide-eyed, wrinkly little charmer named Tulula, died at the veterinary hospital. Another dog, Tito, was still having seizures the next day. Nikki believed that the food caused Tulula's death and Tito's seizures. The dog feed manufacturer, Evanger's, said it would launch an investigation and try to find out what happened.

Meanwhile, Nikki—and plenty of other pet parents in the region—awaited the results of a necropsy on Tulula that would provide more information about what had gotten into her system.

When the answers came in, the news was even more shocking: the substance affecting the pugs was pentobarbital, a barbiturate used to euthanize sick and abandoned animals. Pentobarbital is the euthanasia drug of choice for animal shelters because, as the Humane Society explains in its *Euthanasia Reference Manual*, it's fast-acting and potent, causes minimal pain, is stable in solution, and is inexpensive. It may be a humane method for euthanizing dogs, as far as that goes, but it has no business finding its way into dog food, as it did in this case.[2]

On February 3, Evanger's issued a voluntary recall of five lots of Hunk of Beef Au Jus, including the one containing the cans bought by Nikki Mael. The FDA posted news of this recall on its site, a public service the agency does whenever a company issues a recall, market withdrawal, or safety alert. (These are not FDA investigations but rather postings of companies' actions.) By the time of the Evanger's recall, the lot of twelve-ounce cans that included those Nikki had bought had already been distributed to retail locations and through online sellers in Washington and California; throughout the Midwestern states of Minnesota, Illinois, Indiana, Michigan, Wisconsin, and Ohio; and on the East Coast from Florida to Massachusetts. This batch of dog feed potentially contaminated with lethal amounts of pentobarbital, manufactured in one week in June 2016, found its way to fifteen different states.[3]

More news reports followed, including in *The Seattle Times*. Pet parents shared the news. Evanger's expanded the recall to include other lots and other recipes.[4] Who knows how many lives the recall saved? But for Tulula, it was too late. As Nikki Mael later said, the experience shook her trust in dog food companies. She's taken to making food at home for her remaining dogs. But she misses Tulula.

"Tulula was the leader of the pack," she later said. "She was the boss. She made sure everybody was OK. I think they miss her. They walk around the house looking for her."[5]

But this was not the end of the story. Across the country, reporters at WJLA, the ABC TV news station covering the Washington, D.C., metro area, heard about the case. They decided to do their own investigation. Was this pentobarbital contamination in Evanger's Hunk of Beef Au Jus a freak occurrence, or was it a regular thing with dog food? WJLA partnered with Ellipse Analytics, a lab specializing in food testing, and tested sixty-two samples from over two dozen *other* brands of wet dog feed.

What came back? Nine out of fifteen cans—60 percent—of Gravy Train, a brand not affiliated with Evanger's, also tested positive for pentobarbital. The amount found in these cans was not lethal, according to the FDA.[6] But it was also not legal.

The station shared its findings with its viewers. As with the Oregon news report, pet parents who saw the segment posted it on social media everywhere. Other news outlets followed up, including *People* magazine.[7] Soon pet parents from coast to coast were worrying about pentobarbital in pet feed.

Smucker, the owner of Big Heart Brands, which manufactures Gravy Train, issued a voluntary withdrawal of Gravy Train, and specific lots of other Big Heart Brands, including Kibbles 'N Bits, Skippy, and Ol' Roy. A *withdrawal* is a lesser action than a *recall*, such as the one issued by Evanger's after Tulula died. A withdrawal means a company is removing a product from the stores because of what the FDA considers a "minor violation"—

pentobarbital, in this case, but not enough to kill a dog. A *recall* means something dangerous enough has happened to warrant potential legal action. It's still voluntary, but more serious.

The FDA posted a notice on its site about the Smucker withdrawal, evaluated the company's testing, and said it would keep an eye out for reports of dogs made ill by the product. As this initial FDA notice explained, pentobarbital "should never be present in pet food and products containing any amount of pentobarbital are considered to be adulterated."[8]

Within a month, the FDA upped the pressure on Smucker, saying that the pentobarbital contamination was serious enough to require a recall, not just a withdrawal. Smucker removed at least 107 million cans of dog food from the market.[9] How many dogs had already eaten pentobarbital-laced food? There's no way of knowing for sure. The FDA also got word of yet another problem with a different Smucker product, elevated beef thyroid hormone in Milo's kitchen dog treats—an ingredient that can, and did, make dogs sick. Smucker recalled two varieties of these treats.[10]

All of this FDA involvement might sound like government regulators taking action. But the agency allowed the company to withdraw products from the marketplace on its own rather than shutting down the factory, nor did it issue any fines. The system allows companies to continue doing business as usual—churning out adulterated products while raking in profits, posting notices that pet parents may or may not ever see—while pet parents dish out the feed. Dogs around the nation eagerly wolf it down, never suspecting they might get sick or even die from their own food.

These cases of pentobarbital were not anomalies, nor were they the only time that the FDA had been made aware of the euthanasia drug in dog feed. The same month that Nikki Mael's dogs got sick, three FDA investigators had discovered pentobarbital in pet feed in a factory in Illinois.

During two site visits in January 2017, FDA investigators Lee

Terry Moore, Audrey De La Cruz, and Matthew Buenconsejo noted six instances of adulterated food at Nutripack, a private-label pet feed manufacturer in Markham, Illinois. Specifically, they found pentobarbital in samples they tested of food made for Against the Grain, a gluten- and grain-free boutique brand. The FDA also cited unsanitary conditions at the factory that could lead to food being "contaminated with filth" or "rendered injurious to health."

These violations are detailed in an official memo the investigators filed about their site visits, dated February 14, 2017.[11] This Valentine's Day memo (available for all to see on fda.gov) is a fascinating look at the inner workings of government. Bold letters across the top read: "Department of Health and Human Services: Food and Drug Administration." Boxes below leave room to type in the name of the firm visited, the inspectors' names, and observations. It could be a standardized form for anything, for getting your driver's license or applying to lease an apartment. Only this one lists violations that could end a dog's life.

In a box headed, "During an inspection of your firm, we observed," the inspectors typed:

The following observations were found to be adulterated under the Federal Food, Drug, and Cosmetic Act:
   A food shall be deemed to be adulterated if it bears or contains any added poisonous or added deleterious substance that is unsafe within the meaning of section 402.
   Specifically,
   1.) Your low-acid canned dog food product labeled in part "AGAINST the Grain***GRAIN FREE PULLED BEEF with Gravy***DINNER FOR DOGS***NET WT 12 OZ***" and coded "2415E01ATB12 BEST DEC 2019" was found by chemical analysis to contain the barbiturate drug pentobarbital.

This pentobarbital, as the form states, means this dog feed is legally considered adulterated.

Feed is also considered adulterated if it has been prepared, packed, or held under unsanitary conditions, such as those the inspectors observed, including, among other problems:

> Condensate dripping directly above open cans of the in-process low-acid canned dog food product COOKED CHICKEN LOAF and HAND PACKED CHICKEN.

The FDA issued this memo, a not-so-loving Valentine's Day card. But it was not a notice of legal action against the factory. Against the Grain had actually issued a voluntary recall of one lot of its pulled beef product on February 13. But even in this situation, when federal investigators saw evidence of pentobarbital with their own eyes, the FDA's "action" was to issue a memo to the factory manager—not shut down the plant. As the memo explains, it is not considered a final FDA determination of non-compliance. Instead, it gives instructions for objecting to these findings and for sharing actions taken to remediate the problems.

Nutripack, like everyone else in the commercial pet feed industry, assures the public that its food is safe. Nutripack is a family-owned company, one that, according to the company's website, sources 90 percent of its products from the Chicagoland area, nearly all from slaughterhouses located no more than fifty miles away. By sourcing local, the company says, it can visit suppliers, see what they're doing, and transport the raw ingredients to the plant with their own trucks. And yet Nutripack had pentobarbital in its supply chain (which presumably came in with its own trucks?).

Against the Grain, meanwhile, claims on *its* website that its food is "undisputedly comprised of the highest quality products available" and that "Against the Grain actively participates in the manufacturing of its products."[12]

As it turns out, some of these claims are true, though not actually proof of safety. The same Illinois family owns Nutripack, Against the Grain, and even Evanger's. (The children of the family own Against the Grain.) The pulled beef product recalled by Against the Grain was from the same supplier that Evanger's used for the Hunk of Beef Au Jus that killed Tulula in the Pacific Northwest.[13] This is another example of how "small" doesn't always mean safe and "boutique" doesn't necessarily mean better. Consolidation and inadequate regulation and enforcement run throughout the Big Kibble chain. As this case shows, even "family-owned" isn't always a guarantee of quality when it comes to pet feed.

FARM TO FORK:
THE MEAT HUMANS EAT

We've probably all read or seen pretty horrifying stories about the problems with factory farming: animals living in inhumane conditions, fattened up and fenced in, fed a diet loaded with antibiotics. We know that factory farms are bad for the environment, producing huge amounts of greenhouse gases like methane and contributing to global deforestation. We may have read about multinational agricultural biotechnology corporations like Monsanto making it increasingly impossible for small-scale farmers to compete.

But even with these problems, this list is part of the good side of the meat-production story. The USDA inspection and approval processes safeguarding the meat humans eat are among the best in the world.

The meat humans eat is processed according to strict health and safety standards and carefully tracked from the farm to the table. If you get sick from meat you grill at home, you can track that meal from your plate all the way back to the farmer who raised the animal. This ability for precise backtracking helps ensure the health and safety of consumers, explains John Ward of West Coast Prime Meats, a meat processor and wholesaler in Brea, California, that focuses on humanely raised meat and on working with co-ops and small farms.

As Ward explains, "To process or sell anything into a retail or wholesale establishment, you have to be a USDA-approved processing plant, and have USDA inspections. Once you are approved, you get a USDA plant ID, which means you follow detailed food safety rules and undergo regular USDA inspections. The plant ID number goes on every package you create. This holds everyone accountable along the supply chain."[14]

You can find the meat processor's USDA identification number right on the individual package of meat you buy. (Or the butcher will have the number, if you shop at a butcher's counter.) That processor, meanwhile, will have the USDA identification number of the "fabrication plant" or "harvest plant" (today's words for slaughterhouse), from which it bought the primal—the massive hunk of meat it cuts into smaller portions. The fabrication plant will have a record of the rancher from whom it bought the cow. The rancher will have records of what he fed that animal, how and where it was raised, if it had any illnesses and how they were treated, and how old it was when it was sent to the feedlot (and, from there, to the fabrication plant).

If it seems like Americans still eat a lot of steak and potatoes, well . . . we do. Cattle and calves remain the leading farm commodity in the United States.[15] Cattle are raised for beef in large, corporate-owned farms and also by groups of farmer's cooperatives and individual ranchers. Once they reach a certain weight, they are sent to feedlots for "finishing," then transported to beef fabrication plants around the country. Some thirty-two million cows pass through this commercial cattle-processing system each year.[16] The top cattle-selling state? You guessed it: Texas, accounting for nearly one-fifth of total cow and calf sales in 2017.[17] Half of all commercial red meat production in the United States happens in just four states: Texas, Nebraska, Iowa, and Kansas; cow and calf production generated $77.2 billion in sales in 2017. As of January 2018, there were nearly a thousand animal-fabrication plants in the United States operating under USDA inspection—834, to be exact—an increase of twenty plants from the year before.[18]

After the fabrication plant butchers the cows (and chickens, pigs, goats, lambs—you name it), it generally then ships the primals to a processor—always in refrigerated, sanitary trucks, operating under very strict guidelines. The processor cuts, or "portions," the primals into customer-ready products, then ships the cuts to the store or restaurants, again in refrigerated, sanitary trucks and according to strict guidelines. (Some fabricators do the portioning work themselves in a separate section.)

Specialty meat you might buy, such as organic, grass-fed, hormone- and antibiotic-free, often gets portioned at smaller, boutique processors. These small processors can work with the small, independent farmers focused on specific ethical or health-conscious growing and package and private-label these high-end products. After the portioning process, the packaged meat travels to grocery stores, restaurants, and butchers to be sold to retail customers. The whole process is tracked with amazing efficiency.

When it comes to the "chicken" or "beef" in kibble, however, this comprehensive identification and tracking system doesn't exist. As things stand now, it can't, because the "meat" in that bag doesn't necessarily come from one specific farm, one specific animal, or even one cut of an animal. It may not even come from one species, as you'll see, despite what the label says on the bag. In fact, as a recent study done at Chapman University showed, of fifty-two dog feed products tested, sixteen contained meat species not included on the product label (most often pork).[19]

The journey the "meat" takes from farm to bowl is also very

different from that of a cow to a T-bone, or a chicken to a Cobb salad. The route from farm to dog bowl is more complicated, with more, and stranger, stops. It's a circuitous journey that makes it all too possible for mystery ingredients to work their way in.

FARM TO BOWL:
THE ROUTE "MEAT" TAKES TO BECOME KIBBLE

Farm to Bowl
Step #1: Collect the Carcasses

Unlike meat raised for slaughter for human consumption, the "meat" in a bag produced by Big Kibble isn't generally raised but rather rounded up—including from the discard pile of slaughterhouses. Only about 40 percent of the livestock "grown" (to use the meat industry term) on factory farms makes it into the human food chain. The rest of the animals—the hoofs and beaks, sinews and blood, bones and contents of the intestines—is waste. In the United States, the livestock industry churns out nearly a billion and a half tons of waste each year.[20]

How to get rid of this waste? Some gets buried or burned—or, more recently, composted. Sometimes slaughterhouses send animal waste to an anaerobic digester to turn into usable energy. But much of slaughterhouse waste finds its way into dog food. There's another word for some of this waste: *"by-product."* By-products are the remains of an animal that are not sold as a cut of meat for humans but can have many other profitable uses. By-products are categorized as edible or inedible, and as long ago as the 1920s, these remains could be so profitable as to outperform the actual slabs of meat.[21]

"Meat" is also gathered from "4 D" meat, as in animals that are dead, dying, destroyed, or diseased.[22] (Sometimes 4 D is described as "dead, dying, disabled, or diseased.") Either way, it's disgusting and can be dangerous, as Nikki Mael and others have tragically learned. These are cows, chickens, pigs, and other farm animals that did not take the usual stockyard-to-slaughterhouse-to-processor route because something went very wrong along the way. Maybe a cow got so sick, it died in the feedlot. Maybe a chicken is still alive but too diseased to be legally included in the human food supply. Four D meat cannot be legally included in human food.[23] But in dog food? As an FDA spokesperson recently put it, the agency is aware of the sale of 4 D meat to salvagers (renderers) for use as animal food.[24] In fact, 4 D meat is pretty much always rendered (rather than, say, buried).[25]

Another "D" word you may hear when it comes to animals raised for slaughter: "deadstock." In clothing and other businesses, "deadstock" means unopened unsold items that are removed from the sales floor—new tennis shoes, say, that went out of style before consumers bought them. Deadstock apparel can have a new life as discount merchandise sold through other routes. For a consumer, a store's deadstock can be a big bargain. When it comes to meat, "deadstock" also means dead (live)stock, "products" taken off the sales floor, as in 4 D meat. These are removed from the sales chain of meat for humans. And, like tennis shoes, can find another life as a discount item—protein in processed dog feed.

How toxic is 4 D meat, those downed animals, the deadstock, *really*? Potentially very toxic. The Canadian Food Inspection Agency gives this warning: "Biosecurity is important when transporting deadstock because deadstock can remain infectious long after an animal has died." A disease can jump from a dead animal to a live one, the agency warns. In a decomposing animal, the agency notes, it can happen that "liquefied tissues and bodily fluids escape from the body, these fluids, which may be infectious, can be difficult to contain and can easily contaminate the environment, drivers, equipment and the transport unit."[26]

Sounds scary. And you might think, *If 4 D meat poses a risk to live animals, there must be very strict rules about transporting it.* That thought would be logical. It would also be wrong.

Farm to Bowl
Step #2: Round Up the Remains

On a chilly Tuesday night in late October 2018, outside Montreal, a large cargo truck with an open bed, covered by a few tarps, slammed on the brakes—hard.[27] The truck was owned by Sanimax—a company based in Green Bay, Wisconsin, that collects by-products from the agri-food industry such as slaughterhouse scraps, hides, used cooking oil, and grease. According to Sanimax, every day its team travels more than twenty-five thousand miles to service customers and collect by-products. Each year, Sanimax reclaims nearly 4.4 billion pounds of waste (including slaughterhouse waste). It transports this waste to its own rendering plants, massive cooking facilities where the slaughterhouse scraps, etcetera, get a new life as source material for other products, ranging from soap, paint, tires, and ink to pet feed.[28]

On this particular Tuesday night, something went wrong on the road. When the driver of the truck hit the brakes with sudden force, that action caused the contents of the truck to spill out the back, spewing themselves all over Henri-Bourassa Boulevard, a major east-west street in Montreal. Out came intestines, hearts, animal parts. News cameras swarmed the scene. What they shot was truly disgusting: dismembered cow parts and gutted stomachs being transported in an open, unrefrigerated truck, covered by nothing more than a tarp.

"It was like the set of a zombie film," one observer noted. "Guts everywhere, carcasses everywhere." He described the smell as like vomit mixed with skunk, only ten times worse. "It's a paralyzing smell—you get stopped in your tracks."[29]

Wednesday morning, sticky pink animal guts remained strewn

about the neighborhood, some wrapped around trees. This was after Sanimax had cleaned up. For many people seeing the footage, the accident was the first time they saw not only how the "meat" in their pets' bowls begins but also how it gets transported from the slaughterhouse to the renderers. It's easy to imagine all these Canadian dog lovers sitting on their couches, hands resting on their furry family members, suddenly asking themselves, "Is this really what I've been feeding Farfel?"

We saw the footage, too. But we were not shocked. We looked at the TV and then at each other and said, "Do you think the driver of that truck scraped the remains off the street, reloaded his truck and continued on to the renderer?" He would have been well within his legal rights to do so, if he had.

The Sanimax Montreal general manager insisted that the company was abiding by the rules and regulations governing how slaughterhouse scraps are transported in Quebec. Here's the scary thing: he was.

The Canadian Food Inspection Agency issues recommendations for how deadstock and other material heading to a rendering plant should be transported. Its list of "best practices" includes covering the meat, ideally in leak-, spill-, and scavenger-proof ways.[30] Covering could be a tarp tacked down on either side of the truck bed. There's no requirement that it be transported in a closed truck, nor need it be refrigerated. Also, these are merely recommendations, not rules, a fact made clear by the agency's further suggestion that drivers pack a "spill kit" in case of, well . . . spills, which could happen whether these rules are followed or not. This spill kit should have a shovel, broom, absorbent materials, disinfectant, disposable bags, duct tape, and personal protective gear.[31]

Clearly, the Canadian Food Inspection Agency is anticipating the likelihood of non–spill-proof transportation, such as a truck disgorging dead animal parts all over the road in Montreal.

You might think, *Well, that's Canada. We have stricter rules for transporting animal parts across the highways and byways in the United States.* We say, "No, we don't."

Here in the United States, slaughterhouse scraps and deadstock destined to go to a renderer can sit in the sun outside the slaughterhouse, awaiting pickup—and do. They can be transported in unrefrigerated trucks, sometimes vehicles that most of us would not consider remotely sanitary.

The transport of meat for human consumption gets safer all the time. In 2016, the FDA updated its requirements for loading and transporting human food, in response to the Sanitary Food Transportation Act of 2005 and the Food Safety and Modernization Act of 2011. These were efforts to improve how things were done in human food because, as the updated rules note, back in the 1980s there were press reports of big rigs carrying food from the Midwest to the coasts, then returning with garbage for landfills in those same boxcars.[32] That had to stop, and as a 2016 final ruling explains, states now require trucks and railroad boxcars transporting food for humans to be free of filth and "adequately cleanable" to prevent food from becoming unsafe.[33]

This is not the case when it comes to most of the meat dogs will eat. As this ruling states, these new requirements "should not apply to unprocessed raw materials destined for rendering," such as raw offal and trimmings from animal slaughter, dead animals, and spoiled or outdated meat from retail food establishments because, "requirements related to refrigeration, microbial contamination, decomposition, and adulteration during transportation are not germane to these raw materials destined for further processing and hazard control."[34]

In other words, these materials are going to be cooked into oblivion at the renderer's and kibble factory anyway; why bother protecting them from spoilage and pathogens along the way?

This may sound logical, to some degree. This raw offal, meat trimmings, and spoiled meat *will* be ultraprocessed into little brown bits. But as we've seen with pentobarbital, some contaminants are resistant to processing. The bad stuff can get through. We care about how we transport raw ingredients for our own cooking for this reason—from fresh fish to butter to produce—even when we know we'll be sautéing, baking or grilling. But while the FDA considers canned feed laced with pentobarbital to be "adulterated," it has no problem with meat scraps being transported to a renderer on a hundred-degree day in an unrefrigerated truck. Flies may be following that truck as if it were a Pied Piper for vermin on wheels. If it's going to be rendered, that's good enough.

We think our dogs deserve better, safer meat.

Farm to Bowl

Step #3: Recycle at the Rendering Plant

Los Angeles: Palm trees and celebrities. The crash of the Pacific Ocean and the hum of sports cars. When you think about L.A., you probably don't envision Vernon, an industrial city just southeast of the city, crisscrossed by railroad tracks, a place where tractor trailers are the only action you see on the street and where the skyline is comprised of industrial smokestacks, telephone poles, and the occasional shaggy Washingtonian palm tree peeking up next to an industrial oil storage tank.

Vernon is home to manufacturers, wholesalers, importers, slaughterhouses, and a variety of waste-management facilities. Factories here make chemicals, metal products, food products, furniture, machinery, paper, plastics, and rubber. There are fueling stations for tractor trailers and a huge automotive repair center for broken-down food trucks and tour buses. When it comes to processing waste, Vernon is home to standard waste management services, recyclers of medical products, metal, plastics, glass, corrugated boxes, and textile scraps—and renderers.

Standing on a sidewalk in this hot, windy industrial city, you can see the glass towers of downtown L.A. to the north and the mountains rising through a dusty haze to the east. On a scorching, brilliant Monday in August, bloody-looking meat scraps fall from a green metal chute into a truck at Baker Commodities, one of the town's handful of rendering plants. Steam rises from various spots throughout the Baker complex. You can hear a steady mechanical whir—*shring, shring, shring*—the sound of industry, audible even above the continual roar of eighteen-wheelers picking up and dropping off ingredients for one of the nearly two thousand businesses that operate in Vernon. You can also see seagulls in this town twenty miles inland. They are circling and diving and swooping over Baker Commodities.

Visiting Vernon is like peeking behind the curtain in the *Wizard of Oz* and seeing who's running the show. Or, like the 1976 sci-fi flick *Logan's Run*, in which young, beautiful people are confined to a clean, lovely domed city (and, as it turns out, murdered when they turn thirty). Those who escape find a very different, far less utopian world outside. Similarly, you could live your entire life in Los Angeles and never drive into Vernon.

If you do visit Vernon, however, you might smell the rendering plants before you see them. As with the transportation of raw meat, the rendering of it involves pretty noxious odors. Driving up Indiana Street toward Bandini Boulevard, for example, the odor wafting down the street from Baker Commodities hits you, making you reflexively breathe through your mouth to avoid inhaling the scent of raw meat. If, instead, you park your car at one of the wholesale distributors farther down Bandini and walk up toward Baker, you pass Innovative Waste Transfer. Here, the smell of straight-up trash can make you hold your nose to pass. If you keep walking, the garbage smell gives way to the meat smell—more bloody, warmer—the closer you come to Baker.

For years, the stench from the rendering plants in Vernon

traveled miles to nearby neighborhoods, causing headaches, nausea, and respiratory irritation. The smell was so bad that air-quality regulators finally adopted rules in 2017 requiring these renderers to enclose some of the grounds, limit the amount of time dead animals are left to rot outdoors, and wash out their trucks before leaving to pick up another load. Other states, including Utah, Mississippi, and Texas, have long had odor rules governing rendering plants. With these new laws, California finally took steps to catch up.

As one *Los Angeles Times* article about the new regulations put it, they were sorely needed. "The unanimous vote by the South Coast Air Quality Management District board followed testimony from residents and schoolchildren from Boyle Heights and other communities who complained of odors so putrid they have to cover their mouths and close their doors to avoid nausea and breathing problems."[35]

Though the California law gave renderers in Vernon and other towns three and a half years to enclose odor-emitting areas, by the summer of 2019 there weren't any dead animals visible to passersby at Baker, and you really did have to drive up to the plant, or perhaps park at the nearby SoNice Party, a wholesale party supplier maybe a quarter mile away, to get a whiff of what's going on inside.

Despite the smell and the stories of guts and gore, rendering, in and of itself, is not a bad thing. It's a word used to describe the act of separating the fats from the proteins of discarded meat. Rendering is like the meat version of composting. If you're making a French *salade frisée aux lardons* at home or in a restaurant—curly lettuce topped with extra-crispy bacon—you render the bacon by cooking off much of the fat at a low temperature in a pan. Traditional cooking from around the world relies on home-rendered fats from carcasses, such as lard from pork, tallow from beef, and schmaltz from chicken.

When it comes to large-scale, commercial rendering, however, the raw ingredients, the process, and the final outcome are not quite so homey and delicious.

WHAT GOES IN . . .

For starters, renderers don't use nice slabs of bacon but, rather, the bones and feathers and blood; dead animals that die on farms or en route to somewhere else; and offal—the "protein" that doesn't make it into our food chain.[36] They also use leftovers from grocery stores, butcher shops, and restaurants.[37] Each year, the North American rendering industry "recycles" about sixty billion pounds of animal parts, not only from livestock and poultry but also from aquaculture farming and processing, food processing, supermarkets, and restaurants.[38]

Historically, many states have allowed renderers to process livestock that died of disease, auto collision, or injection with pentobarbital. Both Sanimax and Baker offer deadstock pickup. Sanimax even has an app for scheduling deadstock removal.

The rendering industry has many parts. It's regulated by a variety of state and federal agencies. Laws vary across the states about what kind of animal waste can be accepted by rendering plants. Some states allow renderers to process animals that died in an accident, in a fight with another animal, or in a natural disaster such as the massive flood that drowned pigs and left them out in the fields, rotting, in Missouri recently.

In California, the state's Environmental Protection Agency suggests that, "temporary storage of carcasses for transport to rendering," is the best option for animals that died in a disaster. This offers, ". . . a relatively safe and integrated system that complies with the fundamental requirements of environmental quality and disease control," as an Emergency Animal Disposal Guidance publication advises. [39]

In North Dakota, if an animal dies of an infectious or contagious disease, it can be dumped for pickup by a renderer, as long as it's disposed of within thirty-six hours of its death. [40]

The Humane Society's *Euthanasia Reference Manual* mentions rendering: "One alternative to the landfill is to engage the services of a rendering company, which processes animal carcasses into fertilizers and other products. . . ." Since most people can't stomach the idea of dogs and cats being rendered into pet food or other products, as the manual acknowledges, it suggests that shelters use rendering companies only for the disposal of large animals like horses or livestock. [41]

But euthanized dogs and cats *can* be disposed of at a renderer. There's a very disturbing old news report in which a local TV reporter in Seattle asks the then-president of AAFCO about euthanized animals in pet food. [42] In a now-infamous TV moment, the president, wearing a brown suit and sporting a big mustache, talks about rendering and pet feed labels: "If it says meat and bone meal, you don't know if that's cattle or sheep or horse, or Fluffy," he says. This is a clip that circulates among bloggers clamoring for stricter rules around pet food. No dog or cat remains have ever been found in tests of pet feed, as far as we know. But this old clip is an example of a cavalier attitude about what goes into dog feed that unfortunately persists among some.

Rules around rendering are tightening, and not just when it comes to the stench. In the wake of bovine spongiform encephalopathy, or Mad Cow disease, for example, the FDA established new regulations prohibiting the use of parts from cows older than thirty months, unless the spinal cord and brain are removed first. (Removing the spinal cord and brain can prevent the disease from being passed on.) [43] Still, the pet feed industry is heavily dependent on the recycling-through-rendering process, and the massive slaughterhouses rely on them to cart away waste. As the Wisconsin Department of Agriculture, Trade, and Consumer Protection puts it, while rendering is becoming more expensive and less available, "Rendering remains the best choice to protect the environment, public health, and animal health . . ."[44] To many in Big Kibble, rendered "meat" is too good a source to pass up.

. . . MUST COME OUT

The process of separating the fat from the protein at a commercial renderer also sounds extremely *unlike* crispifying bacon for a French salad. As Mike Rowe, producer of the Discover Channel's Emmy-nominated TV series *Dirty Jobs with Mike Rowe*, recently told ABC News, large-scale, commercial rendering is one of the dirtiest jobs on the planet. "It's a bloodbath. No one wants to see it or talk about it. It took me years to convince a camera crew to go inside a rendering operation. The smell is indescribable; the sights are something out of Kafka."[45]

At a large-scale rendering plant, the raw meat (and bone and beak) take an assembly-line–like ride through various steps from carcass to product for pet feed. Typically, the raw meat gets dumped on a conveyor belt and travels first past a magnet that removes any iron pieces, such as the ear tags that once identified cows. Then it goes onto a grinder that chops the disparate parts into particles of uniform size. These particles ride into a cooking "vessel," or giant-size pot, where they are steam-cooked at 240–90 degrees Fahrenheit (less heat than used to bake a cake or roast a chicken).[46] They cook for forty to ninety minutes, depending on the specific system used and the materials being steamed. The cooked mass is then discharged onto a conveyor belt and moved to another chamber, where the melted fat is separated from the bone meal and other solids by something called a screw press.

Once the fat has been separated out, the remaining solids are called "cracklings," or "crax." These include, according to the National Renderers Association, protein, minerals, and some residual fat. The "cracklings" are then *further* processed to remove more moisture and ground once again. After all this processing, you have the end result: protein meals, the most common of which are meat and bone meal (MBM), meat meal, blood meal, poultry by-product meal, poultry meal, feather meal, and fish meal.

In other words: Voilà! The "meat" in the bag.

If you pick up a bright yellow bag of Pedigree Roasted Chicken and Vegetable Flavor for Big Dogs Complete Nutrition Kibble, you'll see the products from a place like Baker. After "ground whole grain corn," the next ingredient listed is "poultry by-product meal" followed further down on the bag by "meat and bone meal." These are all products from a renderer.

What about premium brands, like Merrick? Take a look at the ingredient list on a bag of Merrick dog feed—say, the Grain-Free Real Texas Beef + Sweet Potato Recipe Dry Dog Food, which, as of spring of 2020, had a beautiful photo on the front of a grilled T-bone steak, freshly cut sweet potato, and bright-green peapod. Then flip over the bag and read the ingredients. Number 2 and 3? Lamb meal and salmon meal. Which came, as you now know, from a renderer.

The Merrick Texas Beef Recipe also lists "deboned beef," as its first ingredient. That beef is not rendered meal, but it's also not a beautifully grilled T-bone. It's most likely mechanically deboned beef, another scrap product from human meat production. After a carcass has been processed for the human food chain, bits of animal muscle remain. This muscle, or meat, can be used. It gets removed from the bones by machines for use in industrial meat production. Some of this can get sold for dog food.

Steve Thomas has been with Darling, one of the world's leading rendering companies, for thirty years. He's now a vice president at Protein Sales, previously having worked in "Fresh and

Frozen"—the company's factories that mechanically process the meat off the carcasses. "We do the collection of coproducts from the meat industry," explains Thomas. "At the processing plant, they are being very efficient and quick, sometimes just taking the breast meat off a broiler and throwing the rest aside. There is a lot of meat left on the breast frame, necks, and lower backs—edible parts of chicken that are not efficient to separate at the processor. So we do it mechanically, freezing the meat, or chilling it into a slurry. Both the frozen blocks and the slurry are used in the extrusion of pet food."[47] With a cow, the spinal column still has meat on it, and the fresh and frozen plant processes this, too. When you see "beef" listed on a pet food bag, it's usually this mechanically removed meat.

Still, most of the "meat" in Big Kibble comes from renderers in the form of meal, a kind of meat powder. As Greg Aldrich, PhD, research professor and pet food program coordinator at Kansas State University and president of the pet food industry consulting firm Pet Food and Ingredient Technology, put it in the book *Essential Rendering*, "Rendered protein meals such as meat and bone meal, poultry by-product meal, and fish meal are almost universally used in pet foods . . . Rendered fats and oils like tallow, lard, poultry fat, and fish oil provide a supplementary source of energy, flavor, texture, and nutrients in pet foods."[48] Or, as the National Renderers Association puts it, "The rendering process converts raw animal tissue into various protein, fat, and mineral products—rich granular-type meals and liquid fats with specific nutritional components."[49]

This "meat" is then stored at the renderer in a feed-bin–like structure or other building, or it's shipped. The fat is stored and transported in tanks.

Sanimax renders and sells nearly three dozen pet food ingredient offerings. These include protein meals, fruit and vegetable powders, and supplements. When you consider the animals and animal parts collected, the way they're transported, the method of cooking and of storage, and the absolutely global scale of pet feed production, it's very hard for anyone to really know for sure what piece of which animal, exactly, went into the bag you're pouring into the bowl. Or what other ingredient (pentobarbital?) may have gone in with it.

FOUR-LEGGED RECYCLING MACHINES

Baker Commodities, founded in 1937 and now in two dozen cities, bills itself as a "completely sustainable company." As Baker literature puts it, the company "recycles" meat trimmings and used cooking oil, turning them into valuable products that can do all kinds of things, including serve as fuel for vehicles and meat and bone meal for pet food. The meat and bone meal does so many things, including serve as "a high protein meal that gives the feed rations of livestock a boost. . . . This additional boost in protein allows farmers to grow their livestock more quickly with less feed, as the cooked MBM is more easily digestible for the livestock's bodies."[50]

Also, as it turns out, meat and bone meal contains high levels of nitrogen and phosphorus, which allow it to be used and labeled as "organic fertilizer."

In some regards, Baker's self-proclaimed position as a "completely sustainable company" makes sense. The waste-to-renderer path *is* an efficient recycling plan. Something has to be done with animal carcasses from our mammoth meat production machine and with all of the other waste we make. Waste is a huge and growing problem globally. Americans throw out more than 250 million tons of municipal solid waste every year.[51] That's almost five pounds of garbage per person, per day. Most of us have seen images of the island of plastic waste floating in the ocean. We've read news stories about the methane gas produced by landfills.

Recycling, or "upcycling," is an important way to divert material away from landfills, and perhaps even to combat the increasingly problematic use-and-toss mentality. Recycling lets us make something new and valuable out of something old. When it comes to animals, the rendering process diverts scrap from the landfill into industry. Every part of the cow is being used.

That all sounds great. Unless, like us, you're concerned about your dog eating that waste and ingesting the potential dangers that come with it.

The farm-to-bowl route essentially uses our dogs and cats as four-legged recycling machines. When the label on a bag of kibble says "Environmentally friendly!" here's one way those words are true: the company is using upcycled slaughterhouse discards and selling them to you to feed to your dog.

But the rendering plant is not the final stop on the dog feed manufacturing express. Before arriving in its bag at the pet specialty store, grocery store, or boutique, this "protein" gets mixed with other ingredients—some certainly healthful, but some moldy, inedible, and hard to pronounce. As we've seen in the news, the grain that's allowed to go into pet feed can be as problematic as the meat.

7

How Mold on Grain—Not Grain—Harms Our Dogs

*The Problem with Mycotoxins . . .
and with the Grain-Free "Solution," or
You Don't Want Grain-Free—
You Want Mycotoxin-Free*

> *The dog has seldom been successful pulling man up to its
> level of sagacity. But man has frequently dragged the dog
> down to his.*
>
> —James Thurber, American author and humorist

Bentley was a happy-go-lucky golden retriever living in Maryland with his pet parents, Tracy and Chris Meyer. Bentley had been eating supposedly high-quality, grain-free kibble his whole life, and he seemed to love it. The Meyers had chosen this particular grain-free kibble in part because the ingredients sounded healthy enough to eat themselves, including peas and red and green lentils. (How many pet parents similarly choose dog feed based on the appealing photos on the bag?)

But then Bentley began refusing his feed. He was waking up early, panting. He had a honking cough and a distended stomach. The Meyers took Bentley to see the vet. But as they got him ready for the visit, bringing him outside to go to the bathroom one more time, he fainted right in front of them and seemed to be foaming at the mouth. These were terrifying behaviors. What on earth was happening to their dog?

Tracy rushed Bentley to the emergency room. The team there told her that Bentley had gone into heart failure. The staff ran his blood levels and discovered that his taurine level was one-quarter of what it should have been. Taurine is an amino sulfonic acid, which the body makes from the amino acids methionine and cysteine. Taurine is needed for healthy heart functioning. Low taurine is often correlated with heart disease and other heart problems.

The veterinary team was able to save Bentley. He survived the heart failure and returned home, albeit with some serious medications in tow. The doctors prescribed a particular heart medication that can cause liver damage if taken long-term but that would help keep him alive. A year and a half later, Bentley was off that medication, but still on two other heart drugs.[1]

When it comes to unexpected heart failure seeming to occur out of the blue, Bentley was one of the lucky ones, as it turns out.

As grain-free diets rose in popularity, veterinarians around the country began seeing something very strange: pet parents were bringing dogs into emergency rooms around the nation with very surprising signs. Dogs showed odd fatigue, had difficulty breathing, and were coughing and fainting. Some dogs died from sudden cardiac arrest; their hearts basically malfunctioned and stopped beating. These dogs were suffering from dilated cardiomyopathy, or DCM, a condition in which the heart muscle weakens and becomes enlarged. As the heart and its chambers expand, the heart struggles to pump. Valves may leak, leading to fluid buildup in the lungs and abdomen. In worst-case scenarios, DCM results in congestive heart failure.[2]

While certain breeds have long been susceptible to DCM,

such as Great Danes and Doberman pinschers, now other breeds began showing signs of this heart disease, from golden retrievers to labradoodles to shih tzus.[3] As in Bentley's case, DCM can be reversed in dogs not genetically prone to it, if they're given the right veterinary intervention in time and switch diets.

On July 12, 2018, the FDA issued an alert citing a potential connection between grain-free diets and dilated cardiomyopathy, or DCM. As Martine Hartogensis, DVM, the FDA's deputy director of its Center for Veterinary Medicine's Office of Surveillance and Compliance, explained, "We are concerned about reports of canine heart disease, known as dilated cardiomyopathy (DCM), in dogs that ate certain pet foods containing peas, lentils, other legumes or potatoes as their main ingredients. These reports are highly unusual as they are occurring in breeds not typically genetically prone to the disease. The FDA is investigating the potential link between DCM and these foods. We encourage pet owners and veterinarians to report DCM cases in dogs who are not predisposed to the disease."[4]

After the FDA alert, more cases of DCM showed up. CVCA, a practice of nineteen veterinary cardiologists in the Baltimore-Washington, D.C., area, alerted the FDA that it was seeing DCM in these unlikely breeds and others. In a survey of 150 recent cases of DCM done by CVCA, the firm discovered that most of the dogs affected had been on grain-free diets.

Between January 2014 and April 2019, the FDA received 524 reports of dilated cardiomyopathy, most in 2018 after the agency's first public announcement. This isn't a lot, compared with the number of dogs eating grain-free feed, but it was a huge spike compared with the number of reports of DCM submitted to the FDA in the past.

In June 2019, the FDA posted an update to its first DCM alert, listing the brands associated with ten cases or more of DCM. Almost all of these were grain-free blends, sold in boutique pet shops and, in some cases, huge pet retailers. They included Acana, Taste of the Wild, Zignature, 4Health, Earthborn Holistic, Blue Buffalo, Kirkland Signature Nature's Domain, Fromm, Merrick, California Natural, Natural Balance, Orijen, Nature's Variety, Nutrisource, Nutro, and Rachael Ray Nutrish.[5]

The affected dogs were mostly eating grain-free kibble, and some had low taurine levels, but as of this writing, it's not clear what, exactly, is causing the DCM. While one study has shown a correlation between grain-free diets and DCM, there haven't been any studies proving that diet *caused* the DCM. Is DCM related to grain-free diets, or is the rise of DCM simply a coincidence that occurred alongside the grain-free trend? The FDA says it's investigating, but it still doesn't know why some dogs eating grain-free kibble have been turning up with signs of heart disease. Nor is it clear why, despite this spike, millions of dogs on grain-free diets are fine.

As *The New York Times* reported in 2018, the FDA speculated that the excessive use of legumes such as chickpeas and lentils and sweet potatoes used in large quantities as a substitute for grains may interfere with some dogs' ability to make and/or absorb taurine. This may have caused a deficiency and thus the DCM.[6] In 2019, the FDA added that the issue was complex, and might involve several factors.

Another concern, at least to us, is the quality of the grain-free formulations on offer. Do all pet feed companies, including the newer, boutique ones, have vets on staff to formulate the food and/or enough solid nutritional research about their formulations to ensure nutritional adequacy? The problem *could be* due to improper formulations lacking taurine, say, rather than to the specific legumes being used or the grains excluded. Or perhaps the reliance on plant sources as proteins, such as peas and lentils, compromised the overall protein content available to the dogs, and the companies' formulations did not account for this. While these legumes do contain protein, that protein is not as bio-available as animal protein, particularly after processing. Perhaps this led to a protein deficiency, which triggered the low taurine and the DCM.

We also think that if these grain-free recipes had been tested in robust feeding trials, deficiencies might have been found *before* the feed was sent out into the world. All pet feed is required to provide a guaranteed analysis (GA) on the bag—largely for regulators who review labels for compliance with nutrient requirements and voluntary label claims. But it is the norm in the pet feed industry for companies to assess the nutritional adequacy of a recipe (on paper) based on the ingredients *before* they've been processed rather than after. Also, there is no legal requirement that the feed actually be tested on dogs, and even when companies do feeding trials, the typical protocol is pretty rudimentary. If companies were required to feed the food to real dogs as part of a systematic, stringent food-quality assessment program—before marketing it—we suspect many dogs' lives would be saved.

Unfortunately, the DCM cases are the "field test" of many of these new recipes. Pet parents around the nation unknowingly use their own dogs as test subjects for diets marketed as "complete and balanced."

There's another problem with the grain-free trend writ large: grains are actually good for dogs. The movement away from grains—and, more recently, the return to so-called "good" grains— are both examples of Big Kibble marketing to pet parents' fears while not actually improving the quality of the feed for dogs.

WHY DOGS NEED GRAINS

The grain-free kibble trend really took off around 2007, about the time that melamine from China was discovered to have found its way into more than a hundred dog food brands. Plenty of dogs eating commercial kibble have mild digestive or skin problems, and pet parents began asking *what else* could be in the food that caused these symptoms? Grain seemed a likely cause. Gluten-free diets for humans had been gaining traction for years, and many pet parents figured that grains were probably bothering their dogs, too.

Grain seemed a particularly likely cause of minor problems given the fact that a year earlier, in 2006, Diamond Pet Foods had recalled nineteen varieties of dog and cat feed after learning that they potentially contained dangerously high levels of afla-toxin, a deadly toxin that comes from mold growing on grain.[7] Aflatoxin can kill dogs, livestock, and humans by causing deadly liver damage and cancer. At least seventy-six dogs died in the United States after eating the contaminated Diamond feed, ac-cording to the FDA. The recalled feed, which was made in one plant in South Carolina, in one day, was also exported to at least twenty-nine countries.[8]

As Steve Shrum, president of the South Carolina Association of Veterinarians, told NBC News at the time, vets around the state began seeing puppies with signs of liver problems usually found only in older dogs. "It takes such a small amount, and there's pretty much nothing you can do with the process that will inactivate that toxin once it gets in the food supply," he said.[9]

This recall and the widely reported melamine disaster that followed it helped create a clamoring for grain-free kibble. Dog food companies responded by making and aggressively marketing grain-free blends. In 2011, grain-free dog feed accounted for just 15 percent of sales in American pet specialty stores, just under $1 billion.[10] By 2015, 45 percent of all new pet food items intro-duced were grain-free, most of this in the form of kibble.[11]

By the beginning of 2019, if you were looking to buy bagged kibble anywhere in the nation, chances are you'd find yourself confronted by a dizzying array of grain-free options. In some places, grain-free would be your only choice. Grain-free diets had become so popular that they became kind of a standing joke among vets. Vets began saying to each other things like, "Oh, I've got a headache! I better go grain-free!"

Some pet parents saw real improvements in their dogs on the grain-free diets—and the pet industry jumped on this fact, in some cases marketing the notion that grains are worthless "fillers." But the problem with this trend is that grains can actually be a good source of carbohydrates, energy, and nutrients. Also, chances are, your dog does not have a grain allergy, even if his health and vitality seem to have improved since switching him to a grain-free blend. Dogs (and humans) can be allergic to protein, such as the gluten found in wheat, but not generally to a carbohydrate itself. As Lisa Freeman, a veterinary nutritionist and researcher with the Cummings School of Veterinary Medicine at Tufts University, told *The New York Times* in 2018, "Contrary to advertising and popular belief, there is no research to demonstrate that grain-free diets offer any health benefits over diets that contain grains. Grains have not been linked to any health problems except in the very rare situation when a pet has an allergy to a specific grain."[12]

But this idea—that grains don't cause any real problems—doesn't match the experience of many pet parents. The grain-free movement wasn't created by Big Kibble out of thin air; it was a business response to the benefits pet parents perceived. So what was going on here? What was causing the digestive distress or skin problems that drove many pet parents to try grain-free blends? It wasn't the grain, it turns out, but rather the use of *moldy grain*.

WAIT! THERE'S MOLD ON THAT GRAIN?

Mold is a living organism and it grows on grain stored in damp, unsanitary conditions and on grain with cracks in the kernels, which is common in the lower-grade grains generally used in pet feed. If mold grows on corn stored in a damp silo, say, it eats that corn and produces toxic waste products, called mycotoxins. Mycotoxins are basically the poop of mold, and they can cause a host of problems. Mycotoxins suppress the immune system, which can lead to diarrhea, vomiting, and weight loss. Many mycotoxins, such as aflatoxin, are carcinogenic and have been linked to tumors and various cancers.

The term "mycotoxin" was coined in 1962 after one hundred thousand turkeys died near London from ingesting peanut meal that had been contaminated with mold. When investigators realized that mold waste caused the deaths, they stumbled upon an entirely new category of toxin. As the National Institutes of Health later put it, this outbreak introduced the idea that "other occult mold metabolites might be deadly."[13]

Soon the term mycotoxin was being used to describe a variety of fungal toxins. As the USDA's *Mycotoxin Handbook* explains, different molds thrive in different conditions, both in fields and in silos. Some molds love heat, high moisture, and humidity, while other types grow in cool, wet climates. You can't see mycotoxins, but according to the United Nations' Food and Agriculture Organization (FAO), a quarter of the world's food crops are affected by them.

The most notorious and studied mycotoxin is aflatoxin, the cancer-causing poison that killed dogs eating Diamond Pet Foods. Aflatoxins have caused aflatoxicosis in livestock, domestic animals, and humans throughout the world. They are unavoidable, to some degree, and can grow even when farmers and manufacturers follow good practices, according to the USDA, which, along with the FDA, monitors peanuts and field corn for aflatoxin here in the United States.[14]

But there are plenty of other mycotoxins, and grain removed from the human food supply due to mycotoxins can be sold for livestock feed, including kibble for our pets. Wenger Feeds, a family-owned poultry and swine feed manufacturer in the mid-Atlantic region and a member of the agricultural company The Wenger Group, explains this fact in a recent blog post: "Wheat available for use in animal feed is typically a 'feed-grade wheat' and is often product rejected for human food production. Low test weight, sprouted grains, and the presence of mycotoxins are all factors which prevent the use of wheat in human foods."[15]

At JustFoodForDogs, we helped fund a study investigating the presence of mycotoxins in grain-containing and grain-free kibble, as well as in wet food. The lead researcher, veterinary toxicologist (and JustFoodForDogs consultant) Dr. John Tegzes, had long hypothesized that something in kibble was acting as an immuno-suppressant. He wanted to investigate the role that mycotoxins might play.

For the study, Tegzes and his team bought grain-containing and grain-free kibble and grain-containing and grain-free wet dog food in Southern California, made by five major U.S. brands. They tested for eleven different mycotoxins on a total of sixty samples. The study, published in 2019 in the journal *Toxicology Communications,* showed mycotoxins present in 75 percent of the grain-containing kibbles tested. (These were not aflatoxins, but other mycotoxins. This lack of aflatoxins may show, as the authors wrote, "how regulatory and control strategies have been effective in reducing the incidence of aflatoxins in dry commercial dog foods.")[16] No mycotoxins showed up in the grain-free kibble or in the wet food. (Canned food can be processed with ammonia—which we think of as something like dousing it in bleach—which kills mycotoxins.)

One way to avoid mycotoxins in your dog's kibble, obviously, is to skip the kibble. What's most disturbing to us about this study's results is that the mycotoxin level found in the kibble is legal—under the concentration limit of 10 ppm set by the FDA for dog food. This FDA guideline is a recommendation, not a law, which is itself a problem. While there have been studies done on acute mycotoxicosis—animals ingesting a huge amount of mycotoxins and having huge problems—there haven't been studies published yet about mycotoxins at this authorized amount. But most of us would prefer no toxins at any level in our food, or in our dogs'. (You wouldn't rub rat poison on your face even if there are no tests showing the risk of doing so.) After considering the problem, we believe that mycotoxin presence under 10 ppm is enough to act as an immunosuppressant on dogs. The prevalence of problems among dogs eating grain-containing kibble is all we have, for now, as a test.

To mitigate the risk of mycotoxin-related illness in pets, the researchers offered a suggestion: "Dog food manufacturers could incorporate grains that are categorized as US No. 1 by the USDA, and therefore less susceptible to mycotoxin formation." The USDA rates corn and other grains using a variety of factors. A number 1 rating has the tightest specifications around damaged kernels, which means they're less likely to grow mycotoxins than a rating of 2 or 3.

Using number 1 grade grain makes sense and is overall a better choice for dogs than eliminating a valuable source of carbohydrates across the board. One grain-industry professional we spoke to said that she's noticed a trend, anecdotally, toward major pet food companies purchasing higher-grade corn to address the concern about mycotoxins. This sounds encouraging, and we hope that more Big Kibble companies will respond to this latest dose of dangerous dog feed by incorporating human-grade ingredients into their recipes. But we're skeptical. We are not convinced that most Big Kibble conglomerates are springing for higher-quality grains across all their brands—particularly since there is no legal requirement to reveal the grade of grain on the label.

What we are seeing is Big Kibble companies focusing on new, improved *marketing*. Fear of DCM created something of a backlash against grain-free diets, and sales of grain-free feed have started to decline a little. The sixteen brands named in the FDA report took the biggest hit, seeing a 10 percent drop in sales, collectively, in the three months after the announcement.[17] Yet, to date, there is not a genuine, industry-wide, holistic focus on the admittedly complicated issues of DCM and mycotoxins and their relationship with grains. Instead, marketing departments have encouraged a simplistic, unhelpful debate: "Grains-good!" versus "Grains-bad!"

Some traditional Big Kibble brands are fanning the *new* fears of grain-free feed, encouraging pet parents to stick to the trusted, old-school brands that had grains all along. Other brands are tweaking the language on the bag. Merrick, for example, added the phrase "healthy grains" to the label on its Merrick Classic recipes in January 2020, an attempt to differentiate its "good" grains from the "bad" grains, such a corn and soy, that pet parents may be trying to avoid. Another term we're seeing is "ancient grains," used to describe "better" grains such as quinoa or barley.

As Jilliann Smith, director of communications for Merrick, has said, "We quickly shifted our innovation plans over the last few months to address the increased interest among pet parents in grain-inclusive recipes for dogs. We just introduced two new limited ingredient diet recipes that feature healthy grains like brown rice, oatmeal and barley. Both recipes—salmon and brown rice and chicken and brown rice—are free of peas, chickpeas and lentils."[18]

Removing peas, chickpeas, and lentils is another marketing move; these ingredients were found in some of the grain-free diets linked to DCM. Rather than including only the highest-quality peas, potatoes, and legumes, kibble companies are just removing them—and then promoting that fact. Superpremium-priced dog feed is following suit. Stella & Chewy's has a new "wholesome grains" raw-coated kibble, which includes oatmeal, brown rice, quinoa, and pearled barley and, as the label on the front assures pet parents, is free of potatoes and legumes. But removing potatoes is not a good solution. A better approach to healthful food for dogs? Using only high-quality potatoes in properly formulated diets that are not ultraprocessed and safely transporting and storing them.

Of course, there's no reason to assume that the potatoes and legumes used by Big Kibble are of any better quality than the grains typically used. Or the other vegetables and fruit—the carrots, corn, chickpeas, or blueberries.

Take carrots. The USDA's Agricultural Marketing Service grades fresh and processed fruits and vegetables (as well as other comestibles).[19] The grade standards for vegetables and fruit are voluntary; their main purpose is to create a uniform language to facilitate trade.[20] As with grains, U.S. number 1 grade carrots have the most desirable characteristics. They are firm, fairly well colored and formed, smooth, not woody, and free from minor damage caused by things like rot, cracks, frost, and insects. These are the carrots we choose for ourselves at the grocery store. U.S. number 2 carrots also must be firm and fairly well colored, but they can have minor damage due to growth cracks, sunburn, freezing, oil spray, insects, and disease.[21] Number 2 carrots cost less and still count as carrots. Since everything must be ground into a powder or emulsified before it enters the extruder (see chapter 8), number 2 carrots would do just fine.

Other vegetables that sound healthy are not actually the same product we eat. Such as corn, a symbol of summer. It's best when so sweet, you can eat it right off the cob, smothered in butter and doused with salt—or with no extra flavorings at all. We might look for sweet corn at a local farmers' market, or if we're lucky enough to have a big garden, pick it ourselves.

But there are actually two types of corn grown in the United

States, the corn we eat and field corn, a bitter-tasting type that is grown on ninety-nine percent of all corn acres in the United States. Field corn sits on the stalk far longer than sweet corn, until it dries out and hardens. Its main purpose is livestock feed. A third of all field corn grown in the United States is made into livestock feed—5.6 billion bushels in 2017—and it is included as a grain, not a vegetable. The other main use for field corn? Ethanol production.

The field corn used for pet feed is often made from "fractionated" corn products rather than whole corn. It is then dry-milled into grits or cones, which can be easily added into an extruder. Field corn is used in many processed food products for humans, including corn starch, corn oil, corn syrup, and corn cereal. Of course, no one thinks of corn syrup as a vegetable.[22]

When it comes to kibble, field corn is a convenient starch that works well in processed food because, as the National Corn Growers Association explains, it has good binding and expansion properties and "toasts well and forms browning reaction products with rich flavor notes." These factors lead to "pleasing kibbles with a desirable texture. In fact, corn is actually preferred over other grains in palatability tests."[23]

It might brown nicely, but that doesn't make it the vegetable that many pet parents assume is in the feed.

Other so-called vegetables in pet feed are the remains of the human-food-production machine. The Association of American Feed Control Officials' *2020 Official Publication* lists "dried potato products" as an ingredient that can go into feed. This is "the dried residue of potato pieces, peeling, culls, etc., obtained from the manufacture of processed potato products for human consumption."[24] Dogs may do just fine ingesting potato peelings, but that's not what most pet parents imagine when they choose a bag of kibble that lists "potatoes"—or what's in the photo on the bag. As with so many ingredients used throughout the history of dog feed, this is basically industrial food waste repackaged, re-labeled, and dumped into our dogs' diet. This already-processed food scrap will then be processed again in the extruder, further diminishing its nutritional value.

Because of these issues, we worry that using industrial food scraps can lead to feed that fails to meet dogs' basic nutritional needs, despite what it says on the label. We also think this may be a factor in the DCM puzzle; lower-grade vegetables and scraps being considered as whole-food ingredients in the recipe formulation, possibly resulting in a nutrition deficiency in the bowl.

Many companies are taking steps to protect dogs from DCM, such as, in Merrick's case, supplementing its limited-ingredient-diet recipes with taurine and DL-methionine to boost the amino acids, which may be helpful for dogs. The boutique Caru Pet Food Company says it only uses FDA-verified human-grade ingredients and adds taurine to help mitigate the DCM risk.[25]

While boosting taurine levels in these blends seems like a reasonable step, we think mitigation isn't the ideal way to ensure the health of our dogs. Amid all this back-and-forth and confusion, one thing is abundantly clear: the grain-versus-grain-free debate ignores the real questions we need to be asking about our dogs' food: What is the quality of the formulations? What is the quality of the grain being shipped to the kibble factory? And, How are ingredients used in kibble manufacturing transported and stored?

These questions are of utmost importance, especially when you begin looking at the other ingredients that wind up in the bag—some of which don't even *sound* like they might be food.

Big Kibble can legally use not only moldy grains and second-rate vegetables and vegetables scraps but also spray-on flavor and outsourced, premade, feed-grade vitamin mixes—one batch of which recently proved deadly.

Is Your Dog's Diet Harming His Heart?

If your dog is eating grain-free kibble, particularly one of the brands cited by the FDA, don't panic. Millions of dogs are eating these recipes and not having heart problems. Also, vets are finding that, if caught in time, diet-related DCM is reversible. If food caused the problem for your dog, chances are it can also help with his recovery. Talk to your veterinarian about your dog's health. You can ask your veterinarian or veterinary cardiologist to test his blood taurine levels and check for early signs of heart disease, such as a heart murmur or abnormal heart rhythm. And watch your dog closely.

Signs of heart disease can include the following:

- weakness
- slowing down on walks
- coughing
- trouble breathing
- fainting
- exercise intolerance

All dogs get fatigued eventually during exercise (just as humans do), but "exercise intolerance" is visible fatigue out of sync with the amount of exercise. For example, if after five or ten minutes of vigorous play, your dog is exhausted, when only a month ago he could have kept chasing a ball for hours, he's showing exercise intolerance. If you observe exercise intolerance or your veterinarian is concerned, you can ask for additional testing, such as X-rays, blood tests, an EKG, or an echocardiogram.

If your dog is diagnosed with DCM, follow these steps:

- Change your dog's diet, as directed by your veterinarian, including giving him any recommended taurine supplementation.
- Return to your veterinarian or veterinary cardiologist for repeat evaluations and other medications, as requested.
- Stick to it, also in consultation with your veterinarian. It can take multiple months to see improvement in many cases of diet-related DCM.

Report your vet's findings to the FDA. Type in this link for information on how to report a pet food complaint: https://www.fda.gov/animal-veterinary/report-problem /how-report-pet-food-complaint.

*Guidelines provided by a UC Davis team comprised of veterinary cardiologists and nutritionists. Adapted and reprinted courtesy of UC Davis School of Veterinary Medicine.

8

Mysterious Mix-Ins, Spray-On Flavor, Ultraprocessing, Oh My!

What Else Enters the Extruder

> Don't accept your dog's admiration as conclusive evidence that you are wonderful.
>
> —*Ann Landers, American advice columnist*

On December 3, 2018, the FDA issued an alert about potentially toxic levels of vitamin D in dry pet feed. Many pet parents were mystified. Aren't vitamins supposed to boost health? How can they be deadly?

Because, as it turns out, while vitamin D is an essential nutrient for dogs, too much dietary vitamin D can lead to a host of problems, from vomiting, thirst, appetite loss, and seizures to kidney failure and even death."[1] The FDA alert named various brands of kibble containing potentially toxic levels of vitamin D, including a number produced by Sunshine Mills such as Old Glory, Evolve, Sportsman's Pride, Triumph, and Abound (a brand made by Sunshine Mills for Kroger and King Soopers), as well as Nature's Promise, Nutrisca, and Natural Life Pet Products. State and private lab testing of the recalled kibble showed as much as seventy times the intended amount of vitamin D.

The next month, January 2019, toxic levels of vitamin D showed up in higher-priced feed: Hill's Science Diet and Hill's Prescription Diet. Hill's, a Colgate-Palmolive subsidiary, issued a voluntary recall of more than two dozen sizes and varieties of its canned feed, including recipes for adult dogs and puppies, those made with chicken and tuna, beef and turkey, barley and rice.[2]

The recall was too late for Maggie, a hound-terrier mix who had been part of Caitlin Gibson's family for thirteen years. Caitlin had begun feeding Maggie the tainted Hill's after her vet prescribed it to help with some digestive issues. *The Washington Post*, where Caitlin works, did a story about the recall and other dogs killed by feed. Fox News also reported on the recall, and on several dogs who died from kidney failure after eating feed with toxic levels of vitamin D—including a four-year-old Italian greyhound in Tennessee, a thirteen-year-old Bichon mix in California, and an eleven-year-old Chesapeake Bay retriever in Michigan.[3]

The stories about Vitamin D poisoning went viral. Reports of sick dogs kept coming. In March 2019, Hill's expanded its recall, bringing the total number of types of recalled canned feed up to thirty-three.[4] Between January and March of 2019, thousands of pet parents said their dogs had been sickened by Hill's, some fatally.

How could so many different brands of kibble and canned feed suddenly contain toxic levels of a supposedly good vitamin in them? Because of another practice of the globalized, consolidated, profits-above-pets Big Kibble machine—the use of premixes.

THE PROBLEM WITH PREMIXES

When you look at the "guaranteed analysis" printed on a bag of kibble, you'll see a host of vitamins listed. Vitamins sound good, but those *particular* vitamins got there, in large part, through a premixed combo of chemicals purchased by Big Kibble from an outside supplier and dumped into feed to make it nutritious—or at least to make it meet a desired nutrition profile on the label. As industry expert Greg Aldrich put it, "Usually, a formula calls for specific ingredients to be included, and most of these vitamins come in a premix."[5]

A lot of human food also has added vitamins, of course, as does fresh, whole food for dogs such as the kind that our company and others in our category make. But FDA-regulated, pharmaceutical-grade vitamin and mineral supplements are very different from what finds its way into much of Big Kibble. Manufacturers across the Big Kibble spectrum use vitamin and mineral premixes that can include industrial chemicals and are allowed to be labeled as vitamins and minerals, according to AAFCO's model definitions, even if they contain heavy metals such as the zinc hydroxychloride mentioned in chapter 5. The mix-ins can come from China or other countries.

As Aldrich says, "No pet food company would add too much of it intentionally to cheapen their product. The pet food companies have a stake in the animals surviving and doing well. Most of the people I know working in pet food companies are emotionally involved in the business from the animal's health and well-being standpoint. They love their pets. They believe in what they're doing." Still, the purchaser of a vitamin premix doesn't always know precisely what's in it.

The toxic vitamin D came from a premix made by a Dutch chemical manufacturer with a U.S. headquarters in New Jersey called DSM Nutritional Products. In January 2019, DSM had issued a voluntary recall of two lots of vitamin premix due to elevated vitamin D. But that recall came after the toxic blend had worked its way into Hill's feed sold across the nation.[6] Hill's assured pet parents it would require DSM to do more quality testing and that it would improve its own testing of incoming ingredients.[7] Unfortunately, this effort was too little, too late for thousands of dogs.

Months later, the president and general counsel of DSM North America, Hugh Welsh, told VIN News Service what happened. Apparently, a seasoned DSM employee accidentally added an extra drum of vitamin D to the premix instead of vitamin E. But now, he assured the news service, the company had instituted better control measures to avoid future mix-ups.[8]

Meanwhile, lawyers filed more than thirty class-action suits on behalf of plaintiffs against Hill's. At the time of this writing, the class-action suits had been consolidated into one federal action to be heard by the United States District Court in Kansas City, Kansas.[9] To date, we don't know of any pet-food–industry lawsuit actually going to trial. They are generally dismissed or settled, which we assume will happen here, with the terms of the settlement undisclosed, as is common.

The Hill's story is particularly upsetting because this feed was formulated especially for dogs that are already sick, or at least compromised somewhat. The manufacturer should be extra careful with the ingredients in it. As Caitlin says, "The standards should be especially high when you're talking about a product marketed for dogs that are medically vulnerable."[10]

We think that if Big Kibble were truly concerned with the health of dogs, it would be paying more attention to how it's supplementing all of its feed *before* tragedy strikes. Better yet, it wouldn't need massive batches of industrially produced vitamin mixes if the feed itself were actually more nutritious.

Of course, a healthy diet involves both good ingredients and proper preparation. The way most kibble is processed saps out some of the nutrition and flavor that the ingredients might have had at their start. This requires, as you probably guessed, yet more mysterious and often artificial ingredients to be put back in.

FOOD OR SHOES? INSIDE A KIBBLE FACTORY

A kibble factory is the last stop before the store in the dog food supply chain. A traditional kibble plant is a huge, windowless, concrete-floored building. When you look around, you know you're in a factory, but you wouldn't know it was manufacturing food. You see operators driving around the plant, attending to the massive machines, but no T-bone steaks piled up next to the extruders. You get the feeling that these hardworking operators, many of whom probably have dogs of their own, could literally be churning out any mass-produced item—plastic bottles, crayons, Pyrex. As in all factories, productivity is job one.

Most kibble plants are in the Midwest. You can't take your family on a tour of a kibble factory, at least not as of this writing. But if you were to enter on official business, as one industry consultant who has visited nearly two dozen such factories explains, you'd be asked to strap on a hard hat, step into cloglike, steel-toed safety "galoshes," and squeeze in earplugs. Kibble factories in the United States are regulated by the Occupational Safety and Health Administration (OSHA), and employees also wear this type of gear to protect their health and safety.

A traditional kibble factory bears no resemblance to a kitchen. But the *smell* inside might give you a clue about what's being made. The air stinks of dog food. It's like stepping into a giant bag of kibble—not a delicious scent, as you know if you've ever put your nose in a bag. The smell of the kibble processing gets in your clothes, making you want to immediately strip them off and toss them in the washing machine the moment you leave.

Then there's the sound. A typical kibble factory might have two to four extrusion production lines, each the size of two eighteen-wheelers parked nose to end. You can hear these massive metal machines before you see them, even with your earplugs firmly in place. The room reverberates with the clanging of metal. It's so loud that if a foreman wants to talk to an operator, they have to step into one of the specially built little soundproof rooms to hear each other.

Some of today's modern factories, sometimes called "kitchens," have food safety standards equivalent to or excelling those of human food facilities, says Galen Rokey, cofounder of Wenger Manufacturing, one of the world's largest extruder makers.[11] Owners of these kibble kitchens aim to be good global citizens, making efforts to minimize processing, maximize energy efficiency, and reduce carbon footprints, "which we call "foodprints," Rokey says.

Probably 90 percent of kibble today is manufactured through extrusion, says Rokey, who currently works as the director of process technology in Wenger's companion animal division. He says that while some pet feed is still baked like a biscuit—as in the early days of Spratt's Patent Meat Fibrine Dog Cakes—the vast majority of the bags on the shelf are filled with extruded feed that is also cooked as part of the extrusion process.

Extrusion means to force something through a small opening to shape it. If you've ever seen a churros maker at a street fair, or even an at-home meat grinder, you have some sense of extrusion. An industrial-food-production extruder looks something like a giant-size, stainless steel version of the Play-Doh Noodle Makin' Mania set with the spaghetti die attached; thick ropes of kibble dough ooze out of multiple holes simultaneously and then are sliced into bits by a massive rotating knife.

In cold-dough extrusion, the ingredients are mixed into a dough, squeezed out through a die, then baked. This is how Milk-Bone is made. But cooking extrusion is the more common kibble-making method. In a cooking extruder, the ingredients are mixed and cooked right in the extrusion barrel, through injected steam and/or friction generated by the screw's paddles. Operators control the amount of steam injected, the temperature, and the speed of the screw. A Wenger extruder, for example, can be programmed to operate from room temperature for cold dough extrusion up to about 220 degrees. "By law, they have to reach a high enough temperature to destroy salmonella or other pathogens, which is around 183 degrees," says Rokey.

In a typical machine, a huge pipe sucks up the still-rubbery shaped bits and drops them onto a conveyor belt for further drying and/or baking. Kibble must be dried to 10 percent moisture in order to have the long shelf life manufacturers desire.

When it comes to kibble, all of the ingredients must be finely ground in a pre-extrusion processing step, both the meat and the carbs. The pre-extrusion mixing generally happens in the "raw" side of the factory, in a separate room from the extruder. Meal arrives ready to go, but meat can arrive pre-emulsified or be done on-site. Grains, vegetables, and fruit may arrive pulverized or be ground on-site. Once the material is all ground, it enters the extruder part of the factory. Operators dump or pump the meat slurry or meal and powdered vegetables and grains into the extrusion barrel. These ingredients get churned and blended by a massive conical crank, called a "screw," until they become a pliable dough. This requirement for such heavy preprocessing is part of the reason that an extruder feels like any other factory; by the time a cow or some carrots reach the extruder, they are generally unrecognizable.

SPRAY-ON FLAVORING

At the end of the kibble-extrusion line comes what you might consider the fun part, if you were a piece of kibble. The sea of cooked kibble is dumped onto another conveyor or into a revolving drum, where the pieces are sprayed under a multiheaded shower with fat and flavoring. The flavoring is called "palatant," as in a coating to make it palatable. The sprayer, like a carwash for kibble, puts back in the flavor and scent that rendering and then churning, steaming, and baking process right out. These sprays impart flavor, much like the super-tart coating on candy, or the flavor coating on Cheetos.

In pet feed, palatants make up only about 1 to 3 percent of the total pet feed formula, according to Kemin, a leading manufacturer of pet food palatants.[12] But they have a big impact when it comes to flavor and scent. Palatants are also used on baked feed, treats, rawhides, and tablets, as well as incorporated into wet feed, drinks, and gravies.

Palatants have another important job: they can add protein, yeast, and antioxidants to the final kibble product, important ingredients that were either lost in the production process or never adequately present in the ingredients. A spray-on flavor can give the final product the nutritional profile a manufacturer seeks by coating the kibble with a protein and/or fat glaze. As one palatant salesperson said, "A pet manufacturer will say, 'Here is our spec. We need a certain amount of protein.' Then we can meet that specification with different products." Or, as a Kemin brochure about its product Palasurance explains, palatants are available in a wide range of pricing and performance levels and "can conform to ingredient restrictions and customer label requirements."

A palatant's protein can come from various sources and be offered in budget and premium varieties. When kibble companies claim that they are not all the same, they could be telling the truth: the palatant, for example, could be made from liver, which costs more and arguably tastes better, or from the less-expensive pea protein. Dried chicken and duck palatants are also more expensive than one with pea protein.

Even kibble labeled "all-natural" might get its flavor from a palatant, such as Kemin's Palteva-brand palatant, made with natural ingredients. AFB International, a global palatant maker headquartered in Missouri with plants in the United States, China, Brazil, Mexico, Argentina, the Netherlands, and Australia, offers natural, grain-free, limited-ingredient, hypoallergenic, and low-fat palatants.[13]

Kemin offers a bar graph showing the palatability and "intake ratio" of kibble with and without topical palatant. In this graph, dogs are nearly ten times more likely to eat the kibble with the palatant.

As Pat Moeller, then–vice president at AFB International, explained to *Popular Science* magazine in 2013, dogs don't naturally want to gobble up hard, dry, largely grain-based pellets. "So, our task is to find ways to entice them to eat enough for it to be nutritionally sufficient."[14]

As in all manufacturing, extrusion equipment makers continually innovate, striving to build machines that are more efficient, more sanitary—and even, as manufacturers claim, able to make tastier kibble. Wenger has introduced a "low-cooking" extruder to improve the texture and palatability of the kibble. The dough is cooked lightly in the extruder barrel and then cooked again, through baking, once it's out. "You have an extruded/baked product, which pets prefer," Rokey explains.

The grain-free craze is also influencing extrusion technology today. There's an increased need for something called "twin-screw" processing to work with the supermushy nongrains in demand today. Some of today's popular ingredients such as peas, lentils, and potatoes become very, very sticky when ground and heated with steam, says Rokey. They stick to the single screw extruder, gumming up the system. Companies offering grain-free recipes increasingly rely on twin-screw extruders, which have self-wiping, intermeshing screws that clean the mush off each other as they churn.

The words used by processed-food equipment makers sound nothing like the language of a chef. The hundred-year-old Illinois-based manufacturer Cozzini, maker of extruders for pet feed and for human food such as hot dogs, promises its industrial customers "the highest quality dumpers, screw loaders and conveyors" as well as "heavy-duty stainless steel cylinders, smoothly ground sanitary welds, and robust framework."[15]

You read that and you think, "Yum!" Well, maybe not.

The final step is packaging. The kibble travels through a strainer-type machine to shake off crumbs. Then it can be stored in a silo until it gets weighed and bagged—into different-sized bags, with photos and names promising all kinds of different things. The bags are shipped all around the nation, in railcars and trucks, and sold to pet parents everywhere. Then they're driven home and poured into the bowls of innocent, hungry pet dogs everywhere. This final step, from bag to bowl, typically takes a few months.

There's also a quality lab at the plant. The employees take swabs from the extruder machine all day to check for salmonella, E. coli, or listeria. At night, all is quiet in the kibble factory. Some nights, a uniformed sanitation crew enters to sweep and sanitize the ovens. They remove the sides and climb in, sweeping away all of the kibble dust that has accumulated. Mounds of sand-like material wind up on the floor. If any uncooked kibble bits remain, they could develop salmonella and poison the next batch of food.

Fresh? No. Natural? No. Healthy? No way. But this process is definitely one thing: efficient.

SUPER SIZE ME, THE CANINE VERSION

Convenience food has one thing going for it: ease. For a few generations, this one feature has played a starring role on tables and in pet bowls around the nation. But the science of nutrition has continued to advance, as have anecdotal accounts of the results of eating too much processed food. If you've seen the movie *Super Size Me*, you know that one *month* of gorging on nothing but fast food can make a human diner have mood swings, heart palpitations, headaches, a loss of energy, and depression.

A 2019 study published in *JAMA Internal Medicine* looked at the impact over eight and a half years of middle-aged human diners getting about 15 percent of their daily intake of food and drink (by weight) from ultraprocessed food, or about 30 percent of their calories. Ultraprocessed is a term now applied to processed foods that are ready-to-eat or ready-when-microwaved. This includes breakfast cereal, frozen foods like chicken nuggets, dried foods such as instant noodles, chips, chocolate bars, and candy. The researchers found a direct statistical connection between consuming more ultraprocessed food and having a heightened risk of early death from all causes, especially from cancer and cardiovascular disease. The researches theorized that the negative health impact of eating ultraprocessed food comes from the fact that it has fewer nutrients and more sugar, salt, saturated fat, and food additives than fresh food. These are all factors that have been linked to an increased risk of various chronic diseases.[16]

Kibble and canned feed definitely meet the criteria for the term "ultraprocessed," and as some veterinary nutritionists point out, like pet parent, like pet. Feeding our dogs highly processed kibble for their entire life spans is like serving them the equivalent of Big Macs and fries—or Doritos and chicken nuggets—at every meal, seven days a week, forever. Except that when it comes to Big Kibble, the ingredients entering the processor, in general, are inferior or even poisonous.

Many veterinary nutritionists don't agree with this comparison to Doritos or even to fast food. Kibble, after all, is formulated to offer complete and balanced nutrition for dogs; that's its whole purpose. Junk food for humans, on the other hand, is generally formulated to offer instant happiness—in the form of salt, sugar, fat (and increasingly "flamin' hot" spices). This is a fair distinction—the problems of the so-called "guaranteed analysis" aside. But ultraprocessing is concerning in and of itself.

Board-certified veterinary nutritionist Donna Raditic, co-founder of the Georgia-based nonprofit Companion Animal Nutrition and Wellness Institute (CANWI), has been taking care of animals for more than three decades. She is troubled by the fact that our pets are not living any longer than they ever did. "We do so many amazing things for dogs now, like vaccines and teeth cleaning. Yet, while we've improved our own life span, we haven't moved the bar for dogs. I've outlived all my patients. Why? What other factors could there be? As a nutritionist, you have to start asking about what they're eating."[17]

Raditic isn't focused primarily on the specific ingredients that go into the extruder but, rather, what happens to any ingredient subject to heat. She points to a specific chemical reaction that occurs during food processing, even at relatively low temperatures. Called a "Maillard reaction," it may be at the root of the problem with processed food. The Maillard reaction, also known as browning, creates "advanced glycation end products," or AGEs.[18] AGEs result from heating ingredients that contain sugars and proteins. Even in benign cooking processes like toasting bread and caramelizing onions, the food undergoes the Maillard reaction and thus contains some dietary AGEs, which we eat.

This doesn't mean you should declare a war on toast. Humans and dogs can excrete a certain amount of dietary AGEs out of our systems. The problem comes from eating too many. If you flood your body with AGEs day in, day out, they build up beyond your ability to excrete them. "This build-up damages various systems in our bodies, causing everything from wrinkles in the skin to disease," Raditic says. Studies link AGEs to all kinds of ills in humans, from inflammation and aging to heart disease, diabetes, kidney failure, and Alzheimer's.[19] This growing body of research on AGEs is a primary reason that nutritionists and dieticians now urge us to cut back on processed foods like cereal, chips, and Hamburger Helper, and to add in more fresh fruit and vegetables to our diet.

Raditic voices the same concern for our pets. "If we humans are working to avoid them, yet most dogs and cats are eating heat-processed pet diets their whole lives, what happens to them? If I put you on a Cocoa Puffs–type cereal for your entire life, what happens to you?" You probably won't be looking or feeling your best. Raditic is involved in the burgeoning effort to investigate the role of AGEs on disease in dogs.

One recent study she points to, for example, measured the AGEs in sixty-seven types of extruded, pelleted, and canned dog and cat feeds. This study showed one particularly concerning result: dogs consume daily, on average, 122 times the amount of one type of AGE called hydroxymethylfurfural (HMF) than adult humans do.[20] HMF is one of the "hottest" AGEs under investigation in human nutrition right now. It is a suspected carcinogen, possibly breaking down into carcinogenic compounds in the body. As another recent study on HMF in humans puts it, HMF is one of two products "mainly formed through Maillard Reaction and can be regarded as the most important heat-induced contaminants occurring in bread and bakery products."[21]

Raditic and her colleagues are looking to answer a few questions about HMF: Could the consumption of AGEs and their metabolites lead to an accumulation of HMF? Is this the mechanism behind ultraprocessed foods' link to chronic disease and the reason that there is so much cancer and disease in our pet population? Is the lack of HMFs in fresh, whole food the reason that so many dogs do so much better when they stop eating kibble?

While we have many studies on the ill effects of AGEs on humans, this research is still to come with dogs. As of now, pet parents are left to wonder if their dogs' health problems are related to diet. But we should have more information about AGEs and dogs specifically soon. Companion Animal Nutrition and Wellness Institute, for example, is currently funding research at the University of Georgia, Athens, on the nutritional impact of different types of pet food processing. The results should be published by the end of 2020, providing some more concrete research on the effects of AGEs on dogs.

If all of this sounds new to you, it is. "There's not a lot of research on whole diets for dogs," explains Raditic. "People have this misconception that we have a wealth of knowledge about pet food, but actually the research we have is the effects of certain ingredients: phosphorus, calcium, wheat gluten. We don't have a lot of data on whole diets themselves."

Professor and industry consultant Greg Aldrich makes a similar point. "People assume we have a massive amount of data on companion animal nutrition that has been supported by their tax dollars, and that is incorrect. We are 50 years behind human food and livestock feed in terms of nutrition information. There are not federal grants for pet food research. Today, the library of knowledge about companion animal nutrition could fill a cardboard box."

Still, when it comes to AGEs, we know they can cause real problems for humans. One conclusion seems obvious to us: we need to take a hard look at what we are putting in our dog's bowls and make it healthier. And as we show in the next chapter, feeding dogs better food can literally save their lives.

PART THREE

Good Friends
Deserve Great Food

9

We Speak for the Dogs

A Return to Fresh, Whole Food for Dogs

Everyone thinks they have the best dog. And none of them are wrong.

—Credited to W. R. Purche

Pet parent Sarah Weibel sent us a thank-you e-mail in 2018. Sarah included "before" and "after" photos of twelve-year-old Chihuahua Ru. In the "before" photo, when Ru was eating canned food, bare patches of pink-and-brown skin cover his neck and sides. His white fur is thin in spots, nonexistent in others. Dark tear stains form circles under his eyes. In the "after" photo, taken once he'd stopped eating canned feed and switched to a diet of fresh, whole, human-grade food, creamy white fur covers his sides and face. His eyes are clear. He looks like a healthy, happy, fluffy (tiny) Chihuahua.

We get letters like this at JustFoodForDogs every day. Literally every single day, and have since we started the business in 2010. Customers write to tell us that their dogs' lives have been improved, and in some cases saved, by switching them to fresh, whole food. These pet parents are so relieved and overjoyed that they feel compelled to write.

We'd like to say it's because of some special, magical formula we've discovered and put in our food, but in truth we have to admit that these dogs aren't doing so much better because of some secret ingredient. We don't have a magic formula. We believe that because kibble can be an immunosuppressant, merely taking your dogs *off* it can immediately improve their health. Our customers are then serving up solid, balanced nutrition that their dogs can easily absorb.

The benefit of fresh, whole food can be most jaw-dropping when seen with sick dogs. These are pets who are seriously suffering and whose immune systems need all the support they can get. Many of these dogs are eating a kibble prescribed by a veterinarian, formulated to address a specific disease or condition—by featuring a novel protein the dog has never tried before, for example, or being made with low protein. These are the bags and cans of feed you might buy at your veterinarian's office with a prescription. But despite the therapeutic formulation, it's still kibble. Diet makes a huge difference in a dog's life. We've seen amazing transformations in dogs who have been switched to food designed to alleviate symptoms or improve conditions—what we call a "veterinary support diet"—when their meals are made from actual human-grade food.

Take Cody, a gray-and-white mixed-breed dog who had developed kidney disease. His disease had progressed so far that his pet parent, Janelle Brown, was feeding him crushed up prescription kibble through a tube. Then Janelle heard about JustFoodFor-Dogs and decided to try it instead. She wrote to us about Cody's improvement, which seemed truly miraculous:

In the Spring, Cody had become so ill, he could hardly walk. But his life was turned around after only one week of the Renal Support Low Protein from Just Food For Dogs. His levels began to improve, and now, three or four months later, he is back to his normal self. The feeding tube has been removed. He loves eating your food. He will be 16 in three weeks, and we are confident that Just Food For Dogs saved his life.

For Cody, our veterinary support diet made such a difference for a few very clear reasons. The kidneys' main job is to process and remove excess toxins, but kibble can introduce more toxins. (You now know why.) So taking him off kibble got rid of that problem. But toxins can also accumulate from metabolizing protein, and renal-support diets like ours are formulated with controlled levels of protein to further lower the toxin load. Our renal-support diet is also low in phosphorus, a mineral that can put additional stress on the kidneys. It also includes anti-inflammatory ingredients, important in slowing the progression of disease. Finally, kidney disease leads to chronic dehydration, and all kibble is dehydrating. For Cody and Janelle, the switch from Big Kibble to whole foods meant more years together.

If reading about what's allowed to be in dog feed surprises you, you're not alone. We work in this industry and still find it hard to believe what companies pass off as "food" when it comes to feeding our four-legged friends. Neither of us ever envisioned running a company selling fresh, whole foods for dogs. This was never on our five-year (or thirty-year plan). How did a serial entrepreneur and a tenure-track professor of veterinary medicine wind up working crazy long days for years on end to develop a new kind of dog food company, changing an entire multibillion-dollar industry in the process?

We developed our interest in fresh, whole foods for dogs in

the same way that so many of our customers have—by seeing
how much happier and healthier our own dogs became once we
started feeding them real food. Our real passion is making the
world better for dogs. Long before fresh, whole food for dogs
became a national movement, we both saw the benefit in our own
dogs, with our own eyes.

Shawn was living in Newport Beach with his girlfriend, Andrea,
and their dog Simon, a Lab-pointer mix he had adopted from the
local shelter in 2001. Simon was Shawn's first dog, a rescue, as have
been all of his subsequent dogs. Shawn and Andrea were feeding
Simon what they believed was a premium dry dog food—certainly
one that was premium priced—a mixture labeled "lamb and rice."

One day, the local Petco was out of the lamb variety. Shawn
reached for a bag of the chicken variety. The price was exactly the
same as it was for the lamb. How could that be? If you go to a
butcher, chicken costs less than lamb. Why wouldn't that price
difference be reflected in dog food? "I looked around at other
brands and discovered that the same thing was true across nearly
every one. The bag might read, 'beef,' or 'chicken,' or 'turkey,' or
'salmon,' but the price was all the same."

Shawn, who'd been an entrepreneur his whole life, was per-
plexed by this pricing issue. It made no sense. He'd just sold his
third business and had some time on his hands. "I started doing
some research about dog food online. I called several brands to
see about getting a tour of a pet food factory." You can tour all
kinds of factories today, from jelly bean makers to coffee roasters.
There's even a website, FactoryToursUSA, that lists public tours,
by state and category. But the dog food companies were not offering tours. "It was surprisingly hard to get good information. It
seemed like a cloak of secrecy existed over the world of dog food,
which also bothered me."

He began to ask other questions about what was in the bag, and to identify a few major issues that explained why the so-called "chicken" and "lamb" cost the same. The first lightbulb moment was the realization that dog food is made from feed-grade ingredients, not human-grade food. These are two very different things. "When I learned about what was allowed to be in dog food, I couldn't believe it. I love dogs, and have since I got my first one. I love all dogs. I think dogs are the best creatures on the planet. I don't have any children, and for me, my dogs are my kids. And yet, at that point, I'd never questioned the quality of what we were feeding Simon."

But now he had plenty of questions. The answers were disturbing. He was shocked to discover that the standards are established by the Association of American Feed Control Officials (AAFCO), not a government agency like the FDA, but rather an association of feed control officials that solicits serious input from trade associations and the kibble industry writ large. "What I learned made me decide I could no longer in good conscience feed our dog this stuff."

Shawn and Andrea decided to make food for Simon at home. They found some recipes online and experimented with ingredients. "Making food for Simon was actually kind of fun. I like to learn new things and to gain knowledge about esoteric topics, like canine nutrition. So for me, it was very cool to figure out now how to cook for my own dog (though Andrea actually did most of the cooking)."

Shawn had no thoughts of starting a business around dog food at the time. He was just cooking for his dog. But Simon's appearance and demeanor improved so dramatically, it was astonishing. He had more energy and was more bright-eyed and sharper. "Honestly, I believe he was thinking better."

Around this same time, Shawn and Andrea also rescued an eight-year-old German shepherd that had been abused and malnourished and named her Nala. She had no fur on her tail. It was brown and leathery like a rat tail. She had such low energy, she could barely hold up her head. These are all results of serious malnutrition. Nala started eating the homemade food right away. "The improvement in her health and appearance was even more striking than in Simon's. Within months, her coat was thick and shiny. Her ears were standing up like they're supposed to. She made a dramatic recovery. She looked like a show dog. We could hardly believe it was the same dog.

"One day, our neighbors Lance and Gretchen stopped us on a walk to ask us about our dogs. 'We've really noticed a big difference with your dogs,' they said. 'Not just Nala, but also Simon. What's going on?'

"We told them about the home-cooked, real food we were making, and that we were no longer using bagged kibble. Lance and Gretchen, who had two dogs of their own, wanted in. Andrea loves cooking and was totally on board with making a double batch."

Then the questions really started coming:

- If fresh, whole food made such a difference in these four dogs, would it improve the health of dogs around the world?
- How could more people feed their dogs fresh food, using the same meats and vegetables humans eat?

And then, of course, there were the questions that come to any entrepreneur:

- Could there be a business here?
- If so, could it be big? Could it become a movement that will disrupt a multibillion-dollar industry in serious need of change?

There had to be a better way to feed the nation's dogs. A pet parent enters a store and confronts fifteen thousand square feet of the same basic product in different packages. Even at a pet boutique, the so-called "premium" kibble is primarily premium in price; much of it is still the same unhealthy, extruded material sourced from factories around the world, made with ingredients that can be deadly. Given the scope of the problems with industrial pet food and the limited options available for concerned pet parents, Shawn decided that the dog food industry was ripe for change. "This is how I became a disrupter in the pet food industry," he says.

"WAIT! DID WE JUST DRIVE PAST A RESTAURANT FOR DOGS?!"

With most new businesses, there's a model to follow—other specialty baked-goods shops, other Internet-marketing programs. When it came to showing American pet parents the dramatic benefits that can come from feeding their dogs fresh, whole food, however, there was no clear "playbook" to follow. No one had done an open-kitchen food business for dogs. (Or cats. Or llamas. Or fish.) Merely passing out samples of homemade food on the street or in a hotel ballroom seemed too small for a business designed to upend the 150-year-old tradition of doling out processed convenience "food" for dogs.

The initial business plan relied heavily on a very substantial market test. The idea was to go ahead and build the world's first dog kitchen in Newport Beach, California. Running a kitchen would mean not only building out the kitchen but also trademarking a name, buying the delivery vehicles, finding the vendors—basically running the business to see if others would have such a dramatic experience switching their dogs to fresh, whole food. It would take a serious amount of money and was a pretty unusual way to start a business. But it seemed necessary. The concept was too unique to do something small, and cooking the food correctly too important to outsource it. Customers needed to see dog food being made in front of them to really "get" it. Part of the success would be the experience, pet parents getting to know the people who are making the food for their dogs, being able to ask questions and make requests.

By early spring 2010, Shawn had the launch team and initial funders set. "Dale Davis, a fantastic graphic artist/branding expert, created the logo, color scheme, packaging and graphics. Simon became the floppy-eared face (and snout) of the brand. Rudy Poe, an entrepreneur and Emmy-winning filmmaker, oversaw the website and general operations. My brother, Todd, pitched in with the store, accounts payable, etcetera. We all really just did whatever needed to be done."

The first JustFoodForDogs kitchen opened in Southern California in January 2011. Within weeks, the positive results began bouncing in, tails held high. The improvement in these dogs was undeniable, week after week. The vision for a national business—and then a movement—was born.

The lack of models meant that during our first five years of growth, we needed to devise novel approaches to all kinds of business challenges—such as cooking in large batches *for dogs*. No one was running a restaurant-size kitchen for dogs. Chefs know how to cook for four hundred *people*; we'd have to do what they do, for dogs.

We went to a restaurant-supply company called Chef Toys, in Fountain Valley, California, to look for some huge mixing bowls, for a start. A very experienced salesperson there, a guy named Wes, got very excited about the concept of a restaurant for dogs. Wes had a dog. He loved his dog. And he knew all about how to cook for large numbers because he'd been in the restaurant industry for years. Wes became one of the first unofficial advisors.

He came out for coffee at a Starbucks and explained the ins and outs of the restaurant-supply business and then connected us to a chef from a Westin Hotel who shared insights on cooking for huge numbers of diners.

Then there was the challenge of opening new brick-and-mortar locations. It's always hard to build a storefront. You have to scout out potential locations, make a bid, negotiate a lease, obtain some basic permits, and build out your space so you can begin operating. But we also had to navigate unique bureaucratic red tape. We didn't fit clearly within an existing category. City officials didn't know which regulations we should follow—those for a restaurant or those for a store? Did we need the parking required for a restaurant? (Which is more than for a retailer.) If so, we couldn't afford to use that location, and the process of looking for a new city for a new location started all over again.

One of the most interesting, and surprising, challenges was working with county health departments and departments of agriculture. Who oversees a kitchen making food for pets? Neither wanted to take responsibility for oversight.

One of the biggest hurdles to clear was finding ingredient suppliers. We'd decided to use only USDA-certified meats and other ingredients fit for humans. Restaurant suppliers sell bulk meat, but when we reached out to one of the largest local restaurant suppliers in our area to set up an account and begin purchasing, the company rejected us as customers. The management didn't want to sell to a dog food company. They also thought it would be a waste of time to establish a relationship with us, assuming, as they told us, that our crazy business idea would fail within a year. Here we were, offering to buy huge amounts of meat and getting turned down. You really have to persevere when trying to do something that upends convention, and not get discouraged.

Eventually, we found a quality meat supplier open to working with us. Today we buy more than two hundred thousand pounds of meat each month.

During that first year, we also decided we wanted JustFoodForDogs to be a veterinary-recommended brand. The way to do that is by running an official feeding trial on the food, following the minimum parameters established by AAFCO. A feeding trial is important because it's the proof that veterinarians need to feel confident that this food is safe. Vets tend to only recommend brands that have successfully run a feeding trial on their dog food. That would have to happen next.

MY DOG IS EATING WHAT?!

When the first JustFoodForDogs opened, Oscar was a university professor with a tenure-track job, teaching veterinary nutrition at Cal Poly Pomona and running the veterinary technician program. Then one day he drove by the new JustFoodForDogs kitchen, which was in his neighborhood. What was this? He pulled into the parking lot in front of the store and walked in.

Shawn was there that day and explained the concept. The idea of a kitchen for dogs was totally new. "I'd certainly talked to many people in the dog feed industry before, but I'd never heard anything like this," Oscar says. "When Shawn offered to give me a tour, I expected to see industrial-size cans of low-quality broccoli, huge pallets of reject produce, things like that. But I saw bunches of fresh broccoli florets sitting on a counter in the kitchen area and real carrots. People were cooking. I could see steam rising from a real stovetop. This was food, for dogs. Not feed."

In Oscar's job, he'd occasionally have representatives from the top pet feed companies come talk to students, a common practice in vet tech programs. He invited Shawn to come in and share his concept, too. The students were intrigued. This was the only pet food representative they'd met using restaurant-grade,

USDA-certified meat and fresh produce approved for human consumption.

A few months later, Shawn reached back out to see if Cal Poly Pomona could help run a feeding trial on the food. While most feeding trials are conducted in USDA-registered laboratories with laboratory dogs, usually with beagles, Shawn, an advocate for dog rescue, proposed instead feeding JustFoodForDogs to pets of faculty and staff, living at home and being loved.

They university agreed to this proposal, but upped the ante. The industry-standard test is pretty rudimentary. It's twenty-six weeks long with eight dogs. The dogs must eat the food being tested and nothing else. Only six of the dogs need to stick with the trial through to the end. At the lab, the techs test the dogs' blood for four pretty basic parameters, before and after the twenty-six-week period. At the end, the dogs need to have maintained good blood values and not have lost more than 15 percent of their body weight individually, or 10 percent as a group. But for the JustFoodForDogs test, Cal Poly Pomona wanted a twelve-month-long trial, not six. They wanted to use thirty dogs, not just eight. They also suggested testing for many biomarkers, not just the typical four. The wanted a complete blood cell count and chemistry panel on every dog at the beginning, middle, and end of the yearlong trial.

It would be very time-consuming and expensive for JustFood-ForDogs to establish and follow the necessary protocol for this extensive testing and research. Why go through all of this, when kibble companies are allowed to run a far easier and less expensive test? "Still, I presented Shawn with these added steps necessary for the university's participation. I didn't know him well yet, and was a little reluctant to present this option," Oscar says.

Shawn agreed immediately. He liked the added requirements. "He said, 'Yeah. Absolutely. We want to know how dogs would do on this kind of test.'"

Oscar contacted Dr. William Burkholder at the FDA to tell him the proposed plan and get guidance on the process. Dr. Burkholder said it could be done; there was nothing in AAFCO against this more exhaustive kind of feeding trial. But the university would have to follow all of the minimum steps in the standard protocol, even if it added more tests and requirements.

"I asked him if we could send him our planned protocol to look at. He said it wasn't necessary, but we could, though it could take months or years for someone at FDA to get to it." The FDA wouldn't provide any official approval, but rather offer comments. "I asked him who oversees feeding trials. He said, basically, no one. There wasn't any FDA or AAFCO approval process for the results of feeding trials. It's up to the companies to run them and also interpret them properly, and for the facility that conducts the feeding trial to sign off on the results."

What? This lack of oversight was shocking. How did that make sense? He also told me that unless someone asks for documentation from the feeding trial, the company never has to show it but should keep it on file. I asked how often an official from AAFCO or the FDA or a state agency asks to see actual feeding trial results. Each state has its own enforcement agency and at that time, he said, in his twenty-five years of doing this, he couldn't recall one instance in which a feeding trial got looked at or questioned by a state official.

This conversation really bothered Oscar. He'd spent his life in veterinary medicine. How could feeding trials for dog food be so unregulated? What if a laboratory got hired by a pet food company to run a feeding trial and the client's feed failed? The lab could risk losing that client in the future, for starters. How do we know that all labs always report honestly? "I'd definitely heard about a laboratory overfeeding dogs to ensure they don't lose weight and to mask nutritional deficiencies in food," he says. "With no regulation protecting the integrity of the results, what else might be going on?" And what else might be happening that's truly awful for the dogs?

The USDA regulates the laboratories in terms of how they treat lab animals, but that has nothing to do with the methodology—or validity—of the studies conducted in them. "In all my years as a veterinary student, practicing vet, and now a professor, I hadn't bothered to question the process behind standard AAFCO feeding trials. If you do pharmaceutical clinical trials for humans, certainly the FDA looks at the results. That's what 'FDA approval' means. This really began to raise some questions for me about the pet feed industry as a whole. What else didn't I know?"

Oscar had a golden retriever named Rey who had been with him for more than a decade. Around this time, Rey was diagnosed with kidney disease. Kidney disease is generally progressive; it will only get worse. Oscar switched Rey to a therapeutic recipe for kidney disease made by Royal Canin, designed to slow down the disease progression. "I was definitely interested in the JustFoodForDogs concept and in the feeding trial, but when it came to my own dog, I was sticking with what I knew, still feeling loyal to Royal Canin."

About six months later, Rey stopped eating the Royal Canin. He just refused to eat. "Golden retrievers rarely say no to food, so I was really worried. He also was going a little senile, staring off into space and forgetting where his food bowl was."

Meanwhile, at the university, the team ran the six-month lab tests on the dogs in the JustFoodForDogs trial. The base-level requirement for success in a feeding trial is that they tolerate the food. The dogs in the JustFoodForDogs trial not only tolerated it but also showed improvement on various blood markers. "This was an amazing result. The dogs were doing great, better than when they started.

"Shawn told me that his company had begun developing veterinary support therapeutic diets for specific problems, including kidney disease. After seeing the results of the lab tests, and not having anywhere else to turn for Rey, I decided to feed Rey the JustFoodForDogs therapeutic diet."

Rey was happy to eat this food. Almost immediately, his health improved. Within weeks, he was doing better. He was lucid again. The episodes of staring out the window or freezing—senior moments for a dog—completely stopped. "Then, when we tested his urine, I saw something even more shocking: his kidneys were concentrating his urine, which is a sign that they're doing their job. His kidneys were working again. This does not happen. Kidney disease, as far as we know, does not reverse. I ran the test again. His kidneys were definitely working. In all my years as a vet and veterinary educator, I had never seen kidney lab values reverse and improve to this extent. Rey actually lived to see his seventeenth birthday. He died peacefully in his sleep, and not of kidney disease.

"Seeing Rey's improvement on the food during those months of the feeding trial, along with the trial's final results, made me rethink my entire career. I realized that JustFoodForDogs was doing something truly transformative. The potential of whole-food nutrition was huge. I was a year away from tenure, from a job for life with a pension. But I'd set a goal for my career as a veterinarian to make a real difference for dogs and for the veterinary profession. I could see that joining JustFoodForDogs would allow me to make an even bigger impact on dogs' health than I otherwise could.

"Everyone thought I was crazy to consider giving up the stability of my job to join a start-up. To me, it was a no-brainer. I resigned from my position at Cal Poly Pomona and joined Just-FoodForDogs full-time."

CHANGING THE HEARTS AND MINDS
OF PROFESSIONALS

From the beginning, working within the veterinarian community was a priority for us. It's a veterinarian's job to help us care for our dogs. They are the first point of information for most pet parents (well, maybe after "Dr. Google"), and we wanted those professionals to fully understand what we were doing. Many of the other new, alternative dog food brands have chosen to bypass vets altogether and market themselves directly to consumers. But cutting vets out of the equation is not a good long-term approach. For a true sea change in food for dogs, vets need to be part of the solution.

Becoming a veterinarian-recommended brand was part of this effort for us. We also offered ourselves up to give "lunch and learn" lectures at area veterinary hospitals. As we explain during these talks to distinguished doctors, a lot has been learned about veterinary medicine and nutrition in general since shelf-stable dry and canned food was developed. Why would we still think this is the healthiest way to feed our four-legged family members?

In 2011, we spoke to the doctors at Southern California Veterinary Specialty Hospital in Irvine, California (which has since become the Blue Pearl Specialty and Emergency, owned by Mars Petcare/Mars Inc). We eventually became the official food for that hospital, and still are. One of the vets working at that location at the time, Dr. Julie Stegeman, became an early supporter of JustFoodForDogs.

Dr. Stegeman is a rock star in the vet world. She graduated top of her class at University of Wisconsin, Madison, with a doctorate in veterinary medicine and then went on to spend three more years studying to become a board-certified internal medicine specialist.

One of her patients, an adorable, twelve-year-old cocker spaniel/poodle mix named Charlie Bahadori—with caramel-colored eyes that seemed to reveal his very soul—was sick with chronic kidney disease and inflammatory bowel disease. Kidney disease is progressive, so he was getting worse with time. But now Charlie wasn't really eating. With renal disease, loss of appetite is not only sad for the dog but also potentially deadly.

Food is almost always an issue with the patients Dr. Stegeman sees. These are very sick dogs that other veterinarians have referred to the specialty hospital for advanced care. "Probably 95 percent of my patients need a special diet. I talk about diet with every client, whether or not they thought about it before coming in," she says. "But there were no commercially available diets that would suit Charlie's nutritional needs, even on paper, much less his finicky taste buds. JFFD gave us an option."

As with Rey, Charlie ate the food and started to improve. Charlie went home, and we worked with Dr. Stegeman to adapt a recipe for Charlie as his needs (and his tastes) changed over time. At one point, we wound up delivering the food to his home ourselves. There he was, sitting on the couch, a kind of scruffy, gentle, supercute dog (though we say that about every single dog we've ever seen). He looked happy.

This dog, who'd been given only months to live, lived for nearly two more years.

Dr. Stegeman went on to prescribe JustFoodForDogs to her other patients. Today, thousands of vets around the country recommend it. Dr. Stegeman says she's found it particularly beneficial for sick dogs that can't digest fat due to pancreatitis or severe forms of intestinal disease. "The diets are especially helpful for patients with inflammatory bowel disease. With that condition, we try to avoid any of the ingredients in the diet they're already eating, because they've acquired a sensitivity to those foods. This usually means finding something that is not chicken, beef, or pork and does not have corn or wheat—the most common ingredients in pet foods. They often haven't eaten fish, so when JustFoodForDogs came out with their fish and sweet potato recipe, it was exactly what I needed. It's become my go-to for patients with severe bowel disease, something I can recommend that they don't have to make themselves." Some pet parents want to cook for their dogs, of course, and this recipe from JustFoodFodDogs is available online, but Dr. Stegeman was grateful for this prepared option for others.

Dr. Stegeman has remained a huge proponent of fresh, whole foods for dogs, for families that can make the switch. She's also been a supporter of our business in general, which is gratifying from a business development/customer service perspective. Before JustFoodForDogs, as she tells it, the only services creating truly custom diets had long wait times and cumbersome recipe-request processes. They wouldn't communicate with pet parents, only with veterinarians, "which just doubled my work," she says. "JustFoodForDogs works closely and directly with the clients to create a truly customized plan which meets their nutritional needs, and the clients love it."

Relationships with professionals like Dr. Stegeman really helped energize our mission in the early days. But convincing vets to rethink so much of what they've been taught is not always easy. We faced pushback from commercial feed makers and even some in the veterinary community. It's difficult to upend a huge, profitable industry, particularly one that has a decades-old manufacturing infrastructure devoted to keeping the status quo. At times it felt like we were having to fend off attacks from industry stakeholders. It wasn't always obvious who had a vested interest in the failure of fresh food for dogs, or why. At one point, we learned that a respected board-certified veterinary nutritionist, who is also a professor, was questioning our overall mission. As an entrepreneur, criticism from an authority like that can make you question your vision at times. Later, we learned that nutritionist was part owner of a small, boutique-style add-in for home-cooked food, and perhaps, like the Big Kibble companies eager for us to disappear, viewed our fledgling company as a threat. It's important, anytime you're starting a new business, to almost expect to meet resistance; ideally, you can harness your frustration into energy to work harder.

Another problem we soon encountered when it came to working with vets was actually working with vets—as in, finding people to hire to formulate our food. We needed people with solid nutrition education to figure out what vitamins and minerals dogs needed. Just feeding dogs human food is not good enough because their nutritional needs differ from ours. (See chapters 10 and 11 for details.)

But when we started looking for veterinarians to come work with us on food formulation, we discovered that they were leaving vet school without knowing how to develop recipes from scratch—and with plenty of misinformation about the benefits of processed food, aka kibble. We decided to create our own nutrition rotation, in partnership with Western University Veterinary School in Pomona, California. We created a clinical rotation for fourth-year vet students focused on creating real-food diets for dogs with special health concerns. This would help us find vets who could formulate food—and we have hired veterinarians from this program, with great success. But it also helps students gain knowledge about an alternative to highly processed feed.

More recently, we initiated several big research projects comparing fresh food to kibble. We've seen the success on literally thousands of dogs ourselves. But we wanted to have the science behind our experience and to be able to share this with the veterinary community.

One study we helped launch, published in the journal *Translational Animal Science* in 2020, tested the digestibility of six of our recipes as a way to assess the general nutrient and amino-acid digestibility of dog food made from fresh, human-grade ingredients. This was the first study done on human-grade dog food, and as the test showed, fresh, human-grade food is highly digestible.[1] This was not surprising, but it is very helpful to us in terms of providing solid science for veterinarians. One common opposition to fresh food that has been voiced by Big Kibble and some veterinary nutritionists is the (very real) lack of research showing benefits to human-grade, fresh, whole diets. This study, and others like it, are beginning to push back against that complaint.

We are involved in a few other studies and are excited to see the results. Like the feeding trial, these university-run, peer-reviewed studies can help us talk to more veterinarians about fresh, whole food and get them as excited about our mission as we are.

These efforts to work within the veterinary community help dogs—and other companies like ours. They can help smooth the way for other fresh food companies that have sprung up and for pet parents wanting to cook for their dogs at home. Whole food is what dogs need, and once the truth gets out, it can't be ignored. The movement away from Big Kibble is gaining steam, and it's not just because of us. Other companies, such as Pet Plate and Farmer's Dog, are also responding to the desire for better food for dogs. The pet food industry has continuously evolved, driven not only by changes in our society and economy and our relationship with dogs but also by market desires. There is a growing market for whole, fresh food for dogs—which we see as great news for pets and the people who love them. Today, more and more vets around the country are recommending a whole-food diet as the right choice for healthy dogs and the first course of action for ill dogs.

ANOTHER FIRST: THE "PERFECT" RECALL

One reason so many pet parents distrust Big Kibble is that they hear about recall after recall on the news. Some in the pet food industry say this increase in recalls is due to tighter monitoring after the melamine scandal. Other people point out that human food gets recalled, too. Human food does get recalled, of course. Recently, we've seen recalls of spoiled romaine lettuce and beef with E. coli, for example. But there are far more recalls in dog food, when you adjust for scale.

In 2018, there were sixty-two recalls in pet food, according to the FDA, more than one per week.[2] This is a typical (and depressing) rate. It's also a pretty massive number, when you consider the relatively small size of the pet food industry as compared to the human food industry. The pet food industry reached $27 billion in 2018, so sixty-two recalls equates to one recall for every $435 million in sales.[3]

Human food, on the other hand, topped sales of $6 *trillion* in the United States in 2018.[4] According to the FDA, there were 703 recalls on human food that year, including those based not on reported illness but on *fear* of contamination risk.[5] This is also a pretty typical rate. Put another way, there was one recall for every $8.6 billion of human food sold in 2018.

Perhaps the best illustration of how pet food is exponentially more dangerous than human food is this: if there were one recall for every $435 million in sales of human food, there would have been a human food recall in the United States at a rate of more than per hour, every day of every week—or a total of 11,284 in 2018.

This would be a public health crisis of monumental scale. News stations would be running recall news twenty-four hours a day. Illness and death from food would be rampant. As it now stands, about 128,000 Americans are hospitalized each year from foodborne illness; 3,000 die, according to the CDC.[6] If human food were adulterated as frequently as pet food currently is, nearly *40,000 people* would be hospitalized due to eating every week, and some 1,000 would die each week from the food supply. Our world would change overnight.

This is the equivalent of what our dogs eat right now. When

we get incensed about Big Kibble—when we compare it with Big Tobacco—this is why.

But, yes, human food does get recalled. And as we discovered early on, dog food made from human-grade ingredients could be included. We voluntarily issued a recall on a special holiday recipe, turkey and duck special, because of a contaminated human-food ingredient. You never want to sell a product that could put any dog or person at risk, of course, and it was a scary moment, trying to figure out what, exactly, had caused the problem. But in a strange turn of events, the incident actually helped us build trust with customers. Our sales rose significantly after it. Recently, a customer met our CEO in the Costa Mesa, California, kitchen and said to him, "Oh, I spoke to you before. We talked for like three hours on the phone, back when you had a recall. Nice to speak to you again."

In November 2018, we got a call from a customer who said her two dogs had gotten sick after eating our turkey and duck special. She believed the food was the culprit. You never know for sure if food is the cause; dogs can get into all kind of things. But two dogs on one food definitely concerned us.

We went into full-investigative mode of the turkey and duck special. We asked the customer to return the unused portion of food. We sent the uneaten turkey and duck special to Certified Labs in Buena Park, California. Certified Labs, founded in 1926 in New York City, is a private, independent food-testing laboratory with four locations. It's the place everyone uses to test food, from mom-and-pop restaurants to national chains. We asked the SoCal lab to run the "fast test" for clostridium, salmonella, E. coli, campylobacter, and listeria—the big five foodborne bacteria. This test can show bacterial DNA markers on the food and get answers to you the next day. Still, even a positive result is considered only "preliminary" evidence of contaminated food, because the bacteria could have gotten on the food from a cooking surface. It may not be actually growing in the food.

The turkey and duck special came back preliminary positive for listeria. But where did the bacteria come from? We immediately swabbed all areas, including drains, in the West Hollywood kitchen where it was made, sent off those swabs, cleaned that kitchen like crazy, and sent samples of all of our other recipes to the lab for the one-day test.

Certified Labs, meanwhile, was also following up on the turkey and duck special with a more thorough five-day test that involves trying to grow the bacteria on the food sample. This test is the real deal. If it comes back positive, that's proof that the listeria came from the food and has to be pulled from the sales floor and from customers' kitchens. We didn't want to get a positive result, of course, but we had to know.

The kitchen test came back clean, but after five days we got the truth on the turkey and duck special: listeria. Something in the food was definitely contaminated. Meanwhile, we also got a presumptive positive of two of our other diets. We cross-referenced the three recipes to see what ingredients they shared. As it turned out, just one: french-cut green beans, which we'd bought from a well-known restaurant-supply company. We decided to test the beans and sent unopened boxes to the lab.

But how to tell customers? We had a positive on the turkey and duck special—and we knew exactly who bought the turkey and duck special because we have direct relationships with our customers. We sent a note to all of our turkey and duck special customers, telling them about the listeria and saying we were recalling it. But we had only a preliminary positive on the other two recipes. Did we wait for proof positive before notifying people about those?

We thought, *The turkey and duck special got confirmed; these will, too.* We decided to send a note to *all* of our customers explaining about the turkey and duck special and about the preliminary positive on these other two diets. We didn't wait for them to get confirmed through the five-day test.

We reached out to an attorney who specializes in FDA compliance, and she thought we were crazy. She said we didn't have a legal obligation to notify anyone about the other two diets unless we had a confirmed positive from the five-day test. The FDA also told us to wait until the listeria was confirmed before telling customers. It wasn't necessary to inform them, and it could cause unnecessary panic if we told them. But to us, dogs' health was on the line.

By the end of the week, the other two diets got confirmed for listeria, too, as did the boxes of green beans that came from the restaurant-supply company. We had a culprit. We sent *another* letter to our customers, offering money back to anyone who had purchased any of these three diets during the specific time period that these beans were used—whether or not their dogs got sick. We put our executives' phone numbers on the letter (which is why our CEO spent a couple hours on the phone with a customer, talking turkey and duck special). We made this money-back offer easy; they could just give us their information via a link we provided, and we'd refund their credit card.

We gave a lot of money back, and mostly to people whose dogs never got sick. No dogs died from the tainted green beans in the special, for which we are grateful, and also lucky. But we wanted to do what we felt was right by the customers and their dogs.

Listeria is not typically harmful to pets, and those two dogs got better. But it can cause serious disease in people. The FDA was very interested in knowing where the green beans came from and in getting the word out about the contamination to human diners. Because we're buying our ingredients from the same suppliers that sell to restaurants and grocery stores, we can track any problem with the speed and specificity available in the human food chain. Those two sick dogs and our testing of dog food ultimately allowed the FDA to protect human green bean eaters in several states.

Throughout the affair, our team came together as pet parents, and we asked ourselves, How would we want this handled from our pet food company, as *pet parents*? Then we spoke to our customers as we'd like to be spoken to ourselves. We approach business decisions *first* in terms of what's good for dogs; profits must come after. There's definitely a movement among many businesses today to design and implement socially responsible, sustainable practices. Corporations are adopting standards known as the "triple bottom line," or the "3 Ps: People, Planet, and Profit." The goal is to do well and do good.

We love this idea, though we are striving to meet a quadruple bottom line, too: *Pets*, People, Planet, and Profits.

A BIG BOX RETAILER SIGNS ON

On a spectacular May day in Manhattan, office workers with crisp collars and creased khakis spring from their cubicles and stream toward the Union Square farmers' market—the city's premier celebration of fresh produce. Under sturdy pop-up tents, vegetables and flowers picked that morning are spread out like jewels: pale green asparagus spears; pointy red radishes, brilliant pink peonies sprouting from plastic tubs. This is where Manhattanites come to remember their connection to nature, to see what's growing in the farms outside the city, and to participate in the celebration of color and health that is farm-fresh produce. Fresh-faced kids chomp on apples. Slim hipsters in fringe-bottomed jeans and tank tops smell basil. Older residents fill cloth bags with tomatoes and berries.

Directly across the street from the market is the city's largest pet supply retailer, Petco. It fills the bottom-floor corner unit in a row of historic buildings lining Union Square North. A pet supply store and a farmers' market might seem like they sit on opposite ends of the fresh-food spectrum. Except, on this day the Petco, too, is brimming with fresh produce and meat.

This is the city's first JustFoodForDogs kitchen, opened inside of a Petco, a traditional pet retailer that has, until now, built its business on kibble and cans. What passersby see inside this traditional brick-and-mortar pet retailer today looks far more like the fresh food extravaganza going on across the street than like anything they're used to seeing in a pet supply store. Peering through the tall windows lining the front of the Union Square Petco, you can see a pile of just-chopped carrots sitting on a butcher-block counter, as bright and fresh as anything on offer at the market across the street. Green apples and rough-skinned russet potatoes are stacked in bins. The Union Square store caters to locals and to tourists and occupies a lot of real estate in the minds of the city's pet parents, physically and psychically. It's not some fancy, epicurean option for dogs; it's just about good health.

Union Square is a prime location for us, and we are thrilled for this chance to bring fresh, whole foods for dogs directly to consumers who care about the connection between food and health. But it also speaks about the future of dog food, loud and clear: it will be freshly made, using human-grade ingredients. It will be good for dogs.

Since finally managing to find a supplier, sign a lease, and open that first store in Southern California, we have now opened freestanding kitchens throughout California as well as in New York, Seattle, and Chicago. We have more than one hundred "pantries" in Petco stores around the nation—each one a small "store within a store" offering fresh, refrigerated food and information, staffed by our own highly trained employees—as well as about one hundred more in veterinary hospitals.

Petco has made prime space for JustFoodForDogs and canceled contracts with other traditional commercial dog food companies to the tune of millions of dollars a year. The Petco arrangement is part of the megaretailer's desire to become known as the brand that stands behind good nutrition.

This is all amazing news for us, and for pet parents everywhere. But we're not the only ones in this business. Our mission and that of other dog-loving dog food makers—as well as the passion of pet parents—are changing the nature of the pet food industry. Fresh, whole foods is a growing segment within the pet food industry, even as we insist on following the standards set for human food—not animal feed. According to one industry analysis, fresh, whole food is projected to expand by more than 24 percent between 2019 and 2023.[7]

We're at the head of the pack, but others are definitely running alongside us, which, again, is great for pets around the nation and the world. In December 2016, PetPlate launched, a home-delivery service similar to Blue Apron.[8] Even Walmart, purveyors of that low-cost kibble Ol' Roy, is getting on the fresh food bandwagon. In 2019, Walmart's delivery service, Jet.com, teamed up with Ollie to offer home-delivered, fresh, human-grade pet food.

After a near decade of fighting against the status quo, people no longer drive by our kitchens, scratching their heads and saying, "Is that a restaurant for *dogs*?" Instead, pet parents all over the country can watch their dogs' food being made in front of them. Many are beginning to expect this as the norm. We're still working to change what people feed their dogs and what the industry considers "food."

Are you ready to join us? We know your dog is.

The Face of Our Brand

My very first dog, Simon, is the face of our brand. But a short time ago, I had the sad job of sending out a letter to those who knew him. Here is an excerpt:

Dear Friends,

Many of you have had the pleasure of meeting the dog behind the concept that has become JustFoodForDogs, my beloved Simon. It means everything to me that his likeness adorns the face of every food package. For me it's like a covenant of what's inside and a reminder of why we created JFFD in the first place.

Sadly, this morning we had to say goodbye to Simon. He was 15 years old. It seems like yesterday that I picked him up at the shelter in Huntington Beach. He was just a lanky ball of energy at six months. His zest was boundless and his spirit even more so. Newport Beach Back Bay was behind the house and he would never tire of chasing the ball in those bushes. Later it was the park in Corona Del Mar and even up until 11 years old he could run up and down the hill there . . . big red Kong ball clenched between his pearly whites.

Even though he lost his leg to cancer at 13 and battled a variety of other diseases including dementia, he remained happy and loving until he was no longer able to carry on.

Much has been said about a dog's unconditional love for us—and it's true, it is both a human and canine essential to be loved . . . but it is also an imperative to give love—and Simon let us love him. For that I will be eternally grateful to him—my very first dog.

Rest in peace my Boo.

Thank you to the fabulous veterinary team that helped him. Andrea and I will be making a donation in each of your names to several charities that benefit dog rescue.

Sincerely,
Shawn Buckley

10

Fact Versus Fiction in Dog Nutrition

Top Ten Nutritional Myths, Debunked

> Some of our greatest historical and artistic treasures
> we place with curators in museums; others we take for
> walks.
>
> —*Roger A. Caras, American writer, wildlife*
> *photographer, and preservationist*

What, exactly, should your dog eat? For starters, real food that's safe for humans. But not every single thing that we humans eat is safe for our dogs. Many of us have picked up myths over the years about what dogs can and can't eat. Some are merely amusing, while others can be downright dangerous. Here, to set the record straight, are the top 10 myths about dog nutrition—and the truth.

BIG MYTH #1: In the wild, dogs eat raw food. Therefore, Raw Food Rules.
THE TRUTH: The dog is a domesticated animal, with a digestive system adapted for cooked food.

While your dog may look like he's in his most natural state running outdoors, tongue flapping in the wind, he's also likely quite at home crashed out on your bed, chewing the remote control. The domestic dog is not a wolf, nor does he have some wild, undomesticated brother whose diet he should model. Even a stray dog, like those you might see in parts of the developing world, would be very happy to come home with you if given the chance. Left alone, dogs don't head into the woods to join their wolf cousins and take down a fifteen-hundred-pound bison, then gnaw on its raw flesh. They hang around towns, waiting for restaurants, stores, and home cooks to toss extras into the trash.

Just as there are no wild dogs demonstrating their "truer" nature, there is no wild, raw diet they should be eating. Dogs evolved away from wolves thousands of years ago, and so did their digestive systems. Like humans, dogs lack gut enzymes needed to digest raw plants. Both of our species need help, such as through cooking and chewing. These processes break down plant-cell walls and enable us to digest them and access their nutrients. But while we humans chew our food, dogs often don't chew much. They scarf down their food, an enthusiastic eating style that can mean raw carrots and tomatoes arrive in their guts nearly whole, then pass right out, bringing their nutrients with them. (For ruminants, such as cows, who spend all day chewing, raw is just fine.)

When it comes to digesting raw meat, an animal needs a lot of stomach acid, which true carnivores have (see below). For us omnivores, once again, cooking helps do the work. Cooking also decreases the chance of getting sick from bacteria that can contaminate raw meat.

BIG MYTH #2: Cooking decreases nutritional value and destroys important enzymes (aka Raw Food Rules).
THE TRUTH: Cooking concentrates nutrients. It also makes food easier to digest.

When it comes to raw food, a lot of the volume is water. Cooking removes some of the water, creating a more nutrient-dense food. Steaming, boiling, sautéing, baking—all of these methods reduce the amount of water and make food more digestible for dogs, safer, and more palatable. The USDA offers minimum recommended temperatures for the safe cooking of meat, generally below two hundred degrees.

But don't just take it from us. The USDA lists the nutritional value of raw versus cooked meat. These can be found on the USDA's 2018 FoodData Central, a source used by dieticians and whole food pet companies like ours.[1]

If you look at the comparison between raw and cooked chicken breast, it's easy to see the benefits of cooking. Take thiamin, also known as B1, an important vitamin for converting carbs into energy and supporting the heart, other muscles, and nerves. B1 is one of the most heat-sensitive vitamins. If cooking "destroyed" nutritional value, as some raw food proponents insist, B1 would be the first to go. But there is more B1 per gram after cooking:

Nutritional Value of Chicken Breast, with skin (per 100 grams)

	RAW	ROASTED
Calories:	172	195
Protein:	20.85 g	29.55 g
Calcium:	11 mg	14 mg
Phosphorus:	174 mg	212 mg
Thiamin (B1):	.063 mg	.065 mg

The nutritional boost of cooking is even more obvious in ground beef. Cooked beef has more calories, more protein, more calcium per gram than raw beef.

Ground Beef 80/20 (per 100 grams)

	RAW	PAN-BROWNED
Calories:	254	272
Protein:	17.17 g	27 g
Calcium:	18 mg	28 mg
Phosphorus:	158 mg	226 mg
Thiamin (B1):	.043	.045

Roast Beef for Rover? Yes!

Safe Temperatures for Cooking Meat

Beef, Veal, Lamb
Whole cuts: 145° F
Ground: 160° F (no rest time needed before eating)

Poultry
Whole or ground: 165° F

Pork
Ground: 160° F
Whole and ham: 145°F

Check the temperature with a food thermometer while the meat is in the oven or pan, then wait three minutes before serving. (Meat continues cooking during this rest period.)[2]

BIG MYTH #3: My dog is a carnivore. All he needs is meat.

THE TRUTH: Dogs are omnivores. They need carbohydrates, too.

Sure, your dog may refuse to leave the kitchen if you're frying bacon for breakfast, but a true carnivore or "obligate carnivore"—as in, a meat-only eater—is rare in the animal kingdom. Only ferrets and cats meet this strict definition, house cats as well as big cats like lions and tigers. Dogs are sometimes referred to as "facultative carnivores"—a meat eater that can also digest plants—or omnivores, like humans.

During digestion, both facultative carnivores and omnivores convert beta-carotene from fruit, vegetables, and other plants into vitamin A in the liver. Vitamin A is critical for the eyes, skin, mucus membranes, and immune system. True carnivores lack liver enzymes to convert beta-carotene. They have a rough life, digestively speaking. Cats consume a huge amount of meat, and those in the wild get their vitamin A by eating the livers of omnivores. With house cats, as we've seen, the huge protein load of a carnivore lifestyle strains their livers and kidneys over time. Many old house cats end up with liver or kidney disease. But for dogs, who can happily digest carbohydrates, a balanced diet is best.

BIG MYTH #4: Any carb in a dog food is an empty filler.
THE TRUTH: Carbohydrates provide important calories and nutrients and help reduce the reliance on protein and fat for calories.

While carbs are called many bad names—from "empty" to "cheap" to "filler"—they actually play some valuable part on our plates and in our bowls. Carbs not only provide beta-carotene but also calories for energy, about 3.5–4 calories per gram, the same as meat. Since it's unhealthy to get all one's calories from meat (or fat) alone, carbs are an essential building block of a balanced meal.

Carbs provide glucose, which our cells need. Without carbs,

the body will break down fat and muscle to extract the glucose. Even if you've had success losing weight on a keto diet, this is a taxing way for the body to get glucose and not how you want your dog to eat.

Finally, carbs contain real nutrients. Potatoes, for example, provide potassium, a mineral that supports the nervous system and the heart, helps muscles contract, regulates fluid and mineral balance, and helps keep blood pressure down by mitigating sodium intake. Feeding your dog a mix of meat *and* potatoes, for example, allows you to provide him the energy and nutrients he needs without overloading on protein.

Russet Potato, Baked with Skin (per 100 grams)

Calories:	95
Carbs:	21.44 g
Protein:	2.63 g
Calcium:	18 mg
Phosphorus:	71 mg
Thiamin (B1):	.067
Potassium:	550 mg

Spinach, also a carb (though with a better reputation), is loaded with calcium and minerals. But its low caloric content means your dog needs other carbs (such as potatoes), for energy.

Spinach, Boiled and Drained (per 100 g)

Calories:	23
Carbs:	3.75
Protein:	2.97
Calcium:	136 mg
Phosphorus:	56 mg
Thiamin (B1):	.095

Cheap fillers *do* exist. Such as sawdust, an insoluble, indigestible filler that can be labeled as "hemicellulose" extract on a bag of kibble. That is a filler no dog needs.

The Truth About "Essential Nutrients"

Nutritionists use the term "essential" to describe nutrients that the body *cannot produce itself.* They are important, and therefore it's "essential" that our food or supplements provide them. Those nutrients not labeled "essential" are critical, but the body can produce them itself. Biologists take it one step further. They say that the nutrients the body produces itself are the most *essential*—so important that our systems don't leave it to chance that we get them.

The most important nutrient that humans and dogs make ourselves? Glucose, which we get from starch (or from breaking down our own muscle and fat, in the absence of starch in our diet). Glucose is indispensable to life and is the most basic unit of carbohydrate. The common misunderstanding of the term "essential nutrients" can lead people to assume that carbs are unnecessary fillers. Nothing could be further from the truth.

BIG MYTH #5: Grains are bad for dogs.
THE TRUTH: Grains are a valuable source of protein and carbs.

Like fruits and vegetables, grains are "good" carbs. They provide calories and protein. Take enriched white rice, a grain that has more calories than a potato and more thiamin than ground beef.

Rice, White, Long-Grain, Regular Enriched, Cooked
(per 100 grams)

Calories:	130
Carbs:	28.17 g
Protein:	2.69 g
Calcium:	10 mg
Phosphorus:	43 mg
Thiamin (B1):	.163 mg

If your dog seems to do better on a grain-free diet, chances are it wasn't the grain that bothered him before but rather mycotoxins, a waste product of mold that can grow on improperly stored grain. Unlike mold, you can't see mycotoxins. But they can be deadly to dogs, have shown up on Big Kibble products made with grain, and have been tracked in at least one recent study of these bagged feeds. (See chapter 7 for an explanation of mycotoxins and the resulting grain-free movement.)

A grain-free diet is safe from moldy grain, but it could also be missing valuable calories and nutrients—especially if the resulting formulations lack nutritional balance. Recently, grain-free diets have been implicated in a rise of dilated cardiomyopathy in dogs. (See chapter 7 for more details on this deadly disease.) Despite the popularity of grain-free diets, grains are good food. Don't deny your dog his rice or wheat; just make sure you're feeding him human-grade grain.

BIG MYTH #6: Different breeds have different nutritional needs.
THE TRUTH: Breed-based blends are marketing, not nutrition. Dogs' nutritional needs can vary with age, activity level, health, and reproductive status, but not by breed.

But wait! What about Mars's Royal Canin brand and its Golden Retriever Adult Dry Dog Food in an entirely different bag than its Black Labrador Adult Dry Dog Food? Or the other brands that offer breed-specific recipes? Don't they matter?

While Royal Canin has actually done some interesting research on the snout shape of different breeds of dogs and cats and how this may impact their ability to scarf up different sizes and shapes of kibble, this is not a nutritional investigation. And let's face it: goldens and Labs are basically the same size and tend to have the same lifestyle. (Fetch! Slobber. Snuggle.) The idea that black Labs and golden retrievers need different food is patently ridiculous.

Still, different dogs do have different caloric needs. A shepherd that is actually shepherding sheep, for example, needs far more calories than one lying around the house watching Dog TV. Puppies need more calories than older dogs. A very ill dog may need more calories than its healthy sibling (to fight critical illness). The variation in caloric need due to these kinds of factors can be even greater in dogs than in humans, and sometimes can align roughly with breeds—working and sporting dogs may actually do more work than those in the toy and nonsporting groups. But every dog has his own personality and style. You need to know your dog's activity level, health, and ideal weight and serve his meals accordingly.

BIG MYTH #7: Dog food is a scam. Dogs can just eat what we eat.
FACT: Dogs need food designed for their nutritional needs, which are different from ours. Some "people food" is toxic for dogs.

Before the invention of dog feed as a category, dogs ate what we ate or scavenged for scraps. But as research into canine physiology has improved, so has our understanding of dogs' specific nutritional needs. While they *can* eat most people food (though not all, see Big Myth #8), a healthy human diet can leave a dog without critical vitamins and minerals.

After a year or so on table scraps alone, with no added vitamins, a dog may lack, most notably:

- **Calcium**, which supports healthy bones, vascular contraction, nerve transmission, muscle functioning, and hormonal secretion.
- **Vitamin D**, which helps with calcium absorption and is needed for bone growth.
- **Vitamin E**, a collective name for a group of compounds with antioxidant properties that support the immune system and metabolism.
- **Choline**, which helps with metabolism, cell integrity, muscle control, and nervous-system functioning.
- **Phosphorus**, which works with calcium to help build bones and contributes to cell signaling and energy production.

If you're cooking for your dog at home, the easiest way to balance his meals is to make sure you're using a recipe created by a veterinarian or veterinary nutritionist and to add a multivitamin mix. The best way to think about this added mix is like this: most of us take vitamins and/or supplements, even *with* food designed to meet our nutritional needs. We also get our nutrient levels tested during routine checkups. And as the master of our own meals, we can respond to cravings, which some research suggests might be a way we address nutritional deficiencies naturally. When it comes to our dogs, it's up to us to ensure proper nutrition.

Nutritional Needs of Dogs, Defined

Dogs need 42 different vitamins, minerals, and fatty acids, in addition to specific levels of protein and fat, for their food to be complete and nutritionally balanced. These include the following:

12 Essential Minerals

Calcium, iron, magnesium, phosphorus, potassium, sodium, zinc, copper, manganese, selenium, chloride, and iodine.

12 Essential Vitamins

Vitamins B1, B2, B3, B5, B6, and B9; choline; vitamin B12, or cobalamin; vitamin A; vitamin E; vitamin D; and vitamin K. (Research shows that bacteria in the dog's gut help produce vitamin K when a dog is eating real food; supplementation is only required in a heavily processed commercial diet.)

5 Essential Fatty Acids

Eicosapentaenoic acid (EPA), docosahexaenoic (DHA), linoleic acid, arachidonic acid, and α-linolenic acid.
Puppies need all five to grow, but adult dogs don't need arachidonic. EPA, DHA, and α-linolenic acid are omega-3 fatty acids, which have an anti-inflammatory effect in the body, like fish oil. Linoleic acid and arachidonic acid are omega-6 fatty acids.

12 Essential Amino Acids

Tryptophan, threonine, isoleucine, leucine, lysine, methionine, cystine, phenylalanine, tyrosine, valine, arginine, and histidine. These are building blocks of protein.

> **Taurine**
>
> While not specifically "required" by most references, most veterinary formulators will also look at taurine levels because taurine deficiency has been linked to the recent spate of heart disease in dogs.

BIG MYTH #8: Table scraps are bad for dogs!
FACT: Dogs can eat what we eat, with some very notable exceptions.

The idea that "people food" is bad for dogs is pervasive and long-standing, and partially the result of very intentional marketing in the early days of Big Kibble. (See chapter 3.) But dogs can eat people food, and probably enjoy it even *more* than we do, given the starring role food plays in their lives. (A cracker can be a high point in a dog's day.)

Things that are good for us are generally good for dogs. Like us, no dog really needs Cronuts, Cheetos, or fried chicken skin. Handing your dog food from your table can train him in the annoying habit of begging while you eat. Instead, instruct him to sit and stay away from the kitchen or the table during your meals and share your food separately.

There are some foods dogs should never eat.

> ## Leave It!
>
> *Foods We Love That Are Bad for Dogs*
> - **Xylitol and Other Artificial Sweeteners.** Think sugar-free candy is the perfect training treat for your dog? Not so fast. Candy, mints, gum, jelly, cereal, baked goods, and even toothpastes can be made with Xylitol, often

billed as a lower-calorie, all-natural sugar substitute (and not always disclosed on the ingredient list). Xylitol can act like a nuclear sugar bomb for a dog, causing the pancreas to release massive amounts of insulin, dropping blood sugar levels dangerously low, and leading to weakness, trembling, seizures, liver destruction, and even death. As little as 0.1 grams of Xylitol per kilogram of a dog's body weight can be lethal. If your dog eats Xylitol, call your nearest veterinary hospital right away. You might be advised to try to induce vomiting immediately. If it's been thirty minutes or more, head to the veterinary clinic or vet hospital right away. New types of sugar substitutes hit the market all the time, and we don't always have adequate research on their impact on dogs. Your safest bet is to avoid them all.

- **Candy.** While Big Kibble may claim that grains are "fillers," candy is the real empty-calorie villain. Dogs, like people, have evolved to seek calories. Just as a child can ruin his dinner by filling up on Skittles and become addicted to candy, so can a dog. Just as humans can become sick from too many sweets and even get diabetes, so can dogs. Finally, the highly processed sugar in candy and other junk food can be hard to digest (for us and them). Your best bet? Keep your pet ignorant of this entire category of comestible.

- **Coffee, Coke, Tea, and Other Caffeinated Substances.** Caffeine raises a dog's heart rate just as it does ours. But their small size means even something small, like an espresso shot, can have a large impact. Too much caffeine can lead to cardiac arrest in dogs. While most dogs will not voluntarily lap up a cup of coffee, they may eagerly eat chocolate-covered espresso beans, a used tea bag left on a table, or Excedrin or caffeine pills dropped on the floor. A dog will show signs of too much caffeine in about thirty to sixty minutes—jittering, restlessness, hyperactivity, and even vomiting and seizures. Take your dog to the veterinary clinic or hospital if you suspect caffeine ingestion.

- **Chocolate, Cocoa Powder.** We humans love chocolate for a lot of reasons. The taste. The texture. The stimulation. (Cacao, the bitter, waxy bean from the cacao tree that is the essence of chocolate, contains theobromine, a stimulant similar to caffeine.) But while caffeine acts on the central nervous system, theobromine is a smooth muscle relaxant and cardiac stimulant, and in dogs it can lead to seizures, arrhythmia, and even death. The good news is that it takes a substantial amount of theobromine to kill a dog. Milk chocolate and cookies tend to have very little real cacao and therefore are less dangerous than many people fear (see Big Myth #9 for details). [3]

- **Onions, Garlic, Chives, Shallots, and Leeks.** The sulfuric compounds in onions and their cousins, called disulfides, reduce the red blood cells' ability to carry oxygen. They can also trick a dog's body into attacking the blood cells as if they were invaders, causing hemolytic anemia. Onions are far more dangerous than garlic. A medium-to-large onion—about 100 grams—can be toxic to a forty-five-pound dog. [4] Onion and garlic powder are even worse. Onion and garlic powder are commonly added to processed snacks; one more reason to keep them away from your dog. Still, one accidental exposure to onions in cooked human food is rarely a problem. Repeated exposure to small amounts of either could cause anemia. [5] Signs of onion and garlic ingestion include lethargy, weakness, decreased appetite, fainting, reddish urine, panting, vomiting, and elevated heart rate. Take your dog to the veterinarian if you're worried.

- **Cinnamon and some spices.** Spices can irritate a dog's mouth, esophagus, and stomach. Dogs love fresh food, no spices needed.
- **Grapes.** Grapes and raisins have been linked to kidney failure in some dogs, though the reason and amount are unclear. Some dogs will experience kidney failure after ingesting just a few grapes, while others may bolt an entire bunch and be fine. Your best bet? Avoid them.
- **Nuts.** Some nuts are theoretically fine; many are risky. Walnuts, pistachios, and pecans often harbor mold and its toxins. Macadamia nuts can cause lethargy, weakening of the legs, vomiting, diarrhea, and fever. Pine nuts and Brazil nuts are so fatty that they can promote pancreatitis. When it comes to nuts for Nipper, just say no.
- **Prescription and nonprescription drugs for humans.** The leading pet toxin, according to the ASPCA? Medications for humans, ingested by dogs. Painkillers, ADHD medication, anti-inflammatory drugs, blood pressure medication, serotonin uptake inhibitors— all the things people take to improve their health and well-being can seriously hurt or kill a dog. Even over-the-counter pain medications like acetaminophen, ibuprofen, and naproxen are toxic for dogs.
- **Marijuana.** Don't feed your dog weed. Marijuana can make dogs anxious, scared, and incontinent—basically a really bad trip for a dog. And one he didn't know he was taking.

BIG MYTH #9: Chocolate = death for dogs.
THE TRUTH: Chocolate can sicken or even kill a dog, but it depends on the cacao percentage in relation to the weight of the dog.

You're eating M&Ms while reading a book, perhaps one about dogs. You get up to pour a cup of coffee and realize, upon returning, that—oh no!—your English mastiff, Matilda, has wolfed down your M&Ms! You have a moment of panic. *Should I call poison control?! Why is she wagging her tail and running around in circles instead of convulsing?*

Because she's a big dog and M&Ms contain very little cacao. Hershey's milk chocolate has only about 11 percent cacao.[6] The rest is milk, cocoa butter, and sugar. As chocolate gets darker, the cacao percentage increases, as does the risk to a dog. Semisweet chocolate, the type used in chocolate chips, contains about 60 percent cacao, and about 0.26 grams of theobromine per ounce. Baker's chocolate, that dark, unsweetened variety, is 100 percent cacao and contains the most theobromine, at 0.45 grams per ounce.[7]

Here's a quick rule: one once of milk chocolate per pound of dog could be lethal.[8] So a 120-pound mastiff would need to eat 120 ounces of M&Ms to get sick enough to die. Even a family-size bag of M&Ms is only nineteen ounces. A five-pound Chihuahua would need to eat five ounces of M&Ms; a single-serving-size bag is 1.7 ounces.

PetMD has a great Dog Chocolate Toxicity Meter where you can enter your dog's weight and the type and amount of chocolate he may have eaten for a quick gauge of severity.[9]

What to do if your dog eats your chocolate and you're worried? Call your veterinary clinic or animal hospital, or the AS-PCA hotline. A vet might help you assess the damage over the phone or suggest you come in immediately to induce vomiting, ideally within an hour of ingesting chocolate (or other harmful substance). If you go to the vet, bring the candy wrapper.

While it may be scary in the moment, take heart: a dog will recover from too much chocolate if caught early and treated properly and suffer no lasting negative affects.

> BIG MYTH #10: Dogs love food, but they don't really love us; they just stick around for the grub.
> THE TRUTH: Dogs love to eat, but they also form very real, intense bonds with humans, otherwise known as love.

Your dog is gazing up at you with big, brown, adoring eyes. You believe you have a genuine bond with this living creature, and yet some part of you wonders, *Is it me, or is it the meals?*

It's you. Interspecies bonds are real. When it comes to dogs and humans, we have a particularly symbiotic connection, and it's not anthropomorphism to talk in terms of genuine affection. As the psychologist/founder of the Canine Science Collaboratory at Arizona State University, Clive Wynne, puts it in his new book, *Dog Is Love: Why and How Your Dog Loves You*, "Dogs have an exaggerated, ebullient, perhaps even excessive capacity to form affectionate relationships." They love more quickly and move on more easily—if, say, they've been abandoned and then adopted by a new family—but that is the dog form of love.[10]

That's what we've been saying all along.

Dogs also prefer certain people over others. If it seems like your dog loves you, tolerates your neighbor, and avoids the neighbor's toddler at all costs, your assessment is probably right. These preferences are also based on more than who gives the best treats, though giving a dog a treat is a good way to initiate a connection.

Where does this skepticism about canine-human love come from? Perhaps it's cynicism from those who don't have dogs or haven't had good relationships with dogs. Or maybe it has more to do with the human trait of (sometimes) forming quid pro quo in relationships, self-serving connections forged strictly for utilitarian reasons. Perhaps it's due to an anxious attachment style on the part of the human, or maybe a specific dog who is on the less snuggly side.

Bottom line: if your dog acts like he loves you, this is one love you can definitely trust.

11

Can My Dog Eat Popcorn?

Real Answers to Common Questions

> The gift which I am sending you is called a dog, and is in fact the most precious and valuable possession of mankind.
>
> —*Theodorus Gaza, fifteenth-century Greek scholar*

When it comes to human food, what, exactly, can your dog eat? And why does he nibble on some nonfood items (shoes, grass)? On our company website, we offer pages of answers to frequently asked questions like these. But of all the FAQs we list, the one that gets the most visitors is about popcorn. "Can my dog eat popcorn?"

Why do so many people want to know this? For years, the popularity of this page baffled us. Who are all these people making popcorn for their dogs? Are they snuggling in for an evening with Netflix, trying to figure out whether their dog prefers butter-flavored popcorn or kettle corn? Who makes popcorn for their dog? We used to ask each other about this all the time.

Then, one night, the answer became clear.

About a year ago, Oscar was watching a movie at home with a few friends. "We were sitting in the living room on the L-shaped sectional in front of the big screen, totally absorbed in the movie, passing a bowl of popcorn back and forth, dropping the occasional popcorn kernel on the floor, as you do when you're focused on a movie and shoveling popcorn into your mouth. My dog, Bruce, was there, too.

"Suddenly, one of my friends said, 'Hey, Oscar! Your dog is eating popcorn. Can dogs eat popcorn?!'"

Bruce had been walking around, scarfing up the dropped pieces. Suddenly, the explanation for the FAQ question was clear! Every evening, millions of Americans around the country are watching TV with their dogs—and dropping popcorn, just as we were. They aren't asking for advice before popping corn for their dogs; they're scrambling for answers *after* their dogs have wolfed down snacks they made for themselves. Americans eat about fourteen billion quarts of popcorn each year, and we grow the bulk of the world's supply. Some of that crop is going to our dogs.[1]

We live with our pets, play with them, sleep with them—watch TV with them—yet many of us have unanswered questions floating in our heads about their diets and some particular habits of our best friends. Here, to answer the burning—or salted and buttered—questions you have about dogs, is our Official Nutritional Q&A.

BURNING QUESTION #1: Can my dog eat popcorn?
OFFICIAL ANSWER: Yes, in small amounts. But skip the butter, salt, and M&Ms.

Popcorn, a starch, contains nutrition and calories, which provide energy dogs need. There are about 30 grams of carbohydrates and 120–50 calories in a serving of popcorn (two tablespoons unpopped, or four to five cups, popped).[2] When sharing this crunchy snack with your dog, avoid adding salt, butter, chocolate, or flavorings containing onion or garlic powder (see why below). And look out for uncooked kernels, which can break a dog's tooth (or a human's), be a choking hazard, and cause an upset stomach. An unpopped kernel could also get lodged in your dog's mouth, possibly causing infection or dental disease.

> BURNING QUESTION #2: Why does my dog eat her own poop?
> OFFICIAL ANSWER: She could be a neat freak. She could be bored or stressed. She could be hungry. She could be ill.

Eating one's own poop, a behavior called "coprophagia" (from the Greek words for "consumption of feces"), is completely revolting to us. But it's not uncommon for dogs or other animals. Rabbits eat excrement to aid metabolism and provide nutrition. Still, it's not an essential part of any dog's daily diet. Since we can't ask dogs what, exactly, they think they're doing, veterinarians have evolved a few working theories.

The Compulsive Cleaning Theory: The most widely accepted behavior-based theory is that some dogs have an obsessive-compulsive–like need to clean up after themselves. Female dogs instinctively keep their bedding area clean for their puppies, these theorists posit, so the "cleaning gene" must be part of the species. Be careful about punishing your dog for "accidents" in the house, because she may decide to "clear the evidence" before you notice—an example of a dog's profound desire to connect with us, gone (nauseatingly) awry. To help curb your dog's extreme need to clean, scoop the poop yourself *before* she does. If you pick up after your dog consistently, she may eventually realize it's not her responsibility and leave well enough alone.

The Boredom or Stress-Eating Theory: If your dog is left home alone all day, she might eat poop for entertainment. (See below for advice on better ways to keep a dog stimulated.) Or, she could be under a lot of stress. Dogs feel stress from many of the same major changes that stress us out—a new baby, an older child moving out, a whole-family relocation. Another cause could be a desire for attention from you. If you respond with a huge amount of emotion, such as yelling, you could reinforce it.

It's frustrating, but recognize that your dog is expressing distress with this behavior. If your otherwise-healthy dog is eating poop, take a look at her daily schedule and its diversions, any stressful changes to it, your own level of attention, and your training tactics. Try adjusting your actions to curb hers.

The Hungry-Dog Theory: If your dog is underfed, she might just eat whatever is in front of her, including her own poop. Similarly, if you cook at home for your dog but aren't getting in the proper nutrients, your dog could try to correct those nutritional deficiencies on her own. Or, if you've switched from kibble to mouth-wateringly delicious, fresh, whole food, she *might* be trying to get more, in any form it comes.

Make sure she's getting enough food, enough calories in that food, and that her meals are properly balanced for a dog's needs.

The Medical Theory: Some diseases increase appetite, such as diabetes mellitus, Cushing's disease, intestinal malabsorption, exocrine pancreatic insufficiency (EPI), and malnutrition. Certain medications also increase appetite. Parasites can compete with your dog for nutrients in her food. In any of these cases, your dog might resort to coprophagia in an effort to feel full or to gain nutrients.

If your dog is scarfing down excrement and shows signs of illness or has greasy, yellow stools, make an appointment with your vet to have it checked out right away.

BURNING QUESTION #3: Why does my dog eat grass?

OFFICIAL ANSWER: Yum!

The term for pets eating nonfood items is "pica." Children manifest pica when they eat dirt or sand, as do dogs when they eat grass (or poop). First, to debunk some common theories: some people believe that dogs eat grass to make themselves throw up, but there is little evidence to support this theory. A dog may throw up after mowing the lawn with his teeth, but it doesn't follow that he was eating grass with this aim. Some people think grass eating may be a way to alleviate boredom, but this theory also seems suspect because many dogs will stop to eat the grass in the middle of a stimulating walk. Another theory holds that grass provides nutrients missing from their food. We don't believe this theory, either, because your lawn may look lovely, but it's not all that nutritious for a dog. Some people believe grass is a source of fiber. We know a poodle that liked to graze on grass during her daily walks; when her pet parents switched her to a high-fiber diet, she stopped. The fiber theory makes some sense, but there's no good evidence backing it.

We conclude that dogs eat grass because they like it—the taste, the texture, or the crunch. On a hot day, some may like the moisture in the blades, especially if there's no water around. Eating grass isn't a problem for dogs. Still, if it happens all the time and worries you or if your dog develops a sudden obsession with grass, take him to the vet to see if there is a gastrointestinal problem such as parasites, inflammatory bowel disease, allergies, or food sensitivities.

BURNING QUESTION #4: My dog eats food I'm not feeding him, like bananas left on the counter or, once, an entire sheet cake. Why?

OFFICIAL ANSWER: Human error.

If your dog is eating food off the counter, you haven't drawn a clear line between what is off-limits—human food on the counter—and what you've put out for him. It may look like he's just too big or too curious for your house or overly obsessed with food, but he's actually unclear about the rules. If you find this behavior funny, he'll pick up on that positive energy and keep doing it.

Instead of laughing or yelling, move your dog off the counter. Stand in front of him and make him sit. (You might even send him to his bed, if he's trained to go to the bed.) If you do this consistently, you're setting a boundary. Also, make sure that he is getting enough food and nutrition in his bowl.

> **BURNING QUESTION #5**: Is freeze-dried food better than canned or kibble?
>
> **OFFICIAL ANSWER**: Possibly. But freeze-drying compromises nutrient content. Contact the manufacturer to find out how they're accounting for that fact.

For the freeze-drying process, companies freeze the food, then dehydrate it. This can be done with fresh, whole food, and some companies are now offering this as an option for dogs. We created a prototype freeze-dried version of our food but chose not to offer it to customers because water-soluble vitamins, such as the B vitamins, need water to exist; freeze-drying destroys them, decreasing the nutritional content of the food. Companies can add nutrients back in after processing, though this can compromise flavor or appearance. AAFCO guidelines don't require companies to verify the nutritional profile after processing, meaning the nutritional profile on freeze-dried food, as on kibble, may not reflect what your dog is actually eating. See if you can find out how, exactly, the company you're considering maintains nutritional integrity of the food. At JustFoodForDogs, we choose to use Tetra Pak technology for a shelf-stable product, rather than freeze-drying.

BURNING QUESTION #6: What should I feed my
  dog when we're traveling?
OFFICIAL ANSWER: Ideally, a portable version of his
  current diet.

Traveling with a dog can enhance your trip, and more and
more Americans are doing it. We take our pups on road trips,
fly with them on airplanes, bring them along while camping.
If you're feeding your dog a whole-food diet, the easiest option
might seem to be to just give him leftovers from your meals or
order him something at a restaurant. But this switch in diet can
lead to indigestion and probably diarrhea, which does not enhance anyone's vacation. You also don't know what, exactly, is in
that food (onion? garlic?).

Dogs, in general, do best on a relatively consistent diet.
At JustFoodForDogs, after we dismissed freeze-drying as an
option for travelers, we decided to use Tetra Pak technology
in order to offer a shelf-stable product, convenient for travel.
Other companies also offer food in Tetra Paks. This is a great
option for travel. Another option, if you're taking a road trip or
a camping trip and currently feed your dog fresh, whole food,
is to bring it along in a cooler (as you would with your own
food). If you're flying, check in advance to see if the fresh-food
company you use is available in your location or can be shipped
there. If you're renting a house or condo or have a hotel with a
kitchen and you cook for your dog, continue cooking for him
as usual.

BURNING QUESTION #7: Is feeding human-grade
  food to dogs sustainable? Don't we need all the food we
  can grow for humans?
OFFICIAL ANSWER: It's not a zero-sum game. Feeding
  dogs real food doesn't cause world hunger.

We actually see this question about the sustainability of real food for dogs as one that is coming, largely, from Big Kibble—a strategy designed to discourage pet parents from turning away from processed feed. The claim is that it's irresponsible to feed our pets healthy, high-quality food because that action removes food from the supply chain available to humans and could significantly raise the cost of ingredients, given the greater market demand.

We love the idea that Big Kibble is taking up the call for sustainability. But while hunger is a serious issue, it is also one with many moving parts, from the presence or lack of arable land and sustainable growing practices to manufacturing processes, distribution routes, macro- and microeconomics, climate, and war. Feeding dogs good food, however, is never going to be a major cause of human hunger.

We don't see ultraprocessed kibble made from the remnants of human food production as ideal for dogs, and so in some ways this could be a larger question about the sustainability of pets. Can the world support pets? We say, "Yes!" Dogs improve our lives in so many ways; we absolutely believe pet ownership is valuable and compatible with a sustainable lifestyle.

We also believe—and hope—that there is enough technology and creativity in the world to grow good food for all humans and for our pets. We think the market will continue to push for real improvements in the pet feed industry, writ large. And we look forward to the day when we can truly call everything our dogs eat "food."

BURNING QUESTION #8: What will happen to the scraps of human-food production if we don't feed them to our dogs?

OFFICIAL ANSWER: Pet food is only one of the many clients served by the rendering industry.

Is it our dogs' job to eat dehydrated chicken poop? No. Our four-legged family members should not be living recycling machines. At this point, renderers provide materials for many other products, including fuel and fertilizer. We're optimistic about the possibilities for scrap materials *other than* feeding them to dogs. We speak for the dogs.

BURNING QUESTION #9: Why is all kibble brown?
OFFICIAL ANSWER: Ah-ha! Good thing you got this book.

Recipes

Healthy Food for the Ones You Love

F eeding your dog nutritious food is surprisingly easy and probably a lot less challenging than trying to cook for a whole family of picky human eaters (each of whom may be following a specific diet that excludes whole categories of food). Making your dog's meals guarantees that he's not getting any harmful additives or mystery ingredients or subsisting on highly processed foods that are like the canine version of eating nothing but Froot Loops at every meal.

Dogs love fresh food. In the early days, we did a lot of tastetasting with dogs and discovered that they tend to love certain ingredients and combinations, such as mixed proteins (which we have in our specials) and scrambled eggs. To create each of these recipes, we came up with an idea of a good combination and then lined up the nutrition data about each ingredient, available on the USDA database, along with nutrition information we have from our own testing or from a supplier, such as the supplier of our fish oil. We chose ingredients that we know are safe for dogs and palatable, then adjusted the various amounts of each until we devised a formulation with the optimal amount of overall nutrition; adding supplements if needed.

We use fresh vegetables at our kitchens and advise you to do the same, when possible. Wash all fruits and vegetables thoroughly before cooking and make sure to choose potatoes that are fully ripe—no green spots. If you must use frozen produce, your dog will still love his dinner. But make sure to choose frozen options with no added salt, sugar, or spices, which can be dangerous for dogs. (See chapter 9 for no-go spices.) All vegetables in these recipes are lightly cooked to jump-start your dog's digestion process and help him absorb nutrients.

Each of these recipes makes about ten pounds. We recommend making this large of a batch, separating it into daily portions, putting whatever you can use in three or four days in the refrigerator and freezing the rest in a Tupperware-style container or zipper bag. (Meat will last four days in the refrigerator; fish three.) For a small dog or a small kitchen, you can cut the recipes in half. You'll likely need some extralarge bowls and big pots and pans to make these recipes.

Note that dogs need to eat different amounts of each recipe. For updated calorie content on each of these recipes, recommended feeding amounts and approximate serving sizes for your own dog, visit out calorie calculator at JustFoodForDogs.com

Why Your Dog Needs to Take His Vitamins

While cooking for your dog can be fun and easy, the trick is to make sure your dog's meals are nutritionally balanced. This generally means adding a nutrient supplement to the recipe. Dogs have different nutritional needs than we do, and over time they can develop deficiencies in calcium, vitamin D, vitamin E, choline, or phosphorus from homemade diets that have *not* been nutritionally balanced for their species.

To ensure proper nutrition, mix in a dog-specific nutrient blend—ideally one that has been tested in feeding trials. You can use one created by JustFoodForDogs or from another reputable company. You can also ask your local compounding pharmacy to create a nutrient blend based on the ingredients in one like ours, though this can get expensive. Each recipe below calls for two to six tablespoons of a multivitamin mix to guarantee that your dog is getting optimal nutrition. Most reputable, balanced recipes you'll find elsewhere do the same.

Each recipe below also includes safflower oil, a great source of linoleic acid, an essential omega-6 fatty acid. Linoleic acid is a precursor to the body's inflammatory response and is critical for healthy immune function. ("Essential" nutrients are those that must be obtained from food rather than made inside the body. See chapter 9 for more information on essential nutrients.)

Another way to think about it is like this: just as we take vitamins to guarantee we're getting *all* the nutrients we need, so should our dogs.

Recipe One

Beef and Russet Potato

The ingredients for this superpopular dish are easy to find and easy to cook. Beef is an excellent source of essential amino acids and essential fats. We use an 80/20 or 80/15 ground beef, so the included fat provides calories. Given the healthy amounts of protein and fat, this recipe is exceedingly palatable (dogs love protein and fat the most in their food). Beef liver is rich in minerals, because the liver is where minerals are stored in the body. Liver is loaded with iron, magnesium, manganese, selenium, copper, and zinc. The carrots provide vitamins C and K, potassium, and dietary fiber. Russet potatoes add vitamin C, vitamin B6, potassium, niacin, fiber, magnesium, and thiamin. Apples are high in antioxidants and fiber and provide some flavor. (Remember to core and remove all seeds before using, since seeds can be harmful and even toxic to dogs if they accumulate in their system.)

Yield: 11.5 pounds

Ingredients:

- 3 lbs., 9 oz. ripe russet potatoes with skin, cubed into bite-size pieces
- 1 lb., 14 oz. sweet potatoes with skin, cubed into bite-size pieces
- 5 lbs. lean ground beef (80/20 or 85/15), raw weight
- 2.5 oz. beef liver, diced or ground, raw weight
- 5 oz. carrots, finely chopped
- 5 oz. green beans, finely chopped
- 2.5 oz. green peas, finely chopped
- 2.5 oz. green or red apples, washed, cored, finely chopped
- 3.75 oz. safflower oil
- 1 tbsp. fish oil (JustFoodForDogs sells it, or use any 18 percent EPA/12 percent DHA)
- 3 tbsp. multivitamin mix like JustFoodForDogs Beef and Russet Potato DIY Nutrient Blend

Cooking:

Boil potatoes and sweet potatoes until cooked (about 10–15 minutes), then plunge in ice bath to stop cooking. Drain and set them aside to cool.

In a nonstick skillet, brown beef and beef liver over medium-high heat, stirring frequently. You do not need to add any butter or oil; the beef will cook in its own fat. When the beef is 50 percent brown and 50 percent pink, add carrots, green beans, peas, and apples. Continue to sauté until beef is fully cooked and vegetables are soft. Do not drain away any of the fat; it is part of the recipe.

Let the mixture cool until warm to the touch. In a very large mixing bowl, combine meat and vegetable mixture with potatoes and sweet potatoes and add the oils. While combining and stirring, slowly sprinkle in the proper amount of the nutrient blend.

Divide into individual serving sizes for your dog in zipper bags or glass or plastic storage containers. Store in refrigerator for four to five days, or up to three months in the freezer.

Recipe Two

Fish and Sweet Potato

This version of fish and chips for dogs can be fed to adult dogs but is also perfect for growing puppies because it is formulated with higher concentrations of vitamins and minerals than a recipe just for adults. Puppies need more calcium and phosphorus than an adult dog because calcium and phosphorus are used to build bone. They also need higher amounts of many essential nutrients, which this recipe provides. Adult dogs can eat growth formula, or "puppy," diets and do just fine. Many companies now offer "all life stage" diets, which basically means that they have the extra vitamins and minerals that puppies need to grow but that adult dogs can healthily store or excrete. (While it may seem as if growing puppies need extra calories, they actually don't unless they are highly, highly active.)

This recipe is also one used by veterinarians to help calm digestive problems like inflammatory bowel disease, or chronic pancreatitis. IBS is a broad term that basically means a reactive gut. Fish and sweet potato are generally highly tolerable and easily digestible even by reactive guts; they're less likely to cause an allergic or other type of reaction than meat or other starches. Pancreatitis is inflammation of the pancreas, an organ that produces enzymes that help digest fat. Fat puts stress on an already inflamed pancreas, so this diet's low fat makes it good for dogs that cannot tolerate too much fat. If your dog suffers with IBS or pancreatitis, talk to your veterinarian about any nutritional change or consideration first.

For this recipe, we use wild-caught Pacific cod, an excellent source of low-fat protein and omega-3 fatty acids, vitamins B12 and B6, niacin, potassium, phosphorus, and selenium.

Using both sweet potatoes and russet potatoes allows us to balance the nutrients between the two ingredients, providing the right amount of vitamin A, as well as other important vitamins, healthy carbohydrates, manganese, copper, dietary fiber, potassium, and iron. Unlike fish and chips for humans, our healthy recipe skips the high-calorie/low-nutrient batter and deep frying and adds in green beans and broccoli as a source of fiber and additional vitamins and minerals.

Yield: 11 lbs.

Ingredients:

4 lbs., 8 oz. Pacific cod, raw weight

6 oz. green beans, finely chopped

6 oz. broccoli, finely chopped

3 lbs., 3 oz. sweet potatoes, with skin, cubed into bite-size pieces

3 lbs., 3 oz. russet potatoes, with skin, cubed into bite-
size pieces

5.75 oz. safflower oil

6 tbsp. multivitamin mix like JustFoodForDogs Fish and
Sweet Potato DIY Nutrient Blend

Cooking:

Preheat oven to 350° F. Place cod on a parchment-lined baking sheet and bake for 15–20 minutes, or until fully cooked. Let cool to touch.

Steam or boil green beans and broccoli until soft. Let cool.

Boil potatoes and sweet potatoes until cooked (about 10–15 minutes). Add ice to stop cooking, drain, and let potatoes cool to touch.

In a large mixing bowl, combine all ingredients, including oil. Slowly sprinkle in the proper amount of the nutrient blend.

Divide into individual serving sizes for your dog and put into zipper bags or glass or plastic containers. Since this is a fish-based recipe, store in the refrigerator for three days, or up to three months in the freezer.

Recipe Three

Venison and Squash

Give your dog a harvest meal with this classic fall recipe. Venison (deer meat) is a perfect protein for a dog who may have scarfed down too many holiday treats, because it's high in protein and iron while relatively low in fat. This novel protein is also rich in vitamins B12 and B6, riboflavin, and niacin and provides all essential amino acids. Look for venison at specialty stores selling fresh, top-quality meats.

Butternut squash is a low-glycemic carbohydrate rich in nutrients, antioxidants, and anti-inflammatory compounds. This is our highest-protein/lowest-glycemic carbohydrate diet, for those looking for this option for their dog. Anytime you can reduce inflammation naturally, that's better for your dog's (and your) health. The unsweetened cranberries provide an excellent source of vitamin C and are high in fiber, manganese, and vitamins E and K. They also add a sweet, tart taste and a holiday feel.

Yield: 11.5 lbs.

Ingredients:

- 3 lbs., 2 oz. butternut squash, cubed into bite-size pieces (unbuttered, no salt)
- 3 lbs., 2 oz. sweet potatoes with skin on, cubed into bite-size pieces
- 4 lbs., 11 oz. ground venison, raw weight
- 15 oz. brussels sprouts, finely chopped
- 2.5 oz. unsweetened cranberries, fresh or frozen, finely chopped
- 4.25 oz. safflower oil
- 1 tsp. fish oil (JustFoodForDogs sells it, or use any 18 percent EPA/12 percent DHA)
- 2.5 tbsp. multivitamin mix like JustFoodForDogs Venison and Squash DIY Nutrient Blend

Cooking:

Boil water. Add squash and sweet potatoes and boil until just cooked (about 10–15 minutes). Plunge into ice bath to stop cooking. Drain and set aside to cool.

In a nonstick skillet, brown venison over medium-high heat, stirring frequently. There is no need to add any butter or oil; the venison will cook in its own fat. When the venison is 50 percent brown and 50 percent pink, add brussels sprouts and cranberries. Stir and cook until all the venison is browned and the vegetables and cranberries are soft.

Let the mixture cool until warm to the touch. In a large mixing bowl, combine with potatoes and sweet potatoes and oils. Slowly sprinkle in the proper amount of the nutrient blend.

Divide into individual serving sizes for your dog and put into zipper bags or glass or plastic storage containers. Store in the refrigerator for four days, or up to three months in the freezer.

Recipe Four

Lamb and Brown Rice

Lamb is a great protein source for aging dogs, or dogs with delicate livers or kidneys. All red meats contain moderate levels of phosphorus, but lamb contains the least. Part of the job of the kidneys is to help get rid of excess phosphorus. Lamb provides all essential amino acids without providing excess phosphorus that the kidneys would have to work hard to get rid of. Lamb liver, ounce for ounce, contains the most concentrated volume of protein and vitamin A of any meat out there. This nutrient-dense food is also a rich source of heme iron (highly absorbent iron from animal protein), copper, folate, riboflavin, niacin, phosphorus, and zinc. Here, it is paired with long-grain brown rice, a complex carbohydrate that offers a good source of calories, B vitamins, magnesium, and zinc. Blueberries add flavor, vitamin K, and fiber.

Yield: 13 lbs.

Ingredients:

2 lbs., 4 oz. long-grain brown rice, dry weight

4 lbs. lean ground lamb (80/20 or 85/15), raw weight

5 oz. lamb liver, diced or ground, raw weight

16 oz. cauliflower, finely chopped

16 oz. carrots, finely chopped

4 oz. spinach, finely chopped

2 oz. blueberries, fresh or frozen

4 tsp. safflower oil

2.5 tbsp. multivitamin mix like JustFoodForDogs Lamb and Brown Rice DIY Nutrient Blend

Cooking:

Cook rice according to usual directions. While rice is cooking, brown lamb and lamb liver in a nonstick skillet over medium-high heat, stirring frequently. While lamb is still slightly pink, add cauliflower, carrots, spinach, and blueberries. Cook until lamb is fully cooked and vegetables are soft. Do not drain away any fat.

Let the mixture cool until warm to the touch. In a large mixing bowl, combine meat and vegetable mixture with cooled brown rice and oils. Slowly sprinkle in the proper amount of the nutrient blend.

Divide into individual serving sizes for your dog and put into zipper bags or glass or plastic storage containers. Store in the refrigerator for four days, or up to three months in the freezer.

Recipe Five

Chicken and White Rice

Your dog can enjoy the comfort food of chicken and rice with this balanced, flavorful, whole-food recipe. We use chicken thighs, an excellent source of protein, vitamins, and minerals, including vitamin B6, iron, pantothenic acid, phosphorus, zinc, selenium, and niacin. Though many North Americans prefer chicken breast, dark meat is the cut of choice in other parts of the world, in part because it actually has higher concentrations of vitamins and minerals. Leaving the skin on some of it, as described here, provides linoleic acid, an essential fat. Fat is actually good for dogs, in the right amount. The chicken fat is also the reason this recipe doesn't require added oil. Don't throw away the giblets. Chicken gizzard is a good source of minerals, while chicken liver is also very dense with nutrients, more so even than the thighs. Long-grain, enriched white rice is easily digestible, high in B complex, iron, calcium, magnesium, zinc, copper, and selenium.

Yield: 9 lbs.

Ingredients:
- 1 lb., 8 oz. enriched long-grain white rice, dry weight (some white rice is not enriched—make sure yours is)
- 2 lbs., 4 oz. chicken thighs, skinless and boneless, diced or ground, raw weight
- 1 lb., 4 oz. chicken thighs, boneless, with skin, diced or ground, raw weight
- 6 oz. chicken gizzard, diced or ground, raw weight
- 5 oz. chicken liver, diced or ground, raw weight
- 8 oz. spinach, finely chopped
- 8 oz. carrots, finely chopped

    8 oz. green or red apples, washed, cored, all seeds
      removed, finely chopped

    4.75 tbsp. multivitamin mix like JustFoodForDogs Chicken
      and White Rice DIY Nutrient Blend

Cooking:

Cook rice according to usual directions. While rice is cooking, brown chicken thighs, chicken gizzards, and chicken liver in a large nonstick skillet over medium-high heat, stirring frequently. While chicken is still slightly pink, add spinach, carrots, and apples. Continue to cook until chicken is fully cooked and vegetables are soft. Do not drain.

Let the mixture cool until warm to the touch. In a large mixing bowl, combine chicken and vegetable mixture with the cooled white rice. Slowly sprinkle in the proper amount of the nutrient blend.

Divide into individual serving sizes for your dog and put into zipper bags or glass or plastic storage containers. Store in the refrigerator for four days, or up to three months in the freezer.

Recipe Six

A Treat!
All-Day Breakfast

Dogs love scrambled eggs, and they can be a fine food for dogs to eat. This recipe isn't nutritionally balanced to serve as a long-term, full-time diet, but it's a great way to give your dog a treat and let him participate in Sunday brunch with the family.

Yield: 11.5 lbs.

Ingredients:

2.5 lbs. white potatoes, with skin, cubed

12.5 oz. dry oats

2.5 lbs. pork tenderloin

2.5 cups fresh, whole eggs (about 12 large eggs)

1 lb., 4 oz. red bell pepper, diced

12.5 oz. spinach, fresh or frozen, chopped

7.5 fl. oz. safflower oil

½ tbsp. fish oil (JustFoodForDogs or any good 18-percent
   EPA/12-percent DHA equivalent)

Cooking:

Boil water. Add potatoes and boil until cooked through (10–15 minutes). Plunge into ice bath to stop cooking. Drain and set aside to cool.

Cook oats and allow to cool.

Preheat oven to 400° F. Line a baking sheet with foil. Without seasoning the pork, place it on the baking sheet. Cook 20–30 minutes, or until a thermometer reads an internal temperature of 145° F. Allow to rest for at least 5 minutes before dicing or cubing into bite-size pieces.

While the tenderloin is cooking, begin to prepare eggs and vegetables. In a very large skillet, scramble the eggs. Once half-cooked, add the bell peppers and spinach and finish scrambling the mixture until fully cooked. Remove from heat and set aside to cool.

In a large mixing bowl, combine all the cooled ingredients and the oils.

Divide into individual serving sizes for your dog and put into zipper bags or glass or plastic containers. Store in the refrigerator for four days, or up to three months in the freezer.

Epilogue: A Better Future for Our Dogs

We are dog lovers, just like you. Making it possible for more people to feed their dogs fresh, whole food is our way of helping improve the lives of dogs. But there are other steps needed to better protect pets and pet parents. Here are six changes we believe are necessary and doable.

Separate Pet Food from Feed.
The Association of American Feed Control Officials should not establish the standards for ingredients in pet food or provide model regulations for its processing and labeling of the food. It's time to separate pet food from livestock feed. We believe that pet food should be overseen by a properly funded and staffed pet food division of the FDA.

This idea, originally proposed by Congress in 2007, has yet to be implemented. We believe its time has come.

Require Honest Labels on Pet Food.
Companies should be required to tell the whole truth on their labels. They shouldn't be allowed to call something "Home-Style Dinner with Beef" if it contains only 3 percent beef or to claim it includes "zinc" if it contains a form of zinc that is not easily absorbed and also has heavy metals. If the bag shows a delicious T-bone steak, the food inside should contain T-bone steak. Pet

food companies also must be *allowed* to tell the whole truth about superior ingredients. Today, if a company uses USDA-certified prime beef in a recipe, it is not allowed to list that fact on the label. Allowing some companies to pass off inferior ingredients as good ones while preventing others from communicating the truly high-quality nature of their ingredients gives an advantage to the companies cutting nutritional corners and leaves pet parents without the facts they need to make educated decisions about what their dogs eat.

We also believe that labeling laws for pet food should be uniform across the states, meaning governed by a national system. Today, regulators in some states will flag a specific label as a problem, while those in other states let it pass.

Create a Pet Food Rating System.

A dedicated FDA pet food division should establish a nationally consistent ABC health and safety rating system for pet food, similar to that which currently exists for restaurants. Products containing inferior ingredients could garner a C or B rating, and pet parents could then choose accordingly. We also think dangerous ingredients such as heavy metals should require a warning on the label, such as currently exists on cigarettes.

End the Legal Definition of Pets as Property.

Legally, dogs (and other pets) are property. But most Americans view their dogs and cats as members of the family. As it stands now, when a mistake is made that harms a pet—or an intentional action is taken that kills one, such as substituting melamine for protein—the guilty party is almost always only liable for the replacement cost of the animal, not the actual harm done to the family from the loss, or even the often-extensive veterinary bills.

Obviously, changing the legal status of pets could have negative economic consequences, such as raising the cost of liability insurance for vets, pet feed makers, and pet product manufacturers. But, on balance, we come out on the side of changing the law to recognize the important role that pets play in our lives.

Extend Tax Benefits to Pet Parents.

Tax laws, writ large, reflect our national values and help guide behavior. Most states don't impose sales tax on grocery food items, and we believe this should be true for dog food as well. Families get a federal tax credit for each child, which can help offset some of the costs of raising a family; tax credits should extend to pet parents, too. Finally, taxpayers can deduct certain medical expenses from their overall earnings; this should be true, too, for medical expenses for companion animals.

Include Pet Education in School.

American educators and parents recognize the benefits of all kinds of extracurricular activities for school-age children, from sports to performing arts to empathy-building programs such as antibullying workshops or restorative-justice circles. We believe that pet education and care should be among these. Learning to care for and interact with dogs helps build empathy, compassion, and self-esteem, and we believe a Pet Education program involving pet care and pet respect is an essential addition to any educational curriculum.

Learning to care for dogs can help kids learn to care for each other, too. The National School Safety Council, the U.S. Department of Education, the American Psychological Association, and the National Crime Prevention Council agree that animal cruelty is a warning sign for at-risk youth. A 2001–04 study by the Chicago Police Department revealed "a startling propensity for offenders charged with crimes against animals to commit other violent offenses toward human victims." Connecting our schoolchildren with our dogs will go a long way toward creating more caring, compassionate adults.

Acknowledgments

Big Kibble is a book, but more than that it is a movement, and it never could have been created (the book or the movement) without the help of countless people who understand the value and the magic of dogs. First and foremost, it needs to be said that there would be no movement, no company, and no book if not for Andrea Parsek, my better half for the past sixteen years and the first one to jump in and start making real food for our beloved dogs Simon and Nala—all those years ago. She has been my thought partner throughout the work on this book but, more important, through the challenges of disrupting a broken industry that has no interest in updating itself.

It is a simple fact that without Wendy Paris, our story never would have been told—at least not in such an articulate, organized, and talented fashion. Thank you, Wendy—we literally could not have done it without you (and we apologize for all the plane rides required to get the research for the book done)! Likewise, our agent, Kirsten Neuhaus, not only believed in us, the story, and the mission to help dogs, she displayed heroic patience in working with Dr. Chavez and me, two novices who had no idea how the publishing world works.

We are deeply grateful to Daniela Rapp, fellow rescue-dog lover and brilliant editor at St. Martin's Press. From the first meeting, she instinctively knew this story needed to be told and was instrumental in doing so. Thank you for believing in us and buying this book, Daniela. "Owned" dogs will benefit because pet parents will wake up to how dogs *should* be fed, and rescue dogs will benefit from our proceeds from this book that Dr. Chavez and I are donating to pet rescue.

Without Julian and Amy Mack, the mission, the company, and therefore this book would not have been as sharply defined or as expeditiously completed. They are not just my business partners and friends but, more important, they are my heroes. Their unfaltering love for older and handicapped dogs is an absolute inspiration, and I stand in awe of their generosity in supporting them. Julian, you are the smartest human being I have ever known, and I am a better person for knowing you.

Carey Tischler is the world-class CEO at the helm of Just-FoodForDogs. When we first met, he immediately saw the prospect of running the business as much more than a money-making opportunity or even than becoming an industry "disruptor"; he knew this was right for dogs, and he knew the idea of real food would be intuitive to pet parents. His knowledge and experience in the traditional pet food business was invaluable in writing this book, and we appreciate his expertise and support.

Without the hundreds of amazing JustFoodForDogs employees and thousands of JustFoodForDogs customers, this experiment never would have had a chance to bloom. We greatly appreciate your feedback, ideas, and collaboration.

Last and certainly not least, I have to recognize the real genius behind our company and this book—my friend, business partner, and the most caring and brilliant vet I have ever known, Dr. Oscar Chavez. He was able to turn the notion of fresh, whole food for pets into something that was real. Something that changed the life of dogs. I simply did not have the skill to make this happen and thus, without him, it would never have come to be. Thank you, Oscar. It is my honor and my privilege to be taking this journey with you.

I started by saying this is more than a book; it is a movement. And ultimately what makes that so is you. Pet parents that care enough to think outside the bag and make an effort to do what is best for their four-legged family. Dogs are perfection. They are love incarnate. We give them a few spare moments each day, and in turn they give us everything they have and everything they are.

—*SHAWN BUCKLEY*

Big Kibble comes after years of work by hundreds of people, and is a part of an ongoing movement to engage thousands more in helping improve the world for dogs. Thanks to everyone who is part of our story. JustFoodForDogs is a team and a family, and I'd like to acknowledge the people who execute our mission every day, from the cooks to the packagers, nutrition consultants, and field managers. This company, and therefore this movement, would not be possible without all of you. Thank you!

Thank you to Wendy Paris, who put our story into words. I knew we had a great story to tell, but I didn't know how to tell it. Wendy captured all the main highlights of a decade of work and helped deliver it in a compelling, accurate, and educational way. Thanks also to our wonderful editor, Daniela Rapp; our agent, Kirsten Neuhaus; and the team at Macmillan. As true dog lovers, you heard our story and came to believe what we believe—that dogs deserve better.

The best part of the JustFoodForDogs adventure has been leading a team of incredible individuals: our veterinary outreach team. Together, we established our department's internal mission:

To establish JustFoodForDogs as the highest standard of practice in veterinary nutrition and vets' first and best recommendation. To elevate nutritional offerings that align with standards for human nutrition, and thereby transform the way pet parents and vets feed their pets. We will achieve this through nutritional consulting and education, always with integrity, even in the face of resistance.

I am proud to say that we're achieving our mission, thanks to their hard work and enthusiasm. You live this mission and bring it to life every day. Thank you! This is your story as much as it is ours.

I'd like to thank my parents, Oscar Chavez Sr. and Rosa Chavez, who always provided any support I requested and allowed me to become my best me. You've set the yardstick for supportive and nurturing parents, a standard I hope to emulate when my time comes. I grew up feeling like anything is possible because of the environment you created. You set the foundation that helped shape my career and that, eventually, is helping transform an industry. I'm not sure how many people get to say this to their parents, but I know I can: You are perfect. (Sorry that I usually wasn't.)

You did a perfect job.

I'd like to sincerely thank the skeptics we met along the way. A few years into the JustFoodForDogs mission, some academic colleagues and prominent members of the veterinary profession discouraged me when I asked tough questions and challenged the status quo.

There is no stronger motivator than a group of naysayers attempting to discourage you. This sort of effort happened repeatedly, in various forms, from different groups, over the past ten years. If you are doing something that matters, as I learned, there will be opposition. If you are doing something potentially transformative, others will try to stop the change. Today we are successful, in part, because of the reverse validation from folks like this.

In contrast, there were thousands of veterinarians who grasped the importance of whole food immediately. You are always a breath of fresh air. As scientists, we have the burden of being "evidence based." We require proof—as in studies—that real food is healthier than processed. But even before the studies were done, enough of you saw the transformation in dogs eating whole food. Thank you.

Finally, I must thank my closest colleague and friend, Shawn Buckley, the best business partner I could ever have. Willing to disagree passionately, but always respectfully, and focus on the greater good, he is probably the strongest strategist I'll ever know. He taught me that you don't have to be good at everything; you just have to be really good at one thing: solving problems. A master strategist shall never starve. I don't know if I'd have the confidence or effectiveness to take on Big Kibble without Shawn. I know for a fact that it wouldn't have been as much fun. Thanks, buddy, for always being slightly more stubborn than I am. You introduced me to a mission and a vision; it's been an honor to play a role in its realization.

—DR. OSCAR CHAVEZ

Many thanks to Shawn Buckley and Oscar Chavez for giving me the opportunity to learn more than I ever knew about dog food, canine nutrition, and industrial food and feed manufacturing. Thank you for trusting me to tell your story and share your passion. Thank you, Kirsten Neuhaus at Foundry, for introducing us and for your belief in this project. Many thanks to Daniela Rapp at Macmillan for providing such thoughtful edits on the content, style, and order. It's so great to work with such a dedicated, thorough editor. Investigative journalist Mark Rivett-Carnac provided invaluable research help throughout this project, and journalist Ellen McCreary Loanes helped get the research started; thanks to both of you for all your help, support, and flexibility, and to Judith Matloff, Columbia University journalism professor and author of *No Friends but the Mountains: Dispatches from the World's Violent Highlands,* for connecting us. Journalists Sony Salzman and Mariella Rudi both jumped in to help with research. And many thanks to Betsy Brown for stepping in at the end for fact-checking.

Friends and family who love dogs (sometimes) love to help do research about them. Many thanks to lawyer/former manufacturing executive/(my mother) Joy Paris for combing through the AAFCO guides and visiting innumerable pet supply stores. My father, Sanford Paris, and his wife, Gina, introduced us to the wonder that is Newtown Feed and Supply. Student Chaya Mushka Telechevsky helped track down news stories of recalls. Writer Annie Murphy Paul, author of *The Extended Mind: The Power of Thinking Outside the Brain,* located articles on dogs and their care from the annuals of midcentury American media. Award-winning investigative reporters/bestselling authors Sheri Fink, author of *Five Days at Memorial: Life and Death in a Storm-Ravaged Hospital,* and Nina Teicholz, author of the *The Big Fat Surprise: Why Butter, Meat and Cheese Belong in a Healthy Diet*, provided guidance and direction. My son, Alexander Paris-Callahan, provided moral support by insisting that our dog needed good food and that this book needed to be written.

Many people in the pet feed industry shared their time, knowledge, and candor, helping to make the case for improving their field, even while working in it. Thanks so much to all of you. Thanks to the National Grain and Feed Association and Pet Food Institute for welcoming us to your annual conference, and to Micky Ruel for making a hot weekend in Kansas City more fun.

—*WENDY PARIS*

Endnotes

Introduction

1 Edie Lau, "Pet owners receive $12.4 million in melamine case," October 12, 2011, VIN News Service. https://news.vin.com/vinnews.aspx?articleId=20025.

2 Tim Wall, "US spends nearly US$33 billion on pet food, treats in 2018," petfoodindustry.com, December 18, 2018, https://www.petfoodindustry.com/articles/7738-us-spent-nearly-us33-billion-on-pet-food-treats-in-2018?v=preview.

3 Debbie Phillips-Donaldson, "Global pet food sales hit $91 billion in 2018," PetfoodIndustry.com, February 18, 2019, https://www.petfoodindustry.com/articles/7899-global-pet-food-sales-hit-91-billion-in-2018.

4 Association of American Feed Control Officials Incorporated, *2018 Official Publication*, 178.

1. Our Longest Love Affair

1 Phone interview with Dr. Amy Kramer and Wendy Paris, April 25, 2019.

2 Mary Ellen Goldberg and Julia E. Tomlinson, *Physical Rehabilitation for Veterinary Technicians and Nurses* (New York: John Wiley and Sons, 2017).

3 "Certified Canine Rehabilitation Therapist," Canine Rehabilitation Institute, accessed June 25, 2019, http://www.caninerehabinstitute.com/CCRT.html.

4 "Home Page," Canine Rehabilitation Institute, accessed April 30, 2019, http://www.caninerehabinstitute.com/.

5 "University of Tennessee Canine Rehab Certificate CCRP," Northeast Seminars/The University of Tennessee, Knoxville, accessed June 25, 2019, https://www.utvetce.com/canine-rehab-ccrp.

6 "Certified Canine Fitness Trainer," Northeast Seminars, accessed June 25, 2019, https://www.utvetce.com/canine-fitness-ccft.

7 *An Era of Change: A Closer Look at Veterinary Education and Practice, 2015*, University of California, Davis, College of Veterinary Medicine, https://www.ucop.edu/uc-health/_files/vet-med-an-era-of-change.pdf.

8 Phone interview with Eva Bitter and Wendy Paris, August 14, 2019.

9 Katie Burns, "Pet Ownership Stable, Veterinary Care Variable," *Journal of the American Veterinary Medical Association* (December 31, 2018).

10 Barbara Natterson-Horowitz, MD, and Kathryn Bowers, *Zoobiquity: The Astonishing Connections Between Human and Animal Health* (New York: Knopf, 2012).

11 Malinda Larkin, "One for the History Books: A Visual History of the AVMA's First 150 Years," *Journal of the American Veterinary Medical Association,* https://www.avma.org/News/JAVMANews/Pages/130715a.aspx.

12 Larkin, "One for the History Books."

13 Interview with Kathryn Bowers and Wendy Paris, Hastings-on-Hudson, New York, May 24, 2019.

2. It's a Dog's Life: 2.0

1 Burns, "Pet Ownership."

2 Michele Tymann, "There Should Be More Dog-Friendly Cafés," *Pet Business,* January 26, 2018, http://www.petbusiness.com/There-Should-Be-More-Dog-Friendly-Cafes/.

3 Morgan Greenwald, "The 20 Most Dog Friendly Countries in the World," Bestlifeonline.com, June 19, 2018.

4 Brittany Shoot, "10 Pet-Friendly Companies Where It's Always Take Your Dog to Work Day," *Fortune,* June 22, 2018, http://fortune.com/2018/06/22/take-your-dog-to-work-day-pet-friendly-companies/.

5 "The Best Dog-Friendly Companies of 2019," Rover.com. https://www.rover.com/blog/best-dog-friendly-companies/.

6 Lisa Wood et al., "The Pet Factor: Companion Animals As a Conduit for Getting to Know People, Friendship Formation and Social Support," PLOS, April 29, 2015, https://journals.plos.org/plosone/article?id=10.1371/journal.pone.0122085.

7 Rosalie R. Radomsky, "POSTINGS: Going Up at 205 East 59th Street; A 27-Floor, Dog-Friendly Condo," *The New York Times,* April 25, 2004, https://www.nytimes.com/2004/04/25/realestate/postings-going-up-at-205-east-59th-street-a-27-floor-dog-friendly-condo.html.

8 Interview with Kerry Brown by Wendy Paris in Manhattan, May 23, 2019.

9 "Pet Industry Market Size and Ownership Statistics," American Pet Products Association, https://www.americanpetproducts.org/press_industrytrends.asp. Accessed March 24, 2020.

10 The State of Global Pet Care: Trends and Growth Opportunities," Euromonitor Research, Market Research Blog, September 28, 2017, https://blog.euromonitor.com/state-global-pet-care-trends/.

11 Burns, "Pet Ownership."

12 Benjamin Gurrentz, PhD, "Millennial Marriage: How Much Does Economic Security Matter to Marriage Rates for Young Adults?" United States Census Bureau Library, Working Paper SEHSD-WP2018-09, April 26, 2018, https://www.census.gov/library/working-papers/2018/demo/SEHSD-WP2018-09.html.

13 United States Census Bureau, "U.S. Census Bureau Releases 2018 Families and Living Arrangements Tables," November 14, 2018, https://www.census .gov/newsroom/press-releases/2018/families.html.

14 Roberto A. Ferdman, "Americans Are Having Dogs Instead of Babies," *Quartz*, April 10, 2014, https://qz.com/197416/americans-are-having-dogs-instead-of -babies/.

15 Rebecca F. Wisch, "Table of State Dog Leash Laws," Michigan State University Animal Legal and Historical Center, 2015, https://www.animallaw.info/topic /table-of-state-dog-leash-laws.

16 Marcello Siniscalchi, Serenella d'Ingeo, and Angelo Quaranta, "Orienting Asymmetries and Physiological Reactivity in Dogs' Response to Human Emotional Faces," *Learning and Behavior* 46, no. 4 (December 2018), https://doi .org/10.3758/s13420-018-0325-2.

17 Juliana Kaminski and Marie Nitzschner, "Do Dogs Get the Point? A Review of Dog-Human Communication Ability," *Learning and Motivation* 44, no. 4 (November 2013): 294, https://www.sciencedirect.com/science/article/abs/pii /S0023969013000325.

18 Julie Hecht, "What's the Point?" thebark.com, June 2016, https://thebark.com /content/whats-point.

19 Amy Cook, Jennifer Arter, and Jucia F. Jacobs, "My Owner, Right or Wrong: The Effect of Familiarity on the Domestic Dog's Behavior in a Food-Choice Task," *Animal Cognition* 17, no. 2 (March 2014): 461, https://doi.org/10.1007 /s10071-013-0677-0.

20 Hannah K. Worsley and Sean J. O'Hara, "Cross-Species Referential Signaling Events in Domestic Dogs (*Canis familiaris*)," *Animal Cognition* 21, no. 4 (July 2018): 457, https://doi.org/10.1007/s10071-018-1181-3.

21 Emily Willingham, "Dogs Detect the Scent of Seizures," *Scientific American*, March 28, 2019, https://www.scientificamerican.com/article/dogs-detect-the -scent-of-seizures/.

22 Lizzy Rosenberg, "Tinkerbelle The Dog's Owner, Sam Carrell, Is The Genius Behind Her Viral Instagram," Elite Daily, November 14, 2018. https://www .elitedaily.com/p/tinkerbelle-the-dogs-owner-sam-carrell-is-the-genius-behind -her-viral-instagram-13109151.

23 *Get Healthy, Get a Dog: The Health Benefits of Canine Companionship*, Harvard Health Publications, https://www.health.harvard.edu/staying-healthy/get -healthy-get-a-dog.

24 M. Nagasawa et al., "Dog's Gaze at Its Owner Increases Owner's Urinary Oxytocin During Social Interaction," *Hormonal Behavior* 55, no. 3 (March 2009): 434, https://www.ncbi.nlm.nih.gov/pubmed/19124024.

25 Darlene A. Kertes et al., "Effect of Pet Dogs on Children's Perceived Stress and Cortisol Stress Response," *Social Development* 26, no. 2 (May 2017): 382–401, https://www.ncbi.nlm.nih.gov/pmc/articles/PMC5400290/.

26 Andy Newman, "World (or at Least Brooklyn) Stops for Lost Dog," *The New York Times*, November 11, 2016, https://www.nytimes.com/2016/11/13 /nyregion/world-or-at-least-brooklyn-stops-for-lost-dog.html.

27 Phone interview with Steven Stosny and Wendy Paris, October 30, 2013.

28 Ed Yong, *A New Origin Story for Dogs, The Atlantic,* June 2, 2016, https://www
.theatlantic.com/science/archive/2016/06/the-origin-of-dogs/484976/.

29 Virginia Morrell, "Why dogs turn to us for help," *Science,* September 15, 2015,
https://www.sciencemag.org/news/2015/09/why-dogs-turn-us-help.

3. A Biscuit in Every Bowl

1   Mary Elizabeth Thurston, *The Lost History of the Canine Race: Our 15,000-Year
Love Affair with Dogs* (New York: Avon Books, 1996), 235.

2   "The History of the Pet Food Industry," Pet Food Institute, https://web.archive
.org/web/20090524005409/http://www.petfoodinstitute.org/petfoodhistory.htm.

3   Katherine Grier, "Provisioning Man's Best Friend: The Early Years of the American Pet Food Industry, 1870–1942," in *Food Chains: From Farmyard to Shop-
ping Cart,* ed. Warren Belasco and Roger Horowitz (Philadelphia: University
of Pennsylvania Press, 2009), 127.

4   "Spratt's Patent," Grace's Guide to British Industrial History, accessed August
20, 2019, https://www.gracesguide.co.uk/Spratt's_Patent.

5   "Explore Our Heritage," Milk-Bone, accessed August 22, 2019, https://www
.milkbone.com/about-us/our-story.

6   Arthur W. Brayley, *Bakers and Baking in Massachusetts, including the Flour, Baking Supply and Kindred Interests, from 1620 to 1909* (Boston: Master Bakers'
Association of Massachusetts, 1909), 236–37, https://books.google.com/books
?id=ZZpPAQAAMAAJ&pg=PR1&lpg=PR1&dq=Bakers+and+baking+in+
Massachusetts,+including+the+flour,+baking+supply+and+kindred+interests,
+from+1620+to+1909&source=bl&ots=1T-GXD6hrB&sig=ACfU3U3LEu-
JwuCiKf_JiVDJzBLslD_rFxg&hl=en&sa=X&ved=2ahUKEwiUmZrsyunk-
AhWLhOAKHSrxAcgQ6AEwBXoECAkQAQ#v=onepage&q=Potter%20
%26%20Wrightington%2Cboston%2C%20began%20canning&f=false.

7   Grier, "Provisioning," 129.

8   "Balm of America: Patent Medicine Collection," National Museum of American
History, accessed August 28, 2019, https://americanhistory.si.edu/collections
/object-groups/balm-of-america-patent-medicine-collection/history.

9   Lee J. DiVita, "Veterinary Antiques: A Lesson in History, the Profession, Advertising, and Collecting," *Journal of the American Veterinary Medical Association News* (October 15, 2001), https://www.avma.org/News/JAVMANews
/Pages/s110101f.aspx.

10 Grier, "Provisioning," 129.

11 Michael K. Guy et al., "The Golden Retriever Lifetime Study: Establishing an
Observational Cohort Study with Translational Relevance for Human Health,"
Philosophical Transactions of the Royal Society of London, series B, Biological
Sciences, 370, no. 1673 (2015), https://doi.org/10.1098/rstb.2014.0230.

12 Linda P. Case et al., *Canine and Feline Nutrition: A Resource for Companion
Animal Professionals,* 3rd ed. (Maryland Heights: Mosby, 2011), 121.

13 Ibid.

14 "Safe Handling of Pet Food in the Home," U.S. Food and Drug Administration, February 20, 2014, https://www.youtube.com/watch?v=_X0F-XYHHxk.

15 "Ralston Purina Company," Encyclopedia.com, https://www.encyclopedia.com/social-sciences-and-law/economics-business-and-labor/businesses-and-occupations/ralston-purina-company.

16 Sara Keckeisen, "The Cost of Conscience: Part One," *Kansas Heritage* 12, no. 2 (Summer 2004): 8, https://www.kshs.org/publicat/heritage/2004summer_keckeisen.pdf.

17 Grier, "Provisioning," 127–28.

18 "Historical Highlights," Westminster Kennel Club, last modified April 15, 2016, https://www.westminsterkennelclub.org/historical-highlights.

19 Thurston, *Lost History*, 236.

20 Old Grist Mill Dog Bread Advertisement, in *Our Dumb Animals*, February 1918, 130. https://books.google.com/books?id=lgtJAQAAMAAJ&pg=PA130&lpg=PA130&dq=potter+and+wrightington+dog+massachusetts&source=bl&ots=kZDb-Dp7ae&sig=ACfU3U2SbCro5myMqoLKC4QJVA0PVo79nA&hl=en&sa=X&ved=2ahUKEwiIqIWH9pbkAhWRmeAKHUPeDe0Q6AEwD3oECAMQAQ#v=onepage&q&f=false.

21 "Spratt's," Grace's Guide to British Industrial History, accessed August 20, 2019, https://www.gracesguide.co.uk/Spratt's_Patent.

22 Grier, "Provisioning," 129.

23 Andrew Nikiforuk, "The Big Shift Last Time: From Horse Dung to Car Smog," *The Tyee*, March 6, 2013, https://thetyee.ca/News/2013/03/06/Horse-Dung-Big-Shift/.

24 Elizabeth Colbert, "Hosed: Is There a Quick Fix for the Climate?" *The New Yorker*, November 16, 2009, https://www.newyorker.com/magazine/2009/11/16/hosed.

25 Joel Levin, "The Internal Combustion Engine Car and the Horse-Drawn Carriage," Plug In America, November 2, 2016, https://pluginamerica.org/the-internal-combustion-engine-car-and-the-horse-drawn-carriage/.

26 "Our History," Ford Motor Company, accessed September 17, 2019, https://corporate.ford.com/history.html.

27 Colbert, "Hosed."

28 Laura Hillenbrand, *Seabiscuit: An American Legend*, (New York: Ballantine, 2001), 9.

29 Michael Price, "Missouri Horses and Mules," Missouri Over There, accessed August 21, 2019, https://missourioverthere.org/explore/articles/missouri-horses-and-mules/.

30 Grier, "Provisioning," 130.

31 Leroy Judson Daniels and Helen S. Herrick, *Tales of an Old Horsetrader: The First Hundred Years* (Iowa City; University of Iowa Press, 1987), 139–44.

32 Paul G. Irwin, "Overview: The State of Animals in 2001," in *The State of the Animals 2001*, ed. Deborah J. Salem and Andrew N. Rowan (Washington, D.C.: Humane Society Press, 2001), 8, https://animalstudiesrepository.org/cgi/viewcontent.cgi?article=1012&context=sota_2001.

33 Andrew Rowan and Tamara Kartal, "Dog Population & Dog Sheltering

Trends in the United States of America," *Animals* 2018, 8(5), 68; https://doi
.org/10.3390/ani8050068.

34 Patrick Watson, "Pet Care Is a Recession-Proof Industry," *Business Insider*,
July 5, 2018, https://www.businessinsider.com/pet-care-is-a-recession-proof
-industry-2018-7.

35 Case et al., *Canine and Feline Nutrition*, 121.

36 Tim Phillips, "Learn from the Past," PetfoodIndustry.com, October 2007,
https://www.petfoodindustry.com/ext/resources/uploadedfiles/PetfoodIndustry
/petfoodindustry200710-dl.pdf.

37 "'Pet Food Boom Originated Here'—1962 article, Chappel Bros., Inc.,
Quaker Oats," Rockford Public Library's Local History, accessed September
17, 2019, https://history.rockfordpubliclibrary.org/localhistory/?p=63566&.

38 Catherine *Dressler,* "Quaker Oats Sells Pet Food Business to H. J. Heinz Co,"
Findarticles.com, 1995, retrieved 2009-08-03.

39 Daniel R. Block and Howard Rosing, *Chicago: A Food Biography* (Lanham,
MD: Rowman and Littlefield, 2015), 141.

40 Andrew Clayman, "Rival Packing Co., est. 1923," Made in Chicago Museum,
accessed September 17, 2019, https://www.madeinchicagomuseum.com
/single-post/rival-packing-co.

41 Susan D. Jones, *Valuing Animals: Veterinarians and Their Patients in Modern
America* (Baltimore: Johns Hopkins University Press, 2003), 119, https://
books.google.com/books?id=1GCJ6hAgt_oC&printsec=frontcover&source
=gbs_ge_summary_r&cad=0#v=onepage&q&f=false.

42 David Herold, "Food Is a Weapon—The Rationing of Goods in US
During World War II," War History Online, June 10, 2017, https://www
.warhistoryonline.com/world-war-ii/wheres-share-gasoline-sugar-rationing
-goods-us_wwii-m.html.

43 Mary Roach, "The Chemistry of Kibble," *Popular Science*, March 25, 2013,
https://www.popsci.com/science/article/2013-03/chemistry-kibble/.

44 *The Toronto Blade*, July 30, 1950, https://news.google.com/newspapers?nid
=1350&dat=19500723&id=XNlOAAAAIBAJ&sjid=KgAEAAAAIBAJ&pg
=1346,3558285&hl=en.

45 Joseph Sjostrom, "DeKalb Horse Abattoir Loses Bid," *Chicago Tribune*,
June 17, 2008, https://www.chicagotribune.com/news/ct-xpm-2008-06-17
-0806160467-story.html.

46 Phyllis Entis, "Evanger's Denied Knowledge of Horse Meat Despite Its License," *Food Safety News*, July 19, 2018, https://www.foodsafetynews.com
/2018/07/evangers-denied-knowledge-of-horse-meat-despite-its-license/.

47 Thurston, *Lost History,* 235.

48 Ibid., 238.

49 "The History of Cheetos," Timeline Maker, last modified May 7, 2014, https://
www.timelinemaker.com/blog/featured-timeline/history-of-cheetos-timeline/.

50 Charles Wilson, "Who Made That Kraft Single?" *The New York Times Magazine*, June 1, 2012, https://www.nytimes.com/2012/06/03/magazine/who
-made-that-kraft-single.html.

51 *Encyclopedia Britannica Online*, s.v. "Ralston Purina Company," accessed September 19, 2019, https://www.britannica.com/topic/Ralston-Purina -Company.

52 John Sutton, *Sunk Costs and Market Structure: Price Competition, Advertising, and the Evolution of Concentration* (Cambridge, MA: MIT Press, 1991), 499.

53 William Shurtleff and Akiko Aoyagi, *History of Modern Soy Protein Ingredients: Isolates, Concentrates, and Textured Soy Protein Products, 1911–2016* (Lafayette, LA: Soyinfo Center, 2016), 1460, http://www.soyinfocenter.com/pdf/190 /Pro1.pdf.

54 Frederick Kaufman, "They Eat What We Are," *The New York Times Magazine*, September 2, 2007, https://www.nytimes.com/2007/09/02/magazine/02pet-t.html.

55 Ibid.

56 Pamela G. Hollie, "Carnation: A Family Company's Evolution," *The New York Times*, September 5, 1984, https://www.nytimes.com/1984/09/05/business /carnation-a-family-company-s-evolution.html.

57 Vartanig G. Vartan, "Tobacco Stocks Gain," *The New York Times*, November 1, 1970, https://www.nytimes.com/1970/11/01/archives/tobacco-stocks-gain -diversity-aiding-cigarette-makers.html.

58 Clare M. Reckert, "Acquisition by Liggett & Myers Adds Pet Foods to Its Products," *The New York Times*, November 20, 1964, https://www.nytimes .com/1964/11/20/archives/acquisition-by-liggett-myers-adds-pet-foods-to-its -products.html.

59 Thurston, *Lost History*, 239.

60 "Your Pets: Killing with Kindness?" *Sioux Falls Argus-Leader*, June 14, 1959.

61 Joe Rice, "Kind to Fido? National Dog Week's Coming Up," *Tallahassee Democrat*, September 3, 1962.

62 Joyce Schuller, "Doggies in Window by Thousands Set for Yule Gifts," United Press International/*Daily World*, December 24, 1961.

63 Thurston, *Lost History*, 243.

64 Steven Greenhouse, "Dogs and Cats—A $2-Billion Market," *The New York Times*, January 27, 1974, https://www.nytimes.com/1974/01/27/archives /dogs-and-catsa-2billion-market-pet-food-producers-in-gourmet-race.html.

65 Thurston, *Lost History*, 243.

4. The Rise of Big Kibble

1 David Lummis, "Has Enough Changed Since the 2007 Pet Food Recalls?" *Pet Product News*, December 5, 2018, http://www.petproductnews.com/Blog /Has-Enough-Changed-Since-the-2007-Pet-Food-Recalls/; "U.S. Pet Market Outlook, 2018–2019," Packaged Facts, August 22, 2018, https://www .packagedfacts.com/Pet-Outlook-11819832/.

2 Greenhouse, "Dogs and Cats."

3 See encyclopedia.com, https://www.encyclopedia.com/books/politics-and -business-magazines/carnation-company.

4 "Tyson's to Buy American Proteins, AMPRO Products assets," *Petfood*

Industry, May 15, 2018, https://www.petfoodindustry.com/articles/7205
-tyson-to-buy-american-proteins-ampro-products-assets.

5 Tim Wall, "51 Mergers and Acquisitions in 2018 Pet Food Industry," *Petfood Industry,* last modified December 27, 2018, https://www.petfoodindustry.com /articles/7756-mergers-and-acquisitions-in-2018-pet-food-industry.

6 "Top Pet Food Companies Current Data," PetfoodIndustry.com, accessed August 21, 2019, https://www.petfoodindustry.com/directories/211-top-pet -food-companies-current-data.

7 Interview with Chase Champlin and Wendy Paris, Newtown, Ohio, July 24, 2019.

8 "FDA Investigates Animal Illnesses Linked to Jerky Pet Treats," United States Food and Drug Administration, last modified August 21, 2018, https://www .fda.gov/animal-veterinary/news-events/fda-investigates-animal-illnesses -linked-jerky-pet-treats.

9 Dvm360.com staff, "Dogswell Jerky Products Recalled for Antibiotic Residue," DVM360, July 31, 2013, http://veterinarynews.dvm360.com/dogswell-jerky -products-recalled-antibiotic-residue.

10 "FDA 101: Product Recalls," U.S. Food and Drug Administration, https:// www.fda.gov/consumers/consumer-updates/fda-101-product-recalls.

11 "List of Medically Important Antimicrobial Drugs Affected by GFI #213," July 30, 2019, https://www.fda.gov/animal-veterinary/judicious-use -antimicrobials/list-medically-important-antimicrobial-drugs-affected-gfi-213.

12 "FDA Investigates Animal Illnesses Linked to Jerky Pet Treats," United States Food and Drug Administration, last modified August 21, 2018, https://www .fda.gov/animal-veterinary/news-events/fda-investigates-animal-illnesses -linked-jerky-pet-treats.

13 Tim Wall, "Pet food labels: Made in the USA," PetfoodIndustry.com, June 21, 2017, https://www.petfoodindustry.com/articles/6514-pet-food-labels-made -in-the-usa.

14 Louis Uchitelle, "Spread of U.S. Plants Abroad Is Slowing Exports," *The New York Times,* March 26, 1989.

15 "Processed Product Spotlight: Pet Food," United States Department of Agri-culture Foreign Agriculture Service, last modified February 20, 2013, https:// www.fas.usda.gov/data/processed-product-spotlight-pet-food.

16 http://www.wrapcompliance.org/, Accessed March 19, 2020.

17 Jane Mosbacher Morris with Wendy Paris, *Buy the Change You Want to See: Use Your Purchasing Power to Make the World a Better Place* (New York: TarcherPer-igee, 2019), 189.

18 Patrick Winn, "Trash Fish: It's Gross, Tainted by Slavery and Possibly in Your Dog Food," PRI, June 18, 2014, https://www.pri.org/stories/2014-06 -18/trash-fish-it-s-gross-tainted-slavery-and-possibly-your-dog-food; "Fish Caught by Slaves May Be Tainting Your Cat Food," PRI, December 30, 2016.

19 Martha Mendoza, "Nestle Confirms Labor Abuse Among Its Thai Seafood Suppliers," *Associated Press,* November 23, 2015, https://www.ap.org/explore

/seafood-from-slaves/nestle-confirms-labor-abuse-among-its-thai-seafood
-suppliers.html.

20 Phone interview Joan Schaffner and Wendy Paris, August 14, 2019.

21 Ibid.

22 "Charge Filed in Contaminated Pet Food Scheme," FDA.gov; http://wayback
.archive-it.org/7993/20170111123153/http://www.fda.gov/ForConsumers
/ConsumerUpdates/ucm048139.htm. Accessed February 12, 2020.

23 Edie Lau, "Pet owners receive $12.4 million in melamine case," October
12, 2011, VIN News Service. https://news.vin.com/vinnews.aspx?articleId
=20025.

24 Amy Nip, "Cancer-Causing Toxin Found in Hong Kong Pet Food Sparks
Alarm," *South China Post,* April 15, 2014, https://www.scmp.com/news/hong
-kong/article/1482845/carcinogen-found-hong-kong-pet-food-consumer
-council.

25 "Processed Product Spotlight: Pet Food," United States Department of Agriculture Foreign Agriculture Service, last modified February 20, 2013, https://
www.fas.usda.gov/data/processed-product-spotlight-pet-food.

26 https://www.nomv.org/. Accessed March 19, 2019.

27 https://iwanttobeaveterinarian.org/how-much-does-it-cost-to-attend
-veterinary-school/. Accessed March 19, 2020.

28 Ryan Lane, "What Is the Average Student Loan Debt for Veterinarians?," Nerd-
wallet, October 30, 2019, https://www.nerdwallet.com/blog/loans/student
-loans/average-student-loan-debt-veterinarians/.

29 US News and World Report Veterinarian Salary, https://money.usnews.com
/careers/best-jobs/veterinarian/salary. Accessed March 19, 2020.

30 "Best Veterinary Schools," U.S. News and World Report, 2019, https://www
.usnews.com/best-graduate-schools/top-health-schools/veterinarian-rankings.

31 "A Partnership in Nutrition," *Advance* (2016): 4, https://www.vetmed.ucdavis
.edu/sites/g/files/dgvnsk491/files/inline-files/VM_Advance_Newsletter
_Spring_16.pdf.

32 "LSU Veterinary School Gets New Nutrition Center Thanks to Generous Donation from Purina," Louisiana State University School of Veterinary Medicine, accessed June 6, 2019, https://www.lsu.edu/vetmed/vet_news/nutrition
_center.php.

33 Phone interview with Mary Thurston and Wendy Paris, September 25, 2019.

34 F. S. Sierles, A. C. Brodkey, L. M. Cleary, et al., Medical Students' Exposure to
and Attitudes About Drug Company Interactions: A National Survey. *JAMA.*
2005;294(9):1034–1042. doi:10.1001/jama.294.9.1034.

35 K. Lieb and A. Scheurich, "Contact between Doctors and the Pharmaceutical Industry, Their Perceptions, and the Effects on Prescribing Habits," *PLOS
ONE* 9, no.10 (2014), https://doi.org/10.1371/journal.pone.0110130.

36 "Curriculum Design," University of California, Davis, College of Veterinary
Medicine, accessed June 6, 2019, https://www.vetmed.ucdavis.edu/dvm/dvm
-curriculum-overview.

37 Cornell University College of Veterinary Medicine, https://www.vet.cornell

.edu/sites/default/files/Curriculum%20Footprint%202018_jkg%20mf%20 005.pdf.

38 Tufts University Cummings School of Veterinary Medicine, https://vet.tufts .edu/education/dvm-program/curriculum-of-the-dvm-program/. Accessed March 19, 2019.

39 University of Tennessee at Knoxville College of Veterinary Medicine, https:// vetmed.tennessee.edu/admissions/Pages/dvm_curriculum_catalog.aspx.

40 Melinda Larkin, "Vet Schools Developing Ethics Policies to Avoid Conflicts of Interest," JAVMA News, November 1, 2011, https://www.avma.org/News /JAVMANews/Pages/111101a.aspx.

5. You Can't Judge a Kibble by Its Cover

1 https://www.aafco.org/Portals/0/SiteContent/Meetings/Annual/2014/FINAL _Assembled_Annual_Agenda.pdf. Accessed April 1, 2020.

2 AAFCO 2014 Annual Meeting Roster, https://www.aafco.org/Portals /0/SiteContent/Meetings/Attendee-Lists/2014_annual_meeting_roster _sacramento.pdf.

3 *AAFCO Pet Food and Specialty Pet Food Labeling Guide* (Association of American Feed Control Officials, revised May 2016), 1.

4 Ibid., introductory page.

5 https://www.fda.gov/animal-veterinary/animal-food-feeds/pet-food.

6 Association of American Feed Control Officials Incorporated, *2020 Official Publication*, 103.

7 Association of American Feed Control Officials, *2018 Official Publication*, 4.

8 Phone interview with Sue Hayes and Wendy Paris, February 11, 2020.

9 Phone interview with Reece Rollins of Southeastern Minerals, February 13, 2020.

10 Association of American Feed Control Officials, *2020 Official Publication*, 418.

11 Interview with Sue Hayes and Wendy Paris, Kansas City, October 1, 2019.

12 Wagner, J. J. et al., "The effects of zinc hydroxychloride and basic copper chloride on growth performance, carcass characteristics, and liver zinc and copper status at slaughter in yearling feedlot steers," *The Professional Animal Scientist,* Vol. 32, Issue 5, 570–79.

13 Association of American Feed Control Officials, *2020 Official Publication*, 418.

14 Roger Govier, "The Canine Cancer Crisis," *Whole Dog Journal*, updated August 1, 2019, https://www.whole-dog-journal.com/health/the-canine-cancer-crisis/.

15 *AAFCO Pet Food and Specialty Pet Food Labeling Guide* (Association of American Feed Control Officials, revised May 2016), 6.

16 Ibid., 50.

17 Ibid., 10.

18 Association of American Feed Control Officials, *2020 Official Publication* 424.

19 Ibid., 451.

20 Ibid., 17.

21 Phone interview with Bob Sullivan and Wendy Paris, November 21, 2019.

22 "Advertising FAQ's: A Guide for Small Businesses," FTC.gov, https://www
.ftc.gov/tips-advice/business-center/guidance/advertising-faqs-guide-small
-business.

23 Ibid.

24 "FTC APPROPRIATION AND FULL-TIME EQUIVALENT (FTE) HISTORY," FTC
.GOV. https://www.ftc.gov/about-ftc/bureaus-offices/office-executive-director
/financial-management-office/ftc-appropriation. Accessed February 13,
2020.

25 https://www.ftc.gov/news-events/press-releases/2016/08/mars-petcare-settles
-false-advertising-charges-related-its. Accessed April 1, 2020.

26 https://www.ftc.gov/news-events/press-releases/2016/12/ftc-approves-final
-order-settling-charges-mars-petcare-made-false; https://www.ftc.gov/system
/files/documents/cases/161212_1523229_mars_petcare_us_decision_and
_order.pdf. Accessed April 1, 2020.

27 Dvm360.com staff, "Dogswell Jerky Products Recalled for Antibiotic Residue,"
DVM360, July 31, 2013, http://veterinarynews.dvm360.com/dogswell-jerky
-products-recalled-antibiotic-residue.

28 Claudine Wilkins and Jessica Rock, "Pet Food Recall," Animal Law Source,
accessed August 21, 2019, animallaw.org.

29 Tim Wall, "Purina and Blue Buffalo Settle Lawsuits After Two Years," November 3, 2016, PetfoodIndustry.com, https://www.petfoodindustry.com/articles
/6113-purina-and-blue-buffalo-settle-lawsuits-after-two-years.

30 General Mills/Blue Buffalo, PetfoodIndustry.com, accessed January 31, 2020,
https://www.petfoodindustry.com/directories/211-top-pet-food-companies
-current-data/listing/13193-general-mills-blue-buffalo.

31 https://blog.theanimalrescuesite.greatergood.com/purina-blue-buffalo-lawsuit/.
Accessed April 1, 2020.

32 "The Truth About Pet Food: Raw Bistro Makes the 2019 List," Raw Bistro,
April 8, 2019, https://rawbistro.com/blogs/raw-bistro/the-truth-about-pet
-food-raw-bistro-makes-the-2019-list.

33 Mollie Morrissette, "Author of Poisoned Pets Creates Art to Help Animals;
Former Fashion Illustrator Creates Portraits of Pets: Poisoned Pets: Pet Food
Safety News," Poisoned Pets: Pet Food Safety News, June 23, 2016, http://
www.poisonedpets.com/author-poisoned-pets-creates-art-help-animals-former
-fashion-illustrator-turns-talents-fund-advocacy-work/.

34 Phone interview with Mollie Morrissette and Sony Salzman, September 12, 2019.

35 Mollie Morrissette, "The 'Mystery' of the Jerky Treat Poisoning in Dogs
Continues to Be Perpetuated in the Media: Poisoned Pets: Pet Food Safety
News," Poisoned Pets: Pet Food Safety News, October 22, 2014, http://
www.poisonedpets.com/reporters-fail-mention-clue-solving-mystery-treat
-poisonings/.

6. When "Meat" Is a Four-Letter Word

1   Bob Heye, "3 Dogs Sickened, Another Dies After Eating Canned Dog Food," KATU News, January 2, 2017, https://katu.com/news/local/3-dogs-get-sick -and-1-dies-after-eating-canned-dog-food.

2   *AVMA Guidelines for the Euthanasia of Animals*, American Veterinary Medical Association, 2013, https://www.avma.org/KB/Policies/Documents/euthanasia .pdf; *Euthanasia Reference Manual*, The Humane Society of the United States, 2013, https://www.animalsheltering.org/sites/default/files/content/euthanasia -reference-manual.pdf.

3   "Evanger's Voluntarily Recalls Hunk of Beef Because of Pentobarbital Expo-sure in One Batch of Food," FDA.gov, February 7, 2018, https://www.fda.gov /safety/recalls-market-withdrawals-safety-alerts/evangers-voluntarily-recalls -hunk-beef-because-pentobarbital-exposure-one-batch-food.

4   "Evanger's Pet Food and Against the Grain Voluntarily Recalls Additional Products Out of Abundance of Caution Due to Potential Adulteration with Pentobarbital," U.S. Food and Drug Administration, February 8, 2018, https://www.fda.gov/safety/recalls-market-withdrawals-safety-alerts/evangers -pet-food-and-against-grain-voluntarily-recalls-additional-products-out -abundance-caution.

5   Adam Littman, "Washougal Woman, Whose Dog Died After Eating Tainted Food, Faces Conspiracy Theories," *The Seattle Times*, February, 23, 2017, https://www.seattletimes.com/life/pets/washougal-woman-whose-dog-died -after-eating-tainted-food-faces-conspiracy-theories/.

6   Lisa Fletcher, "FDA to Investigate after ABC7 Exposes Euthanasia Drug in Dog Food," WJLA-TV, February 8, 2018, https://wjla.com/features/7-on-your -side/fda-to-investigate-after-abc7-exposes-euthanasia-drug-in-dog-food; "FDA Alerts Pet Owners About Potential Pentobarbital Contamination in Canned Dog Food Manufactured by the J. M. Smucker Company, Including Certain Gravy Train, Kibbles 'N Bits, Ol' Roy, and Skippy Products," FDA .gov, February 16, 2018, https://www.fda.gov/animal-veterinary/news-events /fda-alerts-pet-owners-about-potential-pentobarbital-contamination-canned -dog-food-manufactured-jm.

7   Kelli Bender, "Popular Dog Food Brands Recalled After Repeatedly Testing Positive for Euthanasia Drug," *People*, February 18, 2018, https://people.com /pets/dog-food-recall-euthanasia-drug/.

8   Aaron Gould Sheinin, "FDA Warning: Euthanasia Drug Found in Wet Dog Food," WebMD, February 16, 2018, https://pets.webmd.com/news /20180215/pet-alert-euthanasia-drug-found-wet-dog-food.

9   Lisa Fletcher, "J. M. Smucker Company Recalls 5th Pet Food Product in Less Than Month," WJLA, March 26, 2018, https://wjla.com/features/7-on-your -side/jm-smucker-company-voluntarily-recalls-two-varieties-of-milos-kitchen -dog-treats.

10 "FDA Alerts Pet Owners About the Presence of Thyroid Hormones in Certain Milo's Kitchen Pet Treats," FDA.gov, March 27, 2018, https://www.fda.gov

/animal-veterinary/news-events/fda-alerts-pet-owners-about-presence-thyroid
-hormones-certain-milos-kitchen-pet-treats.

11 https://www.fda.gov/media/103064/download. Accessed April 1, 2020.

12 http://www.againstthegrainpetfood.com/about-us/. Accessed February 5, 2020.

13 Corilyn Shropshire, "Some Against the Grain Pet Food Voluntarily Recalled
Over Contamination Fears," *Chicago Tribune,* February 15, 2017, https://www
.chicagotribune.com/business/ct-pet-food-recall-0216-biz-20170215-story
.html.

14 Phone Interview with John Ward and Wendy Paris, July 29, 2019.

15 "FAQs," United States Department of Agriculture Economic Research Service,
accessed August 6, 2019, https://www.ers.usda.gov/faqs/.

16 "Livestock Slaughter 2018 Summary," United States Department of Agriculture National Agricultural Statistics Service, April 2019, https://www.nass.usda
.gov/Publications/Todays_Reports/reports/lsslan19.pdf.

17 "2017 Census of Agriculture Highlights: Farm Economics," United States Department of Agriculture National Agricultural Statistics Service, https://www
.nass.usda.gov/Publications/Highlights/2019/2017Census_Farm_Economics
.pdf, accessed April 1, 2020.

18 "Livestock Slaughter 2017 Summary," United States Department of Agriculture National Agricultural Statistics Service, April 2018, https://www.nass
.usda.gov/Publications/Todays_Reports/reports/lsslan18.pdf, accessed April
1, 2020.

19 Tara A. Okuma and Rosalee S. Hellberg, "Identification of Meat Species
in Pet Foods Using a Real-Time Polymerase Chain Reaction (PCR) Assay,"
Food Control 50, no. 9 (2015), https://doi.org/10.1016/j.foodcont.2014.08
.017.

20 James McWilliams, "The Deadstock Dilemma: Our Toxic Meat Waste," *The
Atlantic*, August 11, 2010.

21 Grier, "Provisioning," 131.

22 *Saunders Comprehensive Veterinary Dictionary,* 3rd ed., s.v. "4D meat."

23 Regulation of Transactions, Transportation, or Importation of 4-D Animals
to Prevent Use as Human Food, 21 U.S.C. § 644, Mar. 4, 1907, ch. 2907,
title II, §204, as added Pub. L. 90–201, §14, Dec. 15, 1967, 81 Stat. 594,
https://uscode.house.gov/view.xhtml?req=granuleid:USC-prelim-title21
-section644&num=0&edition=prelim#sourcecredit.

24 Jennifer Schlesinger and Andrea Day, "What Is Really in the Food Your Dog
or Cat Is Eating?" CNBC, May 6, 2017, https://www.cnbc.com/2017/05/06
/what-is-really-in-the-food-your-dog-or-cat-is-eating.html.

25 Virginia P. Studdert et al., *Comprehensive Veterinary Dictionary* (Elsevier,
2012), loc. 31170–31171, Kindle.

26 "Transport of Deadstock and Rendered Material," Canadian Food Inspection Agency, accessed July 31, 2019, http://www.inspection.gc.ca/animals
/terrestrial-animals/biosecurity/standards-and-principles/transportation/eng
/1519235033628/1519235183948?chap=3.

27 Annabelle Olivier, "'Guts Everywhere': Montreal-Area Residents Furious After Truck Spills Animal Parts on City Street," *Global News,* October 25, 2018, https://globalnews.ca/news/4595198/animal-parts-street-riviere-des-prairies -montreal/.

28 Sanimax.com homepage; "Animal Guts and Entrails Splattered in RDP Af- ter Transport Truck Makes Abrupt Stop," CBC.ca, https://www.cbc.ca/news /canada/montreal/sanimax-truck-collision-1.4877051 https://www.cbc.ca /news/canada/montreal/sanimax-truck-collision-1.4877051.

29 Ibid.

30 "Transport of Deadstock and Rendered Material," Canadian Food Inspec- tion Agency, accessed August 14, 2019, http://www.inspection.gc.ca/animals /terrestrial-animals/biosecurity/standards-and-principles/transportation/eng /1519235033628/1519235183948?chap=3.

31 Ibid.

32 "Sanitary Transportation of Human and Animal Food; Final Rule," 81 *Federal Register* 66 (April 6, 2016), 20095.

33 Ibid., 20128.

34 Ibid.

35 Ibid.

36 D. L. Meeker and J. L. Meisinger, "Rendered Ingredients Significantly Influ- ence Sustainability, Quality, and Safety of Pet Food," *Journal of Animal Science* 93, no. 3 (March 2015): 835, https://doi.org/10.2527/jas.2014-8524.

37 "FAQs," National Renderers Association, accessed August 14, 2019, http:// www.nationalrenderers.org/about/faqs/.

38 Ibid.

39 "Emergency Animal Disposal Guidance," California Environmental Protec- tion Agency, accessed August 14, 2019, https://calepa.ca.gov/disaster/animals/.

40 "Livestock Carcass Disposal," ND Department of Agriculture, accessed August 7, 2019, https://www.nd.gov/ndda/program/animal-health/livestock-carcass -disposal.

41 *Euthanasia Reference Manual,* Humane Society of the United States, 2013, https://www.animalsheltering.org/sites/default/files/content/euthanasia -reference-manual.pdf.

42 https://www.youtube.com/watch?v=RuoSxSJ94RY.

43 James McWilliams, "The Deadstock Dilemma: Our Toxic Meat Waste," *The Atlantic,* August 11, 2010, https://www.theatlantic.com/health/archive/2010 /08/the-deadstock-dilemma-our-toxic-meat-waste/61191/.

44 "Livestock Carcass Disposal," State of Wisconsin Department of Agriculture, Trade, and Consumer Protection, accessed August 14, 2019, https://datcp.wi .gov/Pages/Programs_Services/CarcassDisposal.aspx.

45 Abellin, "The 7 Dirtiest Jobs," ABC News, September 3, 2012, https://abcnews .go.com/Business/dirtiest-jobs/story?id=17130057#2.

46 David L. Meeker, *Essential Rendering: All About the Animal By-Products Industry* (National Renderers Association, 2006).

47 Interview of Steve Thomas by Wendy Paris, Kansas City, October 1, 2019.
48 Meeker, *Essential Rendering*, 159.
49 Ibid.
50 "Our Products—Protein Meal," Baker Commodities, accessed March 20, 2020, https://bakercommodities.com/products/protein-meal/.
51 "National Overview: Facts and Figures on Materials, Wastes and Recycling," United States Environmental Protection Agency, accessed August 14, 2019, https://www.epa.gov/facts-and-figures-about-materials-waste-and-recycling /national-overview-facts-and-figures-materials.

7. How Mold on Grain—Not Grain—Harms Our Dogs

1 Jan Hoffman, "Popular Grain-Free Dog Foods May Be Linked to Heart Disease," *The New York Times*, July 24, 2018, https://www.nytimes.com/2018/07 /24/health/grain-free-dog-food-heart-disease.html.
2 "FDA Investigating Potential Connection Between Diet and Cases of Canine Heart Disease," FDA Center for Veterinary Medicine, July 12, 2018, https:// www.fda.gov/AnimalVeterinary/NewsEvents/CVMUpdates/ucm613305.htm; Trina Wood, "UC Davis Investigates Link Between Dog Diet and Deadly Heart Disease," UC Davis Veterinarian Medicine Blog, July 19, 2018, https:// www.vetmed.ucdavis.edu/news/uc-davis-investigates-link-between-dog-diets -and-deadly-heart-disease.
3 Jan Hoffman, "Popular Grain-Free Dog Foods."
4 "FDA in Brief: FDA Investigates Cases of Canine Heart Disease Potentially Linked to Diet.," https://www.fda.gov/media/128303/download.
5 "FDA Investigation into Potential Link between Certain Diets and Canine Dilated Cardiomyopathy," https://www.fda.gov/animal-veterinary/news-events /fda-investigation-potential-link-between-certain-diets-and-canine-dilated -cardiomyopathy.
6 Jan Hoffman, "Popular Grain-Free Dog Foods."
7 Tainted Pet Food Maker Pays Settlement, CBS News, January 4, 2008, https:// www.cbsnews.com/news/tainted-pet-food-maker-pays-settlement/.
8 Diamond Pet Foods narrows recall after aflatoxin tests, American Veterinary Medical Association, February 15, 2006, https://www.avma.org/javma-news /2006-02-15/diamond-pet-foods-narrows-recall-after-aflatoxin-tests; Department of Health and Human Services Food and Drug Administration Inspection Report, https://www.fda.gov/media/70695/download.
9 "Toxic Pet Food May Have Killed Dozens of Dogs," NBCNews.com, May 10, 2006, http://www.nbcnews.com/id/10771943/ns/health-pet_health/t/toxic -pet-food-may-have-killed-dozens-dogs/#.XhUcuRdKgU0.
10 Jan Hoffman, "Popular Grain-Free Dog Foods."
11 John H. Tegzes, Brian B. Oakley, Greg Brennan, "Comparison of mycotoxin concentrations in grain versus grain-free dry and wet commercial dog foods," Toxicology Communications, Vol. 3, 2019, Issue 1. https://www.tandfonline .com/doi/full/10.1080/24734306.2019.1648636.

12 Jan Hoffman, "Popular Grain-Free Dog Foods."

13 https://www.ncbi.nlm.nih.gov/pmc/articles/PMC164220/.

14 "Molds on Food: Are They Dangerous?" Food Safety and Inspection Service, August 2013, accessed January 7, 2020, https://www.fsis.usda.gov/wps/wcm /connect/a87cdc2c-6ddd-49f0-bd1f-393086742e68/Molds_on_Food.pdf ?MOD=AJPERES.

15 "Wheat for Poultry and Swine Feeds," https://www.wengerfeeds.com/wheat -for-poultry-and-swine-feeds/.

16 Tegzes, Oakley, and Brennan, "Comparison of Mycotoxin."

17 Tim Wall, "'Healthy Grains' Dog Foods Appear in the Wake of DCM," *Petfood Industry*, November 6, 2019, https://www.petfoodindustry.com/articles/8662 -healthy-grains-dog-foods-appear-in-the-wake-of-dcm.

18 Ibid.

19 "Quality Grading and Inspections," USDA Agriculture Marketing Services, accessed January 17, 2020, https://www.ams.usda.gov/services/grading.

20 https://www.ams.usda.gov/grades-standards/vegetables.

21 "Carrots for Processing Grades and Standards," United States Department of Agriculture, accessed January 16, 2020, https://www.ams.usda.gov/grades -standards/carrots-processing-grades-and-standards.

22 "A Tale of Two Corns," National Corn Growers Association. Field corn figures based on U.S. Department of Agriculture, January 2018. https://ncga.com /stay-informed/media/in-the-news/article/2020/03/tale-of-two-corns-pdf. Ac- cessed March 30, 2020.

23 "Corn in Pet Food," National Corn Growers Association, 2020, https://ncga .com/topics/animal-agriculture/petfood.Accessed March 30, 2020.

24 Association of American Feed Control Officials, *2020 Official Publication*, 392.

25 "Our stews are 100% human grade!" http://carupetfood.com/human-grade -verified/. Accessed March 30, 2020.

8. Mysterious Mix-Ins, Spray-On Flavor, Ultraprocessing, Oh My!

1 "FDA Alerts Pet Owners about Potentially Toxic Levels of Vitamin D in Sev- eral Dry Pet Foods," FDA.gov, accessed March 30, 2020, https://www.fda .gov/animal-veterinary/news-events/fda-alerts-pet-owners-about-potentially -toxic-levels-vitamin-d-several-dry-pet-foods?utm_campaign=12-3-2018 -VitaminD&utm_medium=email&utm_source=Eloqua&elqTrackId=B1A4 CFFF6FDEE6DE41FBB7CE16615994&elq=5036556be0c94e5ea7613f5d ac538a1f&elqaid=6140&elqat=1&elqCampaignId=4977.

2 "Hill's Pet Nutrition Voluntarily Recalls Select Canned Dog Food for Excessive Vitamin D," FDA.gov, January 31, 2019, https://www.fda.gov/safety/recalls -market-withdrawals-safety-alerts/hills-pet-nutrition-voluntarily-recalls-select -canned-dog-food-excessive-vitamin-d.

3 Madeline Farber, "Dog Owners Claim 'Toxic' Vitamin D Levels in Recalled

Hill's Pet Nutrition Dog Food Killed Their Pets," Fox News, February 7, 2019, https://www.foxnews.com/health/dog-owners-claim-toxic-vitamin-d-levels-in -recalled-hills-pet-nutrition-dog-food-killed-their-pets.

4 "Hill's Pet Nutrition Expands Voluntary Recall of Select Canned Food for Elevated Vitamin D," FDA.gov, March 20, 2019, accessed January 8, 2020, https://www.fda.gov/safety/recalls-market-withdrawals-safety-alerts/hills -pet-nutrition-expands-voluntary-recall-select-canned-dog-food-elevated -vitamin-d.

5 Jennifer Fiala, "Single Supplier Suspected in Major Pet Food Recall," VIN News Service, December 19, 2018, https://news.vin.com/VINNews.aspx ?articleId=51391.

6 Enforcement Report, FDA, https://www.accessdata.fda.gov/scripts/ires/index .cfm?Product=171929.

7 "Hill's Pet Nutrition Voluntarily Recalls Select Canned Dog Food for Excessive Vitamin D," company announcement, FDA.gov, January 31, 2019, accessed January 7, 2020, https://www.fda.gov/safety/recalls-market-withdrawals-safety -alerts/hills-pet-nutrition-voluntarily-recalls-select-canned-dog-food-excessive -vitamin-d.

8 "Supplier Identified in Hill's Pet Food Vitamin D-Related Recalls." VIN News Service, July 10, 2019, https://news.vin.com/vinnews.aspx?articleId=54144.

9 Tim Wall, "35 Lawsuits Combine Over Hill's Vitamin D Recall," Petfood-Industry.com, December 10, 2019, https://www.petfoodindustry.com/articles /8752-lawsuits-combine-over-hills-vitamin-d-dog-food-recall.

10 Phone interview with Caitlin Gibson and Wendy Paris, January 24, 2020.

11 This and all quotes from Galen Rokey from phone interview with Wendy Paris, December 12, 2019.

12 "Palasurance: Importance of Palatability for Pet Food," Kemin marketing ma-terials, Kemin Industries, 2019.

13 https://afbinternational.com/products/. Accessed March 22, 2020.

14 Mary Roach, "The Chemistry of Kibble," *Popular Science,* March 25, 2013, https://www.popsci.com/science/article/2013-03/chemistry-kibble/.

15 Cozzini website. Accessed March 22, 2020.

16 L. Schnabel et al., "Association Between Ultraprocessed Food Consumption and Risk of Mortality Among Middle-aged Adults in France," *JAMA Internal Medicine* 179, no. 4 (2019): 490–98, https://doi.org/10.1001/jamainternmed .2018.7289.

17 This and all following quotes by Donna Raditic from phone interview with Wendy Paris, May 2, 2019.

18 Mary Jane Brown, "What Are Advanced Glycation End Products (AGEs)?" Healthline, December 22, 2016, https://www.healthline.com/nutrition /advanced-glycation-end-products.

19 R. Singh et al., "Advanced Glycation End-Products: A Review," https://www .ncbi.nlm.nih.gov/pubmed/11270668.

20 Charlotte van Rooijen et al., "Quantitation of Maillard Reaction Products in

Commercially Available Pet Foods," *Journal of Agricultural and Food Chemistry* 62, no. 35 (September 2014): 8883–91, https://doi.org/10.1021/jf502064h.

21 Edoardo Capuano and Vincenzo Fogliano, "Acrylamide and 5-hydroxymethylfurfural (HMF): A Review on Metabolism, Toxicity, Occurrence in Food and Mitigation Strategies," *LWT—Food Science and Technology* 44, no. 4 (May 2011): 793–810.

9. We Speak for the Dogs

1 Patrícia M. Oba et al., "True Nutrient and Amino Acid Digestibility of Dog Foods Made with Human-Grade Ingredients Using the Precision-Fed Cecectomized Rooster Assay," *Translational Animal Science* 4, no. 1 (January 2020), https://doi.org/10.1093/tas/txz175.

2 Recalls and Withdrawals, FDA.gov, accessed April 1, 2020, https://www.fda.gov/animal-veterinary/safety-health/recalls-withdrawals.

3 Tim Wall, "E-commerce Helps US Dog, Cat Food Sales Hit $27 Billion," PetfoodIndustry.com, January 14, 2019, https://www.petfoodindustry.com/articles/7806-e-commerce-helps-us-dog-cat-food-sales-hit-us27-billion?v=preview.

4 Total Retail and Food Service Sales From 1992 to 2018, Statista, February 21, 2020, https://www.statista.com/statistics/197569/annual-retail-and-food-services-sales/.

5 2018 Recalls, Market Withdrawals and Safety Alerts, FDA.gov, accessed April 2, 2020, https://www.fda.gov/safety/archive-recalls-market-withdrawals-safety-alerts/2018-recalls-market-withdrawals-safety-alerts.

6 Foodborne Germs and Illnesses, CDC.gov, accessed April 2, 2020, https://www.cdc.gov/foodsafety/foodborne-germs.html.

7 "Fresh Pet Food Market in US 2019–2023," Infinite Research Limited, July 2019, https://www.reportlinker.com/p05804154/Fresh-Pet-Food-Market-in-US.html?utm_source=PRN.

8 "U.S. Pet Market Outlook, 2018–2019," Packaged Facts, August 22, 2018, https://www.packagedfacts.com/Pet-Outlook-11819832/.

10. Fact Versus Fiction in Dog Nutrition

1 "FoodData Central," USDA Agricultural Research Service, accessed March 24, 2020, https://fdc.nal.usda.gov/.

2 "Safe Minimum Cooking Temperatures Charts," Foodsafety.gov, accessed March 24, 2020, https://www.foodsafety.gov/food-safety-charts/safe-minimum-cooking-temperature.

3 Christina Jason, "Caffeine Versus Chocolate: A Mighty Methel Group," ScienceandFood, September 29, 2015, https://scienceandfooducla.wordpress.com/2015/09/29/caffeine-vs-chocolate-a-mighty-methyl-group/.

4 Anna Burke, "Can Dogs Eat Onions?" American Kennel Club, May 11, 2017. https://www.akc.org/expert-advice/nutrition/can-dogs-eat-onions/.

5 E-mail interview with Wendy Paris and John Tegzes, April 6, 2019.
6 Robert L.Wolke, "Chocolate the Numbers," *The Washington Post*, June 9, 2004, https://www.washingtonpost.com/wp-dyn/articles/A24276-2004Jun8.html.
7 Dawn Hass, "Chocolate Toxicity in Dogs," Pet Health Tips: Toxicity, Purdue University College of Veterinary Medicine, accessed November 17, 2019, https://www.purdue.edu/vet/vth/sapc/toxicity-tips.php#1.
8 https://www.merckvetmanual.com/toxicology/food-hazards/chocolate.
9 https://www.petmd.com/dog/chocolate-toxicity.
10 Karin Brulliard, "What Makes Dogs So Special and Successful? Love," *The Washington Post*, September 25, 2019, https://www.washingtonpost.com/science/2019/09/25/what-makes-dogs-so-special-successful-love/.

11. Can My Dog Eat Popcorn?

1 https://www.popcorn.org/Facts-Fun/Industry-Facts.
2 https://www.healthline.com/health/food-nutrition/carbs-in-popcorn#carbs-per-serving.

Index